# The New Social Democracy

# The New Social Democracy

Edited by

Andrew Gamble and Tony Wright

The Political Quarterly
in association with
the Fabian Society

Blackwell Publishers

Copyright © The Political Quarterly Publishing Co. Ltd.

ISBN 0–631–217657

First published 1999

Blackwell Publishers
108 Cowley Road, Oxford, OX4 1JF, UK.

and
350 Main Street,
Malden, MA 02148, USA.

*British Library Cataloguing in Publication Data*
A catalogue record for this book is available from the British Library

*Library of Congress Cataloging in Publication Data*
Cataloging-in-Publication data applied for

Printed in Great Britain by Whitstable Litho Ltd, Whitstable.

# CONTENTS

Notes on Contributors     vii

Introduction: The New Social Democracy     1
ANDREW GAMBLE AND TONY WRIGHT

Premature Obsequies: Social Democracy Comes in From the Cold     10
DAVID MARQUAND

European Social Democracy and New Labour: Unity in Diversity?     19
DONALD SASSOON

European Social Democracy: Convergence, Divisions, and Shared
Questions     37
FRANK VANDENBROUCKE

Ownership and Social Democracy     53
GERALD HOLTHAM

The Parabola of Working Class Politics     69
COLIN CROUCH

Globalisation and Social Democracy     84
PAUL HIRST

New Keynesianism and New Labour     97
WILL HUTTON

A Response to Will Hutton     103
RUTH KELLY

Environmental Democracy     105
MICHAEL JACOBS

The Helmsman and the Cattle Prod     117
ANNA COOTE

Social Democracy in a Small Country: Political Leadership or
Management Consultancy?     131
JAMES McCORMICK AND GRAHAM LEICESTER

New Approaches to the Welfare State     142
JULIAN LE GRAND

CONTENTS

True Blood or False Genealogy: New Labour and British Social
Democratic Thought                                           151
MICHAEL FREEDEN

'Rights and Responsibilities': A Social Democratic Perspective   166
STUART WHITE

Index                                                        181

# Notes on Contributors

Anna Coote is Director of the Public Health Programme at the King's Fund, London. She was formerly Deputy Director of the Institute for Public Policy Research, the London-based, centre-left think tank (1993–7), and adviser to the Minister for Women (1997–8). Her publications include *Citizens' Juries: Theory into Practice* with J. Lenaghan (IPPR, 1997), *New Agenda for Health*, with D. J. Hunter (IPPR, 1996), *The Welfare of Citizens: Developing new social rights* (IPPR/Rivers Oram Press, 1992), *Sweet Freedom*, with B. Campbell (Basil Blackwell, 1987).

Colin Crouch is a Professor of Sociology at the European University Institute, Florence. He is also an External Scientific member of the Max-Planck Institute for the Study of Society at Cologne. He previously taught at the University of Oxford and the London School of Economics and Political Science.

Michael Freeden is Professor of Politics at Oxford University and Fellow of Mansfield College, Oxford. Among his books are *The New Liberalism* (1978), *Liberalism Divided* (1986), *Rights* (1991) and *Ideologies and Political Theory* (1996). He is editor of the *Journal of Political Ideologies*.

Andrew Gamble is Professor of Politics and Director of the Political Economy Research Centre at the University of Sheffield. He is co-editor of *The Political Quarterly*. His books include *Hayek: The Iron Cage of Liberty* and *The Free Economy and the Strong State*.

Paul Hirst is Professor of Social Theory at Birkbeck College, University of London and Academic Director of the London Consortium Graduate Programme in Humanities and Cultural Studies. His books include: *Associative Democracy* (1994), *Globalisation in Question* (1996), with Grahame Thompson, and *From Statism to Pluralism* (1997).

Gerald Holtham is a former Director of IPPR, former Visiting Fellow of the Brookings Institution, Washington, and former Fellow of Magdalen College, Oxford. As an economist he has worked in the City and at the OECD. He is currently Global Strategist for Norwich Union Investment Management.

Will Hutton is Editor in Chief, *The Observer*. His books include *The State We're In* (1995) and *The State to Come* (1997).

Michael Jacobs is General Secretary of the Fabian Society. An economist, he was formerly Research Fellow in the Department of Geography at the LSE and at the Centre for the Study of Environmental Change and Department of Philosophy at Lancaster University. He is the author of *The Green Economy* (Pluto Press, 1991), *The Politics of the Real World* (Earthscan, 1996), and editor of *Greening the Millennium? The New Politics of the Environment* (*Political Quarterly*, Blackwell, 1997).

Ruth Kelly is Labour MP for Bolton West. Before being elected, she was Deputy Head of the Inflation Report Division at the Bank of England. She has also worked as an economics journalist on the *Guardian* newspaper.

Julian Le Grand is the Richard Titmuss Professor of Social Policy at the London School of Economics. He is the author, co-author or editor of twelve books and over ninety

© The Political Quarterly Publishing Co. Ltd. 1999
Published by Blackwell Publishers, 108 Cowley Road, Oxford OX4 1JF, UK and 350 Main Street, Malden, MA 02148, USA

articles and book chapters on economics, philosophy and social policy, including *Equity and Choice* (1991), *The Economics of Social Problems* (3rd edition, 1992), *Quasi-Markets and Social Policy* (1993) and *Learning from the NHS Internal Market* (1998). He is currently writing a book on the impact of policy and individual behavour, provisionally entitled *Knights, Knaves and Pawns: Public Policy and Human Motivation*.

Graham Leicester is a political consultant and Director of the Scottish Foundation. He launched the Foundation in 1997 with *Things to Come: new thinking for the new Scotland*; and has subsequently written *A Business Guide to Devolution* and *Holistic Government: Options for a Devolved Scotland*. He is a member of the McIntosh Commission on Local Government and the Scottish Parliament. He was previously a member of HM Diplomatic Service, specialising in European Affairs.

James McCormick is Research Director of the Scottish Council Foundation. He is co-author of *Three Nations: Social Exclusion in Scotland* and *Paying for Peace of Mind: Insurance on a Low Income*; and has recently co-edited *Welfare in Working Order* and *Environment Scotland: Prospects for Sustainability*. He was previously a Research Fellow with the IPPR, working for the Commission on Social Justice.

David Marquand was MP for Ashfield 1966–1977, and is now Principal of Mansfield College Oxford and Honorary Professor of Politics at the University of Sheffield. His latest book, *The New Reckoning: Capitalism, States and Citizens* was published by Polity Press in 1997. Weidenfeld and Nicolson will be publishing a second edition of his *Progressive Dilemma* in 1999.

Donald Sassoon is Professor of Comparative European History, Queen Mary and Westfield College, University of London. He is author of *One Hundred Years of Socialism*, and winner of the Deutscher Memorial Prize 1997.

Frank Vandenbroucke is currently Member of the European Parliament. He was Member of the Belgian Parliament from 1985 until 1996, leader of the Flemish Socialists (sister party of Labour in the Flemish region of Belgium) until 1994, and served as Vice-Prime Minister and Minister of Foreign Affairs in the Belgian government.

Stuart White teaches political theory in the Department of Political Science, Massachusetts Institute of Technology. He is currently working on a book, entitled *The Civic Minimum: An Essay on the Rights and Obligations of Economic Citizenship*.

Tony Wright is the Labour Member of Parliament for Cannock Chase and the joint editor of *The Political Quarterly*. He is also Honorary Professor of Politics at the University of Birmingham. His many publications include *Citizens and Subjects* (Routledge, 1994), *Socialisms Old and New* (Routledge, 1996), *Why Vote Labour?* (Penguin, 1997) and *The British Political Process* (Routledge, forthcoming).

# Introduction: The New Social Democracy

ANDREW GAMBLE AND TONY WRIGHT

THERE is a paradox about social democracy at the end of the twentieth century. In Europe social democracy is more electorally successful than it has ever been, forming or participating in governments in a majority of the states of the European Union. Yet, following the ascendancy of neo-liberalism in the 1980s, there has never been such widespread questioning of what social democracy stands for and whether it still offers distinctive policies and goals. This is all the more surprising because the collapse of communism in Europe at the end of the 1980s might have been expected to benefit social democracy as one of the main historical adversaries of centrally planned economies and authoritarian political systems. Instead, at least for a time, it seemed to disorient it. The end of communism cast doubt on all forms of socialism, and called into question whether alternatives to the dominant neo-liberal order were any longer either conceivable or feasible—or even desirable.

In the 1990s social democracy has therefore been forced to redefine itself on a hostile terrain. Conservative commentators have been celebrating the end of history, the final triumph of the principles of free market capitalism as the fundamental and inescapable foundation of democratic order in the modern world. At the same time, changes in the organisation of the global economy—involving systems of production, patterns of work and consumption, and new forms of economic, political and cultural interdependence—have brought into question many of the conditions for social democratic policies which used to be taken for granted, in particular the feasibility of national economic management and the mobilisation of class solidarity.

Some believe that these changes mean that social democracy can now only be spoken of in the past tense. It belongs to a particular era in the development of world politics, an era of relatively protected and sheltered national economies, in which governments of the centre-left were able to create institutions capable of securing full employment, comprehensive welfare provision and extensive regulation of industry. The existence of full employment and of governments committed to using Keynesian principles to maintain it meant a significant shift in the balance of power between labour and capital, weakening the old disciplines of the competitive self-regulating market—bankruptcy and unemployment—and requiring the development of new kinds of co-operation between unions, employers and government to ensure the smooth running of the economy.

Since the 1970s this kind of social democratic regime has been under attack, internally from the ideologues of the new right, and externally because of the

© The Political Quarterly Publishing Co. Ltd. 1999
Published by Blackwell Publishers, 108 Cowley Road, Oxford OX4 1JF, UK and 350 Main Street, Malden, MA 02148, USA

way in which the global economy has developed. Some have proved more vulnerable than others, but a succession of centre-left governments—notably Britain in 1976, France in 1991, and Sweden in 1994—have been forced to change their domestic economic policies significantly in order to maintain the confidence of the financial markets. Many observers have concluded that social democracy of the kind which flourished in the 1950s and 1960s has simply become too costly to sustain. Others fear that trends in the global economy will provoke a race to the bottom in which all countries will be under extreme pressure to accept lower wages and social benefits in order to compete, making the social democracy of western Europe in the 1950s and 1960s seem a golden age of prosperity and tranquillity never to return.

The contributors to this book write from a variety of perspectives, but all of them resist the idea that social democracy is tied to a particular era, or depends on the existence of a closed economy or a particular kind of class structure. Social democracy has always had to change to survive, but it remains an essential tradition for thinking about contemporary politics and the choices open to us. This is because social democracy is not a fixed doctrine but a political movement, as protean as the capitalist economy and society which has given rise to it. It is not a particular historical programme or regime or political party or interest group, or even an unchanging set of values. As a political movement its only fixed point is its constant search to build and sustain political majorities for reforms of economic and social institutions which counter injustice and reduce inequality. What the programme of social democracy should be, and how this should be defined in relation to other parties, is a matter of fierce debate in every generation, and there will always be much room for disagreement, as there is in the pages of this book. But what this book also shows is the vitality and range of social democratic thinking today.

Understood in this way, there have been familiar and recurring tensions in social democracy. One of the most important has been the need to find a balance between developing a programme which will move towards the kind of society social democrats want to bring about, and the compromises they need to make to win votes and assemble a majority electoral coalition in the society as it is. The history of social democratic parties is full of charges that leaders have pursued votes at the expense of abandoning their principles. There has always been a gulf between rhetoric and reality, between the broad and sweeping ideals which define the reforms which need to be carried out, and the narrow and cautious pragmatism of the policies governments pursue. The translation of ideas into workable policies has also been accompanied by perennial charges of betrayal, yet such translation is an essential requirement for initiating a long-lasting process of change and reform. The successful social democratic parties have been those which have been able to find ways of connecting their practical reforms with a larger story of what they stand for and are trying to achieve. One of the difficulties in doing this historically has been the tension between social democracy as the representative and defender of a particular interest or set of interests, and social democracy as a programme to promote the public interest over and above all sectional interests. To establish an organisation based on strong loyalties and shared purposes both are necessary, but the balance between them is not easy to strike. The main sectional interest associated with social democracy in the twentieth century has been organised labour, and this has been both an enormous source of strength and energy, but also at times a source of weakness and inertia.

This era, even in Britain, is now ending. Party leaders are no longer the representatives of a unified, disciplined labour movement, but brokers in an increasingly pluralist and diverse politics. The task confronting the leaders of social democratic parties has always been to find ways of maintaining both the distinctiveness and attractiveness of social democracy as a movement for social change, and its effectiveness as an electoral machine and as an agency of government. In this sense the problems facing social democratic leaders of today and those of fifty years ago are remarkably similar. But the contexts are very different, and so too therefore are the substantive policies (and trade-offs) which are available.

Some of the more apocalyptic versions of the demise of social democracy soon fade away on closer inspection. What social democratic leaders face now, as they have faced in every generation, is the need to modernise and revise their policies and approach in the light of core principles and their understanding of the context in which they operate. Such revisionism is frequently damned as a process of betrayal, in which the original principles and objectives of the movement are diluted until they are unrecognisable, and the party ceases to be a social democratic party at all. This charge has been levelled at 'new' Labour and Tony Blair. Some left-wing critics believe Tony Blair and his allies have adopted a neo-liberal policy and transformed the Labour Party into a second Conservative Party. The tactic may have been crowned with electoral success in 1997, but it has been at the expense of weakening the link with organised labour which gave the party its historical reason for existing, and of emptying the party's policies of any serious socialist or social democratic content.

On this view the 1997 election was confirmation that the Thatcher and Major governments which ruled Britain for eighteen years had succeeded in establishing a new consensus in Britain. It is argued that Labour did not put forward a radical alternative, and failed to challenge the underlying assumptions of Conservative policies. That made it a safe alternative to an unpopular government and helped explain the size of Labour's electoral majority, but it also provided no basis for a radical and reforming government. New Labour was criticised for having a project for the party, but not one for the country. This was why it was content to govern within the parameters it inherited, defining macroeconomic stability in terms of inflation rather than unemployment, pledging not to increase the standard or higher rates of income tax, sticking to the Conservative spending plans for the first two years of the

Parliament, and promising not to reverse either the measures of privatisation or the industrial relations reforms.

Disaffection of intellectuals with social democratic governments is nothing new. It has been a feature of every Labour government in Britain. But there is an extra edge to the criticism this time, a belief that Labour has moved so far to make itself electable that it has abandoned any recognisable social democratic terrain at all. Some of the strongest criticism has come from self-professed guardians of the social democratic tradition, who believe that certain core ideas such as redistribution, universalist welfare and economic regulation, as well as the link between Labour and the trade unions, cannot be abandoned without abandoning social democracy itself. They believe that Labour is becoming in its policies a party that is indistinguishable from a 'One Nation' Conservative party, concerned primarily to manage capitalism humanely rather than to effect any fundamental changes in its social and economic organisation.

Part of the argument turns on what is and is not an acceptable revision of the means and objectives of a political party. In the long dispute over Clause IV of the Labour Party's constitution, those who wanted to keep the original wording argued that if the commitment to common ownership was abandoned, then Labour would no longer be committed to radical change, no longer prepared to challenge the fundamental source of inequality and injustice in capitalist society. Now the argument seems to be that if the commitment to traditional forms of redistribution is lost, Labour similarly will have lost its way. What seems to be overlooked in both cases is that redistribution and public ownership are particular means which social democrats may wish to employ to achieve the society they want. Social democrats have to be free to experiment with different means, and to adapt their programmes in response to the way in which societies are changing. The only real test is whether there is a plausible and intelligent connection between ends and means.

Social democrats need radical thinking and radical exploration in every generation. But being radical means both going to the root of things and being prepared to experiment and adapt. The greatest danger which can beset social democracy is to make a fetish of particular means and to be rhetorical rather than pragmatic in analysing what works and what can be done. Translating such principles as pluralism, efficiency, autonomy, justice and equality into practical policies is long and difficult, and there are certain to be many failures and wrong turnings along the way. Far from dying with the twentieth century, social democracy has new opportunities and new challenges, with left of centre thought having a new vibrancy, freed from the straitjackets of the cold war and the long division of the socialist movement between state collectivists and social democrats.

One of the major consequences of this new intellectual space has been a rethinking of the whole issue of governance and agency. Social democrats are escaping their former fixation with the state and increasingly want to explore the role of different modes of governance, whether state, market, community or household, in delivering the objectives of policy. One key area where social democracy has much to offer, as well as much to reflect upon, is the constitutional arrangements for governance, at the level both of organisations and of political systems. In the past this has been largely neglected. But this is no longer possible. As important powers and functions are transferred away from the nation-state to regional parliaments and assemblies, and to a range of supranational bodies and agencies, the question of the appropriate level at which particular functions should be exercised necessarily comes to the fore. Governance today is inescapably multilevel governance. Governance, the steering capacities of a social system, was traditionally associated with national government and the ways in which it managed the 'mixed economy'. In crucial respects the economy is still both 'mixed' and 'national', but the blurring of the traditional lines between market and state, between public and private, and between the local, regional, national and global, raises new questions about how economies and the private and public organisations within them are governed, how these are changing, and how they might be reformed.

Successful governance is vital both for citizenship and for economic efficiency. A multi-governance world raises questions about what citizens are now citizens of, at what level particular decisions should be taken, accountability assured, and how public involvement and participation should be organised. Can the global economy be governed? And what are the most appropriate organisational forms for such governance? Yet this is not just about macro change. One of the most potent lessons learnt from the right is that a strategy of micro change, paying attention to small details such as the design of institutions, the rights and opportunities available to groups and individuals, frameworks which allow social experimentation, new forms of ownership and association, can be critical in moving society forward, by establishing groups with interests and incentives to support change.

Some critics have argued that multilevel governance poses an insuperable problem for social democracy, because the more that functions are devolved the less possible it becomes for services to be provided on a uniform basis to all citizens. But this is to confine social democracy to national economies and national economic management. Powerful though this model once was it can no longer be sustained in its old form. Some greater degree of diversity is required. But, in conceding this, social democracy is not diluted but strengthened. What is being sought is a constitutional framework which can promote pluralism and diversity, within which the claims of equity can be pursued. The challenge for social democrats is to think through the implications of developing complex multilayer and overlapping forms of jurisdiction and authority. But the need to move faster in this direction to cope with some of the most pressing challenges facing us, such as the threats to the environment, regulation of the global economy and world poverty, is surely clear.

Thus social democratic thought has to renew itself in every generation if it is to remain relevant and practical. Finding ways to make a real difference is what social democratic politics is all about. Concepts such as equality and ownership, the scope of universal provision, the conditions for autonomy, diversity, efficiency and participation, continue to inspire fierce debate and original thinking.

\* \* \* \* \* \* \*

This book reflects this debate and, we believe, contributes some original thinking of its own. The fact that differing views and judgments are to be found here is an indication of the renewed intellectual vitality of social democracy. Our contributors are all recognisably participants in the same conversation, even where there are disagreements, and there is a shared sense of exploration of an uncharted political and intellectual terrain. It is a time for social democrats to learn from each other. There is ample scope for both friendly competition and mutual learning among social democratic parties and governments. The neo-liberal moment may have turned out to be just that, a moment; but it is also clear that the alternative is not simply the resumption of a social democratic politics of a traditional kind. Too much has changed. And too much was wrong.

However, to say this is not to forget about babies and bathwaters. As we began to have discussions among contributors about this book, our initial focus was on prevailing notions of a 'third way' in politics. Yet it soon became clear that, while useful in identifying new territory and opening up new approaches, such ideas could only make sense (and avoid rootless vacuity) if they were securely anchored in the social democratic tradition. In other words, the third way had to be about a new social democracy or it was about nothing. It had to be a new social democracy for new times. But of what kind? That is the question that our contributors were asked to explore—and to which they have responded with a wide range of valuable and suggestive answers.

In suggesting that it is now 'wiser to think of social democracies than of social democracy', David Marquand warns of the vacuities of a 'modernisation' rhetoric that really has nothing to do with a purposive and tough-minded social democratic politics. That requires a clear governing philosophy, that understands the historic weaknesses of social democracy but also is serious about remedying them. This means being serious about market failure and democratic citizenship, but also involves a revised view of how the state should see its role in relation to civil society. Above all, it requires more political imagination than social democrats have often displayed in the past.

Yet while Marquand's argument leads him to think that, at most, Britain now looks like an 'outlier' of European social democracy, Donald Sassoon's careful examination of contemporary currents within the social democratic movements of Europe finds an unprecedented convergence in which (with only a few exceptions) 'Blair's modernisers are part of the mainstream'. It is a mainstream in which neo-liberalism has been halted, intellectual and political confidence restored, but in which social democracy remains in crisis to the extent that it is faced with the task of grappling with the contemporary form of the international organisation of capitalism. It is not a moment for grand visions. Yet it is a moment for understanding that social democracy's traditional mission of domesticating capitalism at the national level now has to be applied to the continental and global levels too.

The general picture of social democratic convergence can be examined in more detail in relation to particular policy areas. Frank Vandenbroucke's analysis of current thinking about the welfare state does just this, in identifying the 'fixed points' that transcend national differences. But this view of the 'intelligent welfare state', which has labour market participation at its centre, does not mean uniform policy prescriptions (or even an unquestioning attitude to traditional values). There is ample scope for experiment and diversity. However, this requires an appropriate economic framework at the European level—an issue on which thinking in Britain does seem to be outside the mainstream—capable of achieving the coordination that is the precondition for convergent welfare reform.

We have become so accustomed to recording the fact that nationalisation is no longer a policy instrument of social democracy that significant issues about ownership have been overlooked. Gerry Holtham shows why ownership still matters and warns against the commercialisation of what should not be commercialised. Arguing that 'public ownership is a protean notion that can embrace very different arrangements', he suggests new forms of public ownership crafted for particular purposes. Social democrats are right to have rejected public ownership as an ideological principle; but it remains an important part of the social democratic armoury if used appropriately and imaginatively.

But used by whom? Clearly not by social democratic parties if they abandon the task of protecting people from market forces. This is the charge levelled by Colin Crouch against new Labour. The validity of this charge (on the evidence so far) is a running debate in several of the contributions here, but in Crouch's piece the argument is linked to an analysis of the changing pattern of class politics. Much will depend upon how the interests of new social forces are defined and articulated, but 'social democrats must get used to the idea that the Party can no longer be the vehicle for reinventing social democracy'. On this view, it can only create the spaces and sites where such reinvention might take place.

The issue of globalisation lies at the centre of all contemporary political debate. It also lends itself to lazy sloganising. As far as social democracy is concerned, globalisation has provided (for those who wanted this) an easy justification for intellectual and political retreat. Yet, as Paul Hirst argues, there is no inevitable 'race to the bottom' and no imperative towards global de-regulation. Nor is there a generalised crisis of the welfare state, as an analysis of particular national circumstances makes clear. What there is, instead, is an agenda for social democrats, both national and supra-national, of regulating markets and (as ever) saving capitalism from itself.

This theme is also taken up by Will Hutton, who believes that new Labour suffers from its lack of any 'fundamental critique of the capitalist system'. New Keynesian theory provides the basis for such a critique, rebuilding social democratic arguments rather than dismantling them, and carrying with it a range of concrete policy implications. Ruth Kelly, continuing the running debate, disputes Hutton's central charge and points to the policy initiatives that are being developed. Perhaps the question is whether, in developing such initiatives, there is also the intellectual and political confidence to articulate what Hutton calls the 'coherent political story' that would give them meaning.

If globalisation has provided one important challenge to traditional social democratic politics, then environmentalism has provided another. For a long time these two traditions seemed to be at odds, both in their analysis and their prescriptions, but this may now be changing. Michael Jacobs argues that 'social democrats and environmentalists are being driven on to the same territory by common economic and cultural changes in the world they confront', and that this territory is largely new to both of them. Revisionist social democracy meets revisionist environmentalism, in a convergence that is both theoretical and practical. Such convergence remains uneven and incomplete, but there is the real prospect of an 'environmental democracy' that draws on the complementary insights of its contributing traditions.

It was suggested earlier that a new attention to issues of governance is a distinguishing feature of contemporary social democracy. Process is integral to product; and the failure to understand this in the past has been a major disability. This whole issue is explored here by Anna Coote in looking at the relationship between those who steer and those who row, between state and civil society, and between social democratic goals and partnerships, public involvement and local action. What is clear is that 'the challenge for a modern social democratic government is to sustain the strength and coherence of its social objectives in the context of a fragmented and dispersed delivery system'.

This line of thinking is explored further by James McCormick and Graham Leicester, in considering to what extent the new political environment in Scotland provides a congenial laboratory for the development of a new model of social democracy. They sound some warnings, but also find grounds for a cautious optimism. The task is to develop 'a form of policy-making which is both guided by a strategic vision and reflects the complexities of the modern world'. Size and traditions combine to make Scotland an interesting place for social democrats to watch. Whatever else, devolution has created new political spaces of the kind that social democracy needs.

It also needs to think radically about the future of the welfare state, another theme that runs through this book. The argument has to go beyond more spending or less, means testing or universalism, voluntarism or compulsion.

From this starting point, Julian Le Grand argues that the idea of partnership offers a way through the familiar dilemmas about how welfare should be financed; and goes on to show in concrete terms how a partnership model might work in relation to long-term care. The details of this example can be debated, but Le Grand rightly castigates the 'fashionable vagueness' of thirdwayism and his insistence on the need for practical and innovative applications of key social democratic concepts is timely.

Yet these concepts themselves develop and mutate. This is necessarily so, as changing circumstances demand new responses and as arguments are expressed in different ways. This is disconcerting to those who prefer the recitation of familiar orthodoxies (which is why social democratic revisionism always occasions the charge of betrayal); but it also makes it important to establish the continuities and connections with what has gone before. Developing a tradition is not the same as abandoning it. There is room for much lively argument on this point, as the final two contributions here demonstrate.

Exploring the genealogy of new Labour in the 'complex series of inter-twined relationships, overlaps and parallel growth' that characterises the history of liberalism and social democracy in Britain, Michael Freeden finds 'important slippages' from this inheritance. By contrast, Stuart White argues that new Labour's emphasis on civic responsibility should be seen as 'rehabilitating an important liberal socialist value', rooted in notions of reciprocity, equal opportunity and autonomy. These are important argu-ments. Whatever else, they reflect the current vitality of social democratic debate.

Perhaps this is the main message to emerge from this book. There is not a singular 'new' social democracy, coherent and fully formed, but there is a clustering of new thinking and policies that reflects a political and intellectual tradition in more confident mood than has been the case in the recent past. The political renaissance of social democracy is accompanied by a renewed vitality of ideas and policies. It is still much too soon to be certain about where this will lead, or what its mature shape will look like. An old social democracy may have been the particular product of the twentieth century; but all the signs are that a new social democracy will make its presence felt in the twenty-first.

# Premature Obsequies: Social Democracy Comes in From the Cold

DAVID MARQUAND

MORE than once in the last twenty-five years, the death notices have appeared in the newspapers, the mourners have assembled in the church, a moving eulogy has been pronounced and the coffin has been carried to the grave-side. And then, at the last moment, the corpse has impudently risen from the dead. The death of social democracy has been proclaimed by luminaries as various as Tony Benn, Ralf Dahrendorf, John Gray and Anthony Giddens. Unfortunately, no one told the voters of Europe. Today, social democrats are in power in most of the member-states of the European Union, including France and Germany—the two leading member-states, which have provided the driving force of the European project since its earliest days.

To be sure, the social-democratic label is not, in itself, very informative. In some moods, at least, the leaders of Britain's 'new' Labour Party describe themselves as social democrats, but their version of social democracy has little in common with that of emblematic British social democrats like Ernest Bevin, Hugh Gaitskell, Anthony Crosland and John Smith—or, for that matter, with those of the ruling French Socialists or of some, if not all, of the key figures in the German SPD. In any case, it is not yet clear what social democracy can or should mean in practice in the economic era through which we are now living—or how the policy implications of the social-democratic tradition now differ from those of other traditions.

Social democrats have always been revisionists. They have always had to modify their doctrines to take account of the latest mutations in an endlessly mutating capitalism. The capitalist renaissance of our time has transformed the terms of political and intellectual debate and the nature of the social and economic terrain. Social democrats would be false to their history, as well as foolish, if they approached it with the instruments and assumptions of the Keynesian golden age which an earlier generation of social democrats did so much to fashion. But reborn capitalism is still a recent phenomenon, as well as an extraordinarily complex and elusive one. There is plenty of room for disagreement about its nature and implications, even among those who share the same values and ideological formation, and the disagreements may cut across doctrinal boundaries. Besides, social democracy is, by nature, heterogeneous. There has never been a single social-democratic orthodoxy, and it would be astonishing if one were to develop in this time of bewildering flux. Now, even more than in previous decades, it is wiser to think of social democracies than of social democracy.

© The Political Quarterly Publishing Co. Ltd. 1999
Published by Blackwell Publishers, 108 Cowley Road, Oxford OX4 1JF, UK and 350 Main Street, Malden, MA 02148, USA

## The Polanyi Pendulum

Yet certain common features stand out. Everywhere, the social-democratic rebirth of the late-1990s is a response to the social and moral dislocation that renascent capitalism has brought in its train. Reborn capitalism and reborn social democracy have appeared on the scene, not simultaneously it is true, but at any rate in close proximity. Fifty years ago, Karl Polanyi famously depicted the 'great transformation' of the nineteenth century as a kind of pendulum, beginning with the social and moral disruption of *laisser-faire* capitalism and ending with a long counter-movement as society spontaneously developed new mechanisms to subject market forces to social needs.[1] Polanyi's pendulum seems to be swinging again, only at much greater speed. So far, at any rate, the chief beneficiaries have been social democrats.

But not necessarily for ever. The people of Europe turned to social democracy because it was there: because it was the most obvious port in which to shelter from the neo-capitalist storm. If the shelter turns out to be illusory reborn social democracy will have no claim on the loyalties of electorates which are, in any case, more volatile than they used to be. The Polanyi pendulum can take a malign, as well as a benign, form. The German social-democratic pioneer, August Bebel, once described anti-Semitism as the 'socialism of fools'. Today, religious and ethnic fundamentalism, xenophobic nationalism, moral authoritarianism and the scape-goating of minorities might be called the fool's social democracy. They too offer shelters—deceptive and dangerous ones, no doubt, but that does not make them less seductive—from the insecurity, injustices and tensions that untamed capitalism brings with it.

As Benjamin Barber puts it, 'Jihad' is the other side of the coin of 'McWorld': cultural tribalism of the global free market.[2] And although 'Jihad' is more prevalent in the former Soviet bloc and the Third World than in North America and western Europe, the moral majority in the United States, the Europhobic nationalists who control the British gutter press, the National Front in France and the Italian neo-Fascists and Lombard League all whistle essentially the same fundamentalist tune as Serbian zealots in Kosovo, Jewish zealots on the West Bank, muslim zealots in Algeria and Hindu zealots in the Indian BJP. It would be wrong to exaggerate. The political cultures and moral economies of present-day Europe are still, by the standards of past history, remarkably tolerant and generous. The current social-democratic rebirth is testimony to that. But if the reborn social democrats betray the trust their electorates have placed in them, and fail to halt the growth of inequality, alienation and anomie against which their victories were a protest, a turn to darker forces could not be ruled out.

More positively, this is the nearest thing to a social-democratic moment in European history. Communism is dead. Fundamentalist left socialism is discredited. The political Right is in retreat, and in some places in disarray. The European project, which social democrats have done much to nurture, has just taken a huge step up; and most of the regimes which will be called upon to exploit the opportunities that this has created are social-democratic, or at any rate led by social democrats. It is a daunting moment, of course. Courage, skill, leadership and luck will all be needed if reborn social democracy is to keep faith with the societies that now look to it to re-tame the newly untamed capitalism of our time. But if it succeeds, it will deserve as well of the present generation as the architects of the post-war settlement deserved of theirs.

## New Labour—Or Not Conservative?

Against that background, new Labour's hesitant gropings for ideological *terra firma* take on a rather alarming hue. At first sight, Britain is, once again, Europe's odd-man-out. Doctrinally, new Labour is, at most, an outlier of European social democracy. But that is only part of the story. In spite of the endlessly-repeated ministerial mantra—'we were elected as new Labour and we intend to govern as new Labour'—the forces that put it into power were remarkably similar to the forces that made Lionel Jospin prime minister of France and Gerhard Schröder Chancellor of Germany. The truth is that new Labour did not win as new Labour. Nor did it win as old Labour. It won as Not Conservative.

Like the continental social-democratic parties, it seemed the best available port in the free-market storm. It bent over backwards to promise as little as possible, but the minimalism of its election manifesto is no guide to the real meaning of its victory. Blair offered security and hope to an anxious country, reeling from the effects of nearly twenty years of neo-liberalism. Now new Labour has to deliver, not only on the cautious offers it knew it was making, but on the nebulous, yet insistent hopes that the leader evoked by being himself. To do so, it will need more than a heterogeneous rag-bag of detailed policies—welfare to work here; Scottish devolution there; elected Mayors in one corner; ferocious centralisation in education in another. It will need a coherent broad approach, a governing philosophy, an ideological compass. And so far it has nothing of the kind.

What it has is a myth, or perhaps a rhetoric: a myth of youth, modern-isation and the future. But that is not a substitute for a governing philosophy. Youth does not last; modernisation is a Humpty-Dumpty word that means whatever the user wants it to mean; the future is indeterminate and unforeseeable. The real meaning of new Labour's modernisation rhetoric is that Blair and his associates have absorbed some of the central tenets of the neo-liberalism of the recent past—the propositions that there is one modern condition, which all rational people will recognise once it is pointed out to them; that the renascent capitalism of our day embodies that condition; and that resistance to it is futile. The most that public policy can do is to help the society and economy to 'adapt' to this condition with as little pain and as much competitive edge as possible. These propositions are classic examples of the social determinism that Isaiah Berlin once savaged as a 'theodicy'.[3] They are designed to justify what might otherwise appear to be evils by an appeal to a higher power—no longer God, but history. They offer a route out of the painful realm of choice and moral argument, and into the comforting realm of necessity. As such, they are a negation of the commitment to human autonomy which has differentiated the social-democratic tradition from mechanistic Marxism on the one hand and High Tory traditionalism on the other.

They also falsify the recent history of the British left. Long before Blair became leader of the Labour Party, indeed well before the 1992 election, the capitalist renaissance was beginning to inspire a counter-movement in the radical intelligentsia. As the old battle between capitalism and socialism became a thing of the past, and as the implications of the restive, masterless, productivity-enhancing but community-destroying new capitalism sank in, new questions began to arrive on the agenda. Granted that capitalism had won its battle with socialism, which of the many varieties of capitalism was to be preferred? Granted that the capitalist renaissance was world-wide, what changes were needed in global economic governance to bring it to heel? How could the undoubted dynamism of the capitalist free market be combined with social cohesion? How could an invasive cash nexus be prevented from eroding the social capital of community loyalty and mutual trust? Should the public domain of citizenship and service be ring-fenced from the market domain of buying and selling and, if so, how?

To these questions, the bleak certainties of the New Right could offer no answers, not the least of the reasons why the anxious middle classes of so-called 'Middle England' turned decisively against the Conservatives once 'Black Wednesday' had destroyed their claim to superior economic competence. Well before Tony Blair's accession to the Labour Party leadership, however, they had become the stuff of vigorous debate on the left and centre-left. Writers like Will Hutton, John Gray, John Kay, Ralf Dahrendorf and Harold Perkin slowly began to grope their way towards a new intellectual and political paradigm, combining insights from traditional social liberalism and traditional social democracy, and centred on the notions of a 'stake-holder' economy, a public domain and a pluralist polity. The Independent Commission on Social Justice, set up by John Smith, and the 'Dahrendorf' Commission on Wealth Creation and Social Cohesion, set up by Paddy Ashdown, struck essentially the same chords.[4] In a different, but equally important sphere, Charter 88 mobilised a surprisingly wide-ranging consti-tuency behind a programme of radical constitutional reform, designed to create a series of pluralistic checks and balances to protect civil society from an overmighty central state.

The emerging new paradigm was necessarily inchoate, and in places distinctly fuzzy; but five key features stood out with reasonable clarity. It was broadly liberal in politics, but broadly social-democratic in economics. It was for capitalism against socialism, but it implied profound changes in the architecture of British capitalism and a concomitant challenge to powerful corporate interests. Though it drew heavily on American academic writing, its vision of the political and moral economy was much closer to those of mainland Europe than to that of the United States. In the British context, at any rate, it was new—newer than anything offered subsequently by new Labour. Above all, it was pluralistic. It implied a multiplicity of power centres, economic and political; and it rejected the notion of a single modern condition to which there was a single route.

The tentative, half-formed new paradigm of the early 1990s was not a fully-fledged alternative to Blairism. The point is simply that new Labour's claim to have discovered the sole path to the future does not stand up to careful scrutiny. There were other paths, which it could have explored. Instead, it closed them off.

## Social Democracy for the Next Century

It is time to re-open them. The notion that today's renascent capitalism is an inescapable part of an inexorable and irresistible modernity, and that all other economic systems are archaic and obsolete, rests on a tendentious reading of the economic history of the last 200 years. It is true that the world of the 1990s and 2000s differs radically from that of the Keynesian 'golden age', as Eric Hobsbawm calls it, which is still the unconscious reference point for most people over the age of 45, and that some of the characteristic policy approaches of that era now lead nowhere. But although the global economy of the 1990s and 2000s is far removed from its benign and stable predecessor of the 1950s and 1960s, it has a great deal in common with that of the nineteenth century and something in common with that of the interwar period. Keynes may be dead, but Marx, Malthus and Ricardo have had a new lease of life. No governing philosophy for the late-twentieth and early-twenty-first centuries will do the work it needs to do if it ignores the central reality of our time, that capitalism has gone back on its tracks and that the latest mutation in its long history can be understood only in the context of its past.

It is not difficult to describe the broad outlines of a governing philosophy that might address that reality. The classic social-democratic theme of market failure should be amplified and re-phrased, and its connections with the equally classic social-democratic theme of democratic citizenship should be re-emphasised. Markets fail; and their failures are systemic, not accidental. They have to be supplemented and regulated; and only public power can supplement and regulate them. The relationship between democratic self-government and the capitalist free market is not easy and harmonious, as western shock therapists imagined after the fall of Communism: it is tense and problematic. As Hayek knew well, the promise of equal citizenship, which is fundamental to democracy, is inevitably in tension with the inequality which is no less fundamental to capitalism. Either democracy has to be tamed for the sake of capitalism, or capitalism has to be tamed for the sake of democracy. The capitalist market economy is a marvellous servant, but for democrats it is an oppressive, even vicious master. The task is to return it to the servitude which the builders of the post-war mixed economy imposed on it, and from which it has now escaped.

To that end, the public domain of citizenship and service should be safeguarded from incursions by the market domain of buying and selling, from what Michael Walzer has called 'market imperialism'.[5] In the public domain, goods should not be treated as commodities or proxy commodities. The language of buyer and seller, producer and customer, does not belong in the public domain and nor do the relationships which that language implies. Doctors and nurses do not 'sell' medical services; students are not 'customers' of their teachers; policemen and policewomen do not 'produce' public order. The attempt to force these relationships into a market mould undermines the service ethic, hollows out the institutions that embody them and robs the notion of common citizenship of part of its meaning.

That much is already implicit in the British social-democratic tradition; it builds on old approaches, rather than developing new ones. In two important respects, however, a social-democratic governing philosophy for the turn of the century would have to enter new territory. It would also focus on the institutional architecture of the private sector, and ensure that enterprises take account of stakeholders as well as owners. By the same token, it would abandon the economism which has constricted social-democratic imaginations so narrowly in the last forty years, and insist that wealth should be redefined to include well-being. Well-being should be defined to include obvious indicators like environmental sustainability and a fair distribution of life chances; but it should also include the social capital represented by, and embodied in, a diverse, pluralistic, tolerant civil society, culturally and ethnically heterogeneous and rich in intermediate institutions.

For a new social democracy would borrow heavily from the old Christian Democratic principle of subsidiarity: the principle that decisions should be taken on the lowest level of government appropriate to the issue concerned. Many of the policies needed to restore social capital are best carried out by localities and regions. Some can be made effective only by the institutions of the European Union. Economic and social regeneration of the sort pursued by a number of old industrial cities are examples of the former. Policies to curb the kind of social dumping implied by the neo-liberal (and new Labour) fetish of 'flexible labour markets', to prevent exchange-rate instability and to discipline the world's financial markets—all crucial to a politics of citizenship and social cohesion—are examples of the latter. The only force capable of countervailing the sovereignty of the global market-place is the sovereignty of a federal Europe, as Oskar Lafontaine had realised. But part of the point of European Union is to safeguard the quintessential European values of variety, autonomy and democracy. European federalism would therefore transfer authority and competence downwards to regions and localities as well as upwards to the Union; and it would also correct the notorious democratic deficit in the Union's own institutions.

## Surgeons and Patients

This is only the tip of the iceberg. As long ago as the 1970s, the 'revisionist' social democracy of Anthony Crosland and Hugh Gaitskell—the tacit governing philosophy which had guided the Labour leadership since the closing years of the post-war Labour Government—was in serious disarray. Revisionist social democrats were adrift in seas which their philosophy had not charted, and through which it could not guide them. There was nothing wrong with their values, but the instruments with which they tried to realise them broke in their hands. That was why they lost the battle with the neo-liberal new right, and almost lost the battle with the neo-socialist new left. If the reborn social democracy of our time is to cope with the problems that face it, it must learn from their failures.

They were failures of process, rather than of policy. The problem was not that social-democratic ministers did not know what to do. It was that they did not know how to do it—or, to put it more precisely, how to encourage and enable others to do it. At its heart lay a certain attitude of mind. It was a venerable attitude, the roots of which can be traced back to Peter Clarke's distinction between 'moral' and 'mechanical' reform.[6] The New Liberals, Clarke suggested, were essentially 'moral' reformers. They believed that reform came, in the last resort, from inner changes of value and belief, and therefore put their faith in argument and persuasion. The early Fabians, by contrast, put theirs in 'mechanical' reform, pushed through by the coercive power of the state. Revisionist social democracy was the child of New Liberalism as well as of Fabianism, of course; but the Fabian element in its inheritance had gradually swamped the New Liberal element.

Despite the humanity and generosity of its founders, it degenerated, in practice, into a system of social engineering, perilously dependent on the positivist social sciences of the day. Social scientists, it was assumed, knew or could easily find out what levers the engineers would have to pull in order to put their values into practice. The engineers could then pull the levers in the knowledge that the machine would respond as they wished. There was no doubt that society could be changed by social engineering from the top: there was also no doubt that it was right to change it from the top. Social democrats wanted to do good, but they were more anxious to do good to others than to help others to do good to themselves. As they saw it, the role of public intervention was to provide, to manipulate, or to instruct, rather than to empower. They reorganised the school system instead of trying to foster an appetite for learning. They tried to maintain full employment by macro-economic manipulation from the centre, instead of by giving local communities the instruments with which to develop their economies. They sought to dispense medical care, instead of trying to help people become less dependent on medicine. In spite of its commitment to personal freedom, social democracy in practice gave a lower priority to spontaneity, creativity and autonomy than to efficiency, tidiness and uniformity. Perhaps because of this, or perhaps because the social scientists on which it relied often thought in this way themselves, it also gave more weight to the quantitative and the measurable than to the qualitative and the intangible.

Hand in hand with all this went a curiously simplistic attitude to the state and to the relationship between the state and the intermediate institutions and voluntary associations of civil society. The state was seen as an instrument (or set of instruments) which social democratic ministers could use as they wished. Civil society was seen, all too often, not as an agent, but as a patient: an inert body, lying on an operating table, undergoing social democratic surgery. The surgeons acted for the best, of course, but they acted on the patient from without; the patient merely received their ministrations. But in reality, of course, governments cannot behave like surgeons. Here, at any rate, Hayek was right. It is not possible to re-make society in accordance with a grand design, since no conceivable grand design can do justice to the complexity and reflexivity of human behaviour. Nor is civil society much like a patient. Even in Stalin's Russia and Hitler's Germany, it turned out to have a mind (or minds) of its own, which could not be bent to the dictator's will. In Britain, it was far more recalcitrant. Instead of lying passively on the operating table, it insisted on arguing with the surgeon, or at least trying to do so. Employers, trade unionists, parents, doctors, teachers, civil servants, investors—none of these were content to abide by the decisions which social democratic ministers took on their behalf. And because revisionist social democracy had no place for the notion of civil society, the surgeons were hopelessly disorientated by this behaviour.

Behind all this lay a deep-rooted failure of political imagination. Revisionist social democracy was concerned with outcomes rather than with processes; with results rather than with the methods by which they were pursued. It forgot that, in the real world, process and policy are inextricably entangled; that good policies are likely to be twisted out of shape by bad methods. At its heart lay the old, social liberal notion of positive freedom; of freedom to; of self-fulfilment. But because it concentrated on policy and underestimated process, it failed to see that positive freedom could not be handed out from on high to a grateful society, like chocolate bars at a children's party; that its vision of a fairer and freer society, in which autonomy, dignity and positive liberty would be enhanced and the human personality would flower, could be realised only in action and by the members of the society themselves.

A revised revisionism would link policy with process. It would be a philosophy of facilitators rather than of blueprint-makers: of listeners and negotiators rather than of commanders or manipulators. Like new Labour it would appeal to a communitarian ethic of mutuality and common citizenship, but where new Labour's conception of community and community loyalties is shot through with a disciplinarian paternalism reminiscent of Sidney and

Beatrice Webb, the new revisionism would see them as the products of pluralistic negotiation and debate. It would abandon the dream of a new society, engineered from above by a reforming Government. It would break with the victory-at-all-costs, winner-takes-all mentality which is as fundamental to new Labour as it was to the New Right. Indeed, it would jettison the whole notion of winners and losers, and seek to replace majoritarian democracy on the traditional British model with the consensual model that most continental social-democratic parties take for granted. It would seek the widest possible diffusion of responsibility and power in what John Stuart Mill once called 'the business of life'; and to that end, it would do everything in its power to strengthen the autonomous institutions of civil society and to protect them from the power-hogging tendencies endemic in the central state. In place of the chilling mixture of technocracy and populism that suffuses new Labour's vision of modernisation and modernity it would put the vision of a pluralistic, diverse Open Society, based on Karl Popper's own symbiosis between security and freedom.[7] The cultural and intellectual resources for such a vision exist within the British social-democratic tradition, but they would have to be rediscovered and mobilised. At the moment of writing the prospects do not look particularly encouraging; but it would be wrong to despair on that account. The price of liberty has always been eternal vigilance.

## Notes

1 Karl Polanyi, *The Great Transformation, the political and economic origins of our time*, Boston, Beacon Press, Beacon paperback edition, 1957.
2 Benjamin R. Barber, *Jihad vs. McWorld*, New York, Times Books, 1995.
3 Isaiah Berlin, *Historical Inevitability*, Oxford, Oxford University Press, 1954.
4 Will Hutton, *The State We're In*, London, Jonathan Cape, 1995; John Gray, *The Undoing of Conservatism*, London, Social Market Foundation, 1994; John Kay, *Foundations of Corporate Success, How business strategies add value*, Oxford, Oxford University Press, 1993; Ralf Dahrendorf, *The Modern Social Conflict: an essay on the politics of liberty*, London, Weidenfeld and Nicolson, 1988; Harold Perkin, *The Third Revolution, Professional elites in the Modern World*, London and New York, Routledge, 1996; *Social Justice, Strategies for National Renewal, Report of the Commission on Social Justice*, London, Vintage, 1994; *Report on Wealth Creation and Social Cohesion in a Free Society (the Dahrendorf Report)*, London, 1995.
5 Michael Walzer, *Spheres of Justice. A Defence of Pluralism and Equality*, New York, Basic Books, 1983.
6 Peter Clarke, *Liberals and Social Democrats*, Cambridge, Cambridge University Press, 1978, pp. 1–8.
7 Karl Popper, *The Open Society and its Enemies*, vol. 1, *The Spell of Plato*, London, Routledge and Kegan Paul, 1952 (2nd edn.), pp. 200–1.

# European Social Democracy and New Labour: Unity in Diversity?

DONALD SASSOON

## Introduction

Until recently any scrutiny of the European Left began with an evaluation of its crisis. The ensuing diagnosis was that the Left was dead, or moribund, or had nothing to say; one needed to move on, go beyond, and leave it behind.

Various explanations were tendered, usually concerned with the disappearance of something or other, such as the industrial proletariat or the nation-state. Either way, it could not explain electoral behaviour. People don't switch their vote from Left to Right because they have lost confidence in Keynesianism, or socialism, or the nation-state or because they realise that governments cannot control international money markets. In reality voters don't switch much. The stability of the West European electorates since the end of the second world war has been impressive. The European Left, year in year out, averages about forty per cent of the vote and so does the Right. The voters in the middle, by definition, switch around and determine who is Up and who is Down.

By the late 1990s the European Left was on the ascendancy, notching up a spectacular and unprecedented number of victories. For the first time ever it was in power in no less than twelve European Union states including—another historic first—the four largest countries: Germany, Britain, France and Italy. It is worth setting this in historical perspective. The years 1945–47 had been years of left advance with national unity governments (including both socialists and communists) in France, Italy, Finland, Belgium, Holland, and Austria, and left governments in Britain, Sweden and Norway. Excluded from this advance was Germany (under Allied occupation), Greece (civil war), Spain and Portugal (right-wing dictatorship).

This period was followed by the Boring Fifties, an era of generalised Left retreat except in the Nordic countries. The mid-sixties saw a shift to the Left in Britain (the Wilson governments of 1964–70), in Germany (Grand Coalition 1966–69, followed by social democratic hegemony lasting until 1982) and Italy (entry of the Socialist Party into the Christian Democratic-led coalition).

By the early 1980s the Left was out of power and in crisis (parties out of power are usually in crisis) in Britain and Germany, but it was stronger than ever throughout southern Europe: in France with François Mitterrand, in Greece with Andreas Papandreou, in Spain with Felipe González and in Italy with Bettino Craxi.

When the Berlin Wall was brought down, hasty commentators read the

© The Political Quarterly Publishing Co. Ltd. 1999
Published by Blackwell Publishers, 108 Cowley Road, Oxford OX4 1JF, UK and 350 Main Street, Malden, MA 02148, USA

event as the definitive confirmation that socialism—in both its Soviet and western versions—was dead. According to this view, the collapse of communism had somehow implicated the West European brand of socialism even though it had never advocated central planning, or a one-party state, or the suspension of civil liberties. Yet a significant proportion of the electorate of eastern and central Europe voted for their post-communist parties. Some were even returned to power. Nowhere else in Europe is the 'Left' as strong as in the former DDR where sixty per cent of the vote went to former communists, SPD and Greens.

The commentators failed to notice a well-established historical pattern: parties respond to crises—and to the changed circumstances which led to them—by changing their policies and adapting to new environments. They thus live and fight another day. The rural-based conservative parties survived handsomely the euthanasia of the peasantry and, no doubt, the parties of the Left will outlive the near-disappearance of the factory proletariat.

What was required was a pronounced bout of revisionism and the unloading of much ideological baggage. As recently as the early 1980s the Labour Party was arguing that 'only socialist policies' would stop Britain's long-term decline. The French Socialist Party won the 1981 election explicitly promising to 'break with capitalism' by developing a third way between a social democratic compromise with capitalism and the soviet model. The Italian communists under Enrico Berlinguer also called for a *terza via* between social democracy and soviet communism. In Sweden, social democrats were debating the Meidner Plan aimed at transferring ownership from the private sector to democratically controlled workers' funds.

By the late 1980s such radicalism had melted like snow. One by one, in a more or less uncoordinated manner, more or less gradually, and more or less ostentatiously, the parties of the West European Left adopted more or less novel strategies. In some cases, these represented a clearer definition of policies and principles which had been in the offing for some time. For instance, the idea that socialism should no longer be defined as an end-state, that is as a post-capitalist society, had been pioneered by the SPD as early as 1959 (the Bad Godesberg Programme). The Labour Party's dumping of the old Clause Four in 1995 must thus be seen as a late falling into line with a position already widely held on the continent.

## The Image

The end of the 'teleology of the final aim' (as Willy Brandt put it) was only one aspect of a much wider convergence. In politics, as in religion, nomenclature and images have always had an important role. Less than twenty years ago the tag 'social-democrat' was a term of abuse among Southern European socialists and those Labour supporters who called themselves 'democratic socialists'. Now the term 'socialist' is seldom used. Even the Italian post-communists have eschewed the term, turning themselves first into the

Democratic Party of the Left (PDS) and then into the even more generic Left Democrats (Democratici di sinistra or DS). Inside the mainstream socialist parties, those on the left have found the once-despised label of social democrat more acceptable than the terminology used by the neo-revisionists. Social Democracy has, after all, incontrovertible historical roots which inevitably appeal to those dismayed by the speed with which the left is discarding its heritage.

Those not so dismayed have embraced novelty with great relish. None more so than Tony Blair and the virtually renamed new Labour. But the lure of the new is rather old hat. For over one hundred years modernity has had substantial appeal, hence the proliferation of the term: the New Imperialism, the New Woman, the New Liberalism and, later, the New Order (Hitler), the New State (Salazar), the New Deal (Roosevelt), the New Freedom (Woodrow Wilson), the New Economic Policy (Lenin), down to the now-forgotten New World Order (George Bush) and the *nouveau concert européen* (Jacques Delors), the New Right, the New Left, the New Age, the nouveaux philosophes, the New Economics, etc. Tony Blair's 1996 speech *New Britain: my vision for a young country* echoed Harold Wilson's 1964 *The New Britain*. On the continent we have had, since the mid-1980s, *les nouveaux realistes* in Belgium, the *renovadores* in Spain, and Craxi's *nuovi riformisti* in Italy; after the U-turn of 1982–3 the French socialists called for *la modernisation* against those who were *vieux jeu* and *déjà vu*, and, of course, Kinnock's supporters used the label 'modernisers' with great enthusiasm.

The present-day 'new-ists' or neo-revisionists have little time for their own history. Traditionally, left-wing parties have presented every major change in strategy as a development of what went on before. They stressed continuity. Now they no longer re-write history. They prefer to forget it. This *is* new. Kinnock's crucial role in the transformation of the Labour Party is overlooked. Jospin's image (principled integrity seasoned with a dash of puritanism) is made to contrast as much as possible to that of Mitterrand (crafty liar with a murky past). Simitis's supporters, or *synchronists* distance themselves from Papandreou and D'Alema's from Berlinguer.

Some of the neo-revisionists seek to re-establish a link not only with the liberal tradition of social reforms but also with its commitment to competition. Thus the leader of the Finnish Social Democratic Party, Paavo Lipponen, after losing the general election in 1991, embraced market reforms and declared that he was a liberal 'in the sense that I believe people have really suffered because of lack of competition. We need a real paradigm change . . .' He won the following elections. D'Alema declared in 1995 that he was a European socialist who had embraced liberal policies, attacked the Italian bourgeoisie for its congenital étatisme and looked forward to building a 'normal' country with a 'genuinely competitive market'. In 1998 he became Prime Minister. In Holland, the Labour leader Wim Kok leads a coalition which includes the free-market liberal VVD (and the left-liberals of *Democraten '66*), and excludes the more socially concerned religious-based parties.

In Belgium, where elections are due in 1999, the socialists, who are losing ground to the Liberals, are aware that they are more likely to be the preferred partners of a Liberal-led coalition than the Christian Democrats. Clearly, Blair is not alone in claiming the mantle of the liberal reformist tradition.

Image-making, a necessary part of politics, remains one of the most 'national' forms of communication. It is, after all, about signalling policies and identities using words and symbols which do not have the same resonance from country to country. In France, there is a radical language of republican values which is commonly employed by both the Left and the Gaullist Right. Rising unemployment was opposed not only because it caused distress but also because it was endangering national 'social cohesion'; the term was first coined in France and used by Chirac throughout his successful presidential campaign in 1995. Racism is condemned not only for moral reasons but because it breaks with the universalist principles of the French Revolution. Thus Le Pen's National Front is seen as xenophobic *and* anti-French. Anti-Americanism is a defence of shared cultural values, not the prerogative of left-wing head-bangers. Conversely, in Spain and Italy, nationalism is regarded as part and parcel of Francoism and fascism which in turn are associated with political and economic backwardness; surrendering sovereignty is not viewed as a major catastrophe; Europeanism is central to progressive modernity.

When making comparisons it is imperative to bear in mind not only such cultural differences but also distinct political contexts. It is one thing to point out that twelve out of fifteen EU governments are 'centre-left': Belgium and Luxembourg, however, are led by Christian Democrats. It is another to be so mesmerised by this fact not to notice that only two social democratic prime ministers have an overall majority: Costas Simitis of Greece and Tony Blair. And only Blair's majority is truly secure. Simitis's achievement in bringing Greece within sight of joining the euro may be astounding, but his party, PASOK, is not solidly behind him. There is a significant populist faction led by the Defence minister, Akis Tsohatzopoulos, which harks back to Papandreou's heritage and who are ready to pounce should Simitis ever falter. Moreover, the opposition New Democracy party, unlike the demoralised Tories, is not far behind in the opinion polls.

Elsewhere coalition is the normal state of affairs and Blair's colleagues have to make concessions to allies on their right or, more usually, on their left. In France, Lionel Jospin has communists in his government and cohabits with Jacques Chirac; in Germany Gerhard Schröder, not the darling of his party, having lost Oskar Lafontaine, who was, cannot afford to alienate the Greens, his coalition partners. Elsewhere (Denmark, Sweden and, outside the EU, Norway) the mainstream social-democratic party is supported by left-socialists who want to 'tax-and-spend' and are unenthusiastic about the euro-currency. In Italy, the situation is more complicated than ever. Massimo D'Alema has succeeded in constructing a government unusual even by Italian standards. His eight-party coalition (or seven, there is a debate on this) stretches from the partially 'unreconstructed' communists led by Armando Cossuta (who in turn split from the totally unreconstructed Bertinotti) to former Christian Democrats led by Cossiga whose ambition is to supplant Berlusconi as head of a new centre-right party.

In Britain the Prime Minister is far less fettered. His majority is unassailable. His party is solidly behind him, or pretends to be. All intelligent Liberal-Democrats suck up to him hoping he will deliver PR. The press is more friendly than it has been to any previous Labour prime minister. Meanwhile, search parties are regularly sent out to determine the whereabouts of Her Majesty's Opposition, suspected of whiling away the hours by shooting itself in both feet simultaneously—an exploit once brilliantly performed by Labour.

On the continent the pressure from coalition partners should pull the social democrats to the left, yet they have followed policies not so dissimilar from those pursued by new Labour, as I will show. Nevertheless, they are under greater pressure to offer occasional left-wing justifications and to present policies in terms which sound more radical than they really are. They 'spin' to the left, Labour to the right. But spinning is not everything. Behind the spin are real and more complex issues. On European and international matters, the contrast between Labour and the continental socialists is at its widest, but it is far from endemic; there are significant pressures towards convergence, and these are likely to multiply as we get nearer to the inevitable British decision to jump off the fence and join the euro. There are also significant differences over relations with the USA. How these will evolve will depend on the international situation and on whether the USA will ever get round to formulating something which looks like a foreign policy. Finally, there are differences in the attitude towards trade unions with Labour as the Left government least favourable to the unions. On most other issues, the general direction is one of overall convergence.

## Europe and the World

It took over four decades for the whole of the European Left to become whole-heartedly Europeanist. Initially only the French, Belgian and Dutch socialist parties were pro-European. They were joined by the SPD in the late 1950s, the Italian PSI in the early 1960s, the Italian Communists and the Spanish and Portuguese socialists in the 1970s, the Greek PASOK in the late 1980s along with the Swedes, Norwegians, Austrians, Finns, and Danes. As for the Labour Party, only relatively recently has an overt pro-Europeanism been one of its distinguishing features. Nevertheless, new Labour is quite far from 'leading in Europe', as the spin doctors' shallow slogan would have it. Labour started out in a reactive mode, following a well-established principle of Britain's European policy: oppose any novelty, stall, let everyone come up with plans, ideas and proposals and then, when all the decisions have been taken, the policy framework established, the road traced, only then, join belatedly, grudgingly, while complaining that everyone is ganging up against you.

Labour's original indication of where Europe should go—the mantra of flexible markets—could not possibly have constituted a European policy. Europe has been built through positive integration, by doing more, not less. Strategies have consisted in determining the next step and assembling a coalition of interests behind it. The construction of the single market has been followed by the single currency. The single currency will be followed by fiscal co-ordination and regional policies: that is, by deepening integration, and this will be followed by widening to eastern and central Europe.

Newly elected social democratic leaders in the two countries that have always led in Europe, France and Germany, started out by talking big and settled for something less; but they made a difference and this because they discussed new stages of integration. Jospin (and his finance minister Dominique Strauss-Kahn) did not obtain the major reform of Maastricht and of the European Central Bank they wanted, but the ECB is now likely to be more responsive to the issue of jobs and economic growth than the Bundesbank clone envisaged at Maastricht. The SPD's argument is that there should be coordination between an anti-inflationary monetary policy and a fiscal policy aimed at balancing budgets over the economic cycle. This is a legitimate response to past German mistakes: after unification, Kohl expanded the economy by deficit spending but this caused the automatic reaction of the Bundesbank which raised interest rates to ten per cent. Monetary and fiscal policies were pulling in opposite directions. Hence the pressure for greater coordination from the politicians while the central bankers demur.

Oskar Lafontaine had kicked off by putting on the agenda the issue of eliminating unfair tax competition and introducing majority voting on EU tax policy. This was announced with all the bluster necessary to hit the headlines, one of Lafontaine's least endearing skills. Labour responded with excessive alarm, supported only by the Spanish government, one of the last conservative administrations remaining in Europe. The key factor, here, was not ideology but the low level of business taxation in Britain and Spain. Everyone has known for quite a while that the single market under a single currency will dictate some convergence on taxation. This is why we have economic as well as monetary union. Someone should have explained this to Mrs. Thatcher when she signed up to the single market and to John Major when he signed the Treaty of Maastricht.

Negotiations and disputes over harmonisation start with a great rhetorical flourish about European unity and always end up with countries haggling over how to preserve the competitive advantage of one's own national capitalism. This presents the Labour Government with a particular difficulty. After eighteen years of Conservative government, the distinctive competitive advantages of British industry are low wages, low taxes, weak trade unions, poor working conditions, a flexible labour force, limited job security. One way of defending British capitalism is to ensure that harmonisation does not eliminate these 'advantages'. This was the Conservative strategy. But the Labour Party is committed to a high wage, high skill economy. This requires cooperating with business. The problem is that the current definition of pro-business has been constructed by the Conservatives, and Labour does not know how to re-define the term without reverting to 'old' Labour. The result is a contradictory strategy difficult to handle.

Paris and Bonn's European initiatives—not regarded on the continent as unusual or eccentric—have been depicted by a section of the British press (that owned by Conrad Black and Rupert Murdoch) as so many dastardly foreign plots to do us down. This is unavoidable as long as Europe remains a matter of intense debate. Anti-Europeans are bound to use any new proposal as further evidence that the EU is on the slippery slope to a federal state. The pro-Europeans are usually on the defensive. Though politically strong, Blair's ability to develop a distinct European policy is significantly hampered by the strength—real or perceived—of the eurosceptics and a morbid preoccupation with the Murdoch press. Of course, there are also tactical considerations: the longer a decision on the euro is delayed, the longer will the Conservative Party wallow in its own euro-torments. Other social democrats in countries outside the euro are more constrained than Labour; for instance in Sweden and Denmark public opinion is against the single currency, as are the Left Socialist parties on whose support the social democrats rely.

However, Labour's European and international policy is in constant evolution. Its learning curve is rising steeply, thanks, in part, to its abysmally low starting-point. At the EU Vienna council of ministers (December 1998) Labour negotiated hard (including trivial but popular issues such as the retention of duty-free), but avoided the outraged tones of past British governments and ensured that it was never isolated. Ninety per cent of Euro-politics consists in maximising the number of friends and minimising the number of enemies. This has always been hard to swallow for British governments so accustomed to confrontational politics.

The general direction of Labour policy towards Europe is unmistakably towards convergence. This is plain in defence policy. The traditional British posture was to oppose any defence role for the European Union out of fear that it would undermine NATO. The Anglo-French declaration of December 1998 constituted a historic reversal of that position. Britain—having secured US support—has now accepted the arguments of the Germans and the French that Europe should take on some defence responsibilities—arguments once opposed by the Conservatives at Maastricht and, more recently, by Blair himself in Amsterdam.

## The USA

Though this was a major step forward towards redrawing Europe's security system, it does not follow that Labour is prepared to abandon its 'special relationship' with the USA, a term which describes the automatic British backing for any American initiatives. British foreign policy has been schizophrenic. On the one hand it dreams of terminating the Franco-German entente—the real axis of European integration—by transforming it into a triangular partnership. It then proceeds as if that dream will never come true and resorts to the 'special relationship' not only to find a role in the world, but also to prevent the USA from establishing a preferential relationship with Germany. From Washington's point of view it is quite clear that if the USA is going to have a special relationship with anyone it should be with Germany: it is the largest country in Europe, it is economically much the strongest, it has the greatest influence in eastern and central Europe and with the Russian Federation, it has a direct line with Paris. Britain has therefore to raise the courtship stakes all the time by demonstrating its total subservience, in the hope of dampening the German policy of the USA. In doing so Britain consigns any ambition of 'leading in Europe' with the French and the Germans to the world of dreams.

Herein lies the major difference between Blair and his European colleagues. British pro-Americanism, particularly when it comes to the use of force, has no real equivalent in Europe, at least among social democrats. It is a constant source of puzzlement. The Labour Government participated in the US aerial bombing of Iraq without reservations, apparently content to allow Washington to decide whether and when to strike. No other European government even entertained such a move.

This is not to say that continental social democrats are anti-Americans. Only in France is there a systematic suspicion of American intentions, and, as I suggested, this is connected to cultural preoccupations which transcend the left-right divide. Otherwise anti-Americanism tends to be confined to leftist parties: the Left Socialists in the Nordic countries, the communists in Spain, France and Italy, the Greens in Germany. Among social democrats, since the end of the Cold War, there has been a growth of pro-American feelings. In Greece Simitis has reversed the strong anti-Americanism of his predecessor, Andreas Papandreou, who, originally, had advocated leaving NATO. In Spain González was instrumental in getting Spain to join the Atlantic Alliance. Walter Veltroni, D'Alema's successor as leader of the Left Democrats, and leading exponent of the Kennedy cult in Italy, had even advocated transforming Italy's post-communists into a local version of the American Democratic Party. In Holland, where public opinion tends towards pacifism, the foreign minister is the Liberal Jozias van Aartsen who is enthusiastically pro-American. Last but not least, and a telling illustration of the constraints of office, Joschka Fischer, the leader of the pacifist and once anti-NATO Greens and Foreign minister of the Federal Republic of Germany supported, albeit unenthusiastically, both the expansion of NATO to eastern Europe and the US air strikes in Iraq in December 1998.

Yet there is little doubt that all continental social democrats regard European unity and a European common voice in world affairs of greater consequence than Atlantic solidarity. None of them, with the possible exception of Veltroni, follow Tony Blair's lead in regarding Clinton's

Democrats as part of a common broad international centre-left 'third way' project. And on this issue, neither Blair nor Veltroni appear to be representative of their respective parties.

This is no small matter. To wish to social-democratise the American Democratic Party may be utopian, but it is not an ignoble aim. It is the perfectly legitimate aspiration of much of the left-liberal US intelligentsia. It may even have been Clinton's aim during his first heroic attempts to reform healthcare. However, to seek to align the European Left, and implicitly the European model of social cohesion and welfare capitalism, to the American one, would be a total surrender. The social-democratic European project, if it has any meaning at all, must be to recast at a global level its own model of capitalist management, its greatest achievement so far. This is crucial not only for the future of West European unity, but for the future of the whole of Europe. The post-communist set-up in eastern and central Europe (excluding the Russian Federation) resembles the political systems of western Europe far more than that of the USA. The survival in a reformed and social-democratic form of the post-communist parties is the clearest indication that the preservation and/or enhancement of the West European model of social protection is regarded as a priority throughout our continent. The electoral defeat of neo-liberalism, temporary as it may turn out to be, is a signal that a significant proportion of European citizens, on both sides of what was the Cold War divide, are profoundly attached to social democracy or to its achievements

This will become even more important in the years to come as the crisis of the other great alternative to US capitalism, the Asian model, unfolds. Japan may resolve its own crisis by adopting the American model and adapting itself to it, accelerating the end of its lifetime employment system and accepting the principles of labour mobility and flexibility. In the absence of a sturdy welfare state, this might give rise to a US-style 'underclass' with its associated social strife and high crime rates. How Japan, hitherto an uncommonly cohesive society, would cope with such a transformation is impossible to tell. How this might impact on the evolution of China is equally unfathomable.

Blair's Clintonism, however, should not, at this stage, be regarded as part of a grand design. Far from being a hallmark of new Labour, it appears to be a leftover of traditional Labour Atlanticism and would be easily recognisable as such by Ernest Bevin, Clement Attlee, Hugh Gaitskell, Harold Wilson and James Callaghan. Traditionally, the political function of such magnified Atlanticism was to provide Britain with an extra-European perspective. Self-excluded from European affairs, and realising the impossibility of developing a truly independent world role, Britain harnessed herself to the US. By involving itself seriously in European integration, Labour may find the strength and courage to develop a truly 'new' policy towards the USA, one of friendship, not of subservience. This re-alignment will take place on the terrain of global governance of the economy. The indication is that, on this issue, Britain is lining up with the Europeans insisting that new mechanisms must be set up, including a reform of the IMF and the World Bank. This is paralleled by Britain signing the new Rome treaty on a permanent court for human rights and the agreement banning landmines, leaving the USA isolated on both counts.

## The Economy

Assessing the extent to which Labour diverges from its continental counter-parts in economic policy is no easy task. It is not sufficient, as some commentators do, to list the differences and the similarities. The degree of convergence achieved by the West European economies over the last ten years or so may be unprecedented, but is largely limited to the Maastricht indicators. The economies still exhibit significant differences in growth rates, employment levels, welfare policies, labour market legislation, female participation rates, taxation and so on. Some differences in policies simply reflect such variations and are not an indicator of ideological contrast. A case in point is labour market flexibility, an area where the divergence between Labour and the others has been magnified.

In fact, there is general agreement on both left and right throughout Europe that labour markets should be more flexible. This is so in Göran Persson's Sweden as well as in Schröder's Germany, where wage costs are twice the level of the UK, labour markets are rigid, large companies must establish supervisory boards with almost equal proportion of workers' and employers' representatives, and many work seven-and-half hours shifts from Monday to Thursday and five hours on Friday. Even the trade unions federation (DGB) agreed at their historic Dresden Congress (1996) to greater flexibility over the issue of regional wage contracts. Trade union reluctance is due to their justified suspicion that entrepreneurs see flexibility as freedom to fire. Countries with a high rate of unemployment are less likely to be soft on this kind of flexibility and many are not convinced that labour market rigidity is a major cause of joblessness. Austria has one of the least flexible labour markets in Europe, a large public sector, the highest wage costs, one of the world's lowest average retirement age, yet she has also the lowest rate of unemployment in Europe (after Luxembourg), has attracted huge inward investment, has inflation at one per cent—and needs no lessons on economic management from the British or the Americans. Italy has highly inflexible markets, high non-wage labour costs and a high level of unemployment, but its considerable 'black' economy is, by definition, highly flexible and tax-free. Britain has a high proportion of part-time workers (which helps flexibility), but its average productivity is far lower. The league table of inward investment does not reflect labour market flexibility: in absolute figures, the UK and France (whose labour markets are very different) were the largest recipients of foreign direct investments in 1997 in the industrialised world after the USA.

Just as all parties of the Left pay at least lip service to the concept of flexibility, all of them use (and abuse) the concept of globalisation. This is often taken to mean nothing more startling that it is necessary to be globally competitive, sell more cheaply, produce more efficiently and find a more favourable position in the international division of labour. Globalisation is often used as a convenient scapegoat to justify inaction (can't go against the markets) or simply to convince left-wing followers to accept unpalatable policies.

Similarly, all parties of the Left have committed themselves to the principle that inflation is the number one enemy. This, in fact, has long been an article of faith throughout the political establishment (left and right), unsurprisingly, as inflation, unlike unemployment, impacts on the entire electorate. It is likely that the development of the single market, the growth of intra-European trade and, above all, the single currency, will make an integrated Europe able to tolerate slightly higher levels of inflation than in the past. There are already signs that the obsession with inflation is receding.

All parties of the Left have sought to discard their image of 'tax-and-spend'. When it comes to direct taxation, they are unanimous: further increases, if they are to occur at all, will be limited to indirect taxation. The era of distribution via high income taxation, once the hallmark of the Left, appears to be over. It is not yet clear what have been the structural as well as political changes which have led to the creation of this major shift in consensus. It should also be said that British direct taxes are now among the lowest in Europe and that no alternative has been found to what remains the fairest and most redistributive way of raising state revenue. Business taxes are another matter. One of Blair's first actions was the windfall tax on public utilities. Jospin made a very similar move. In Germany the SPD and the Greens are committed to energy taxes. In Holland Wim Kok's Labour government will increase business taxes.

Resorting to subsidies and incentives to create employment for the younger generation is a further common trait of the western European Left. In many countries, including France, Britain, Germany and Sweden, business and windfall taxes have been used for this purpose.

All parties of the Left have recognised that there are major problems with funding the welfare state, all have put welfare reform at the centre of their agenda and are all encountering difficulties with it. This issue—dealt with in greater depth by Frank Vandenbroucke in his contribution to this volume—presents far greater difficulties for the parties of the Left than for those of the Right. They cannot politically justify cutting welfare budgets on simple budgetary grounds; when they do (as did Labour with the saga of payments to lone parents at the end of 1997) they incur the wrath of their supporters. Some social democratic parties, such as the Swedish, have been elected on an explicit pledge to increase unemployment benefits, sick-pay, child benefits and pensions and reduce charges for nurseries and childcare costs. In France there is a far higher commitment to high quality public services than in the

UK, hence their popularity. In any case, it is more difficult to achieve a reform when the main motivation is to reduce expenditure quickly. Some reforms entail spending more money in the short term in order to achieve greater savings later on. The constraints are also rather similar: unemployment in a welfare state is costly, advances in medical care make healthcare more expensive, prevention through intelligent and farsighted public health programmes do not come cheap (and the saving is far from assured: heart attacks among men in their early sixties is a cost effective way of cutting down on pensions and long-term care). Welfare 'problems' are far from identical from country to country. In Britain the issue of lone parents has been to the fore for many years, reflecting a 'crisis of the family' far more pronounced in the UK than elsewhere. In Holland the welfare problem took the form of the widespread use of invalidity pensions in the 1980s to resolve—with the complicity of doctors—what was, in practice, an unemployment problem. A similar development occurred in the UK in the 1990s. In most European countries pensions are more generous than in the UK either in monetary terms or in the number of years' contributions required. In Italy a school teacher can become a pensioner after only twenty years' work. In Greece a public sector bank manager can retire in his late forties with a pension equal to 120 per cent of his last salary, find employment in a private bank, earn more money and finish at 65 with a golden handshake. In France state pensions are generous—between two-thirds and three-quarters of last salary—and men retire at 60.

A further—and striking—element of convergence is that the issue of nationalisation no longer divides social democrats. They have all abandoned it. Some—in Germany and the Nordic countries—had done so over forty years ago it. In Italy, the possession of a large public sector was associated more with the fascist economic interventionism of the 1930s and the clientelist policies of the Christian Democrats than with the Left. In France, nationalisation was seen as a bulwark against foreign take-overs. Traditionally only the French and British Left were seriously committed to an extension of the public sector. Now this division between nationalisers and non-nationalisers has evaporated as has the Left's prejudice against privatisation.

On this issue too, Blair's modernisers are part of the mainstream. In fact, because privatisation under the conservatives has been so extensive, Labour could now be classified among the most cautious. The Government has decided to retain the Post Office within the public sector (a notable success for the Communication Workers Union and one of the rare union victories) while Schröder will continue with the privatisation of Deutsche Post. In Italy the programme of privatisation started by the centre-left Prodi government is being accelerated by his successor Massimo D'Alema. In France Lionel Jospin has begun to privatise where his Gaullist predecessors have been timid: he pushed through a reduction of the state share of Thomson-CSF group, achieved a successful sale of the first tranche of French Telecom (which Alain Juppé had postponed), then sold a tranche of the aluminium giant Pechiney as well as two-thirds of CIC, France's fifth largest bank, and announced the partial privatisation of Aerospatiale. Further continental privatisations are far more likely to be inhibited by stock market turbulence than by traditional socialist ideology.

Before the general election new Labour had undertaken to become a truly pro-business party. It has kept its promise, bringing businessmen into the government, flattering them, and appointing them to various agencies and positions of responsibility. Such beatification of private enterprise is all the more surprising as Britain has one of the best and most efficient public sectors in Europe, a competent and honest civil service, excellent higher education (well ahead of France and Germany) and an outstanding state broadcasting system. Though old Labour—when in power—was never anti-business, it did not exhibit the positive outlook towards the world of industry and finance which has characterised new Labour. Blair, Brown and company have actually behaved as if they really liked businessmen far more than workers—and they probably do. What is less known is that, on the continent, the courtship of business proceeds in much the same way.

The Italian post-communist leaders Achille Occhetto and Massimo D'Alema have both travelled to the City of London to provide the Italian press with many column inches indicating that they are 'approved' by international financial circles. D'Alema has, of course, representatives of business directly in the government as leading ministers: Lamberto Dini (Foreign Minister and former banker) and Carlo Azeglio Ciampi (Treasury Minister and former chairman of the central bank). He is actively supported by the Italian equivalent of the CBI and is regularly praised by the chief executives of the largest companies, including FIAT and Olivetti.

Lionel Jospin, that scourge of capitalism, has turned out to be far more pro-business than was expected. His 1998 budget was more generous to enterprises than to households, and less redistributive than the spending plans and tax policies Brown announced in July 1998 and March 1999. In opposition, the French socialists had argued that it was necessary to target aid to industry to achieve higher employment, having identified a lack of demand as the principal problem of the French economy. They had objected to Edouard Balladur's programme of fiscal aid to enterprises, on the ground that these lacked customers, not funds. This analysis was far from mistaken. In 1998, though foreign demand decreased, French growth was remarkable, thanks to a sustained domestic demand. This was the result of the socialists' demand-boosting policies (increase in the minimum wage, and in the Contribution Sociale Généralisée) and appropriate to the continental European cycle. This shows how wrong was the rather superficial analysis which contrasted Labour's commitment to upholding Conservative spending limits to the allegedly populist spendthrift initiatives of the profligate French. The truth of the matter is that Labour, having found the British economy at a different point in the cycle, was determined to bring it into line with that of the continent. This is a necessary precondition for joining the single currency and locking Britain, irrevocably, into the European cycle.

Not all policy changes are an indication that past ones were wrong. It does happen, occasionally, that changes in policies reflect changed circumstances (as politicians would do well to remind journalists eternally chasing after great U-turns). Thus now the French Treasury minister, Dominique Strauss-Kahn, probably impressed by US growth, has decided that it is more important to encourage investment by lowering business taxes. Supply-led growth is back in France as it is in Britain. Boosting demand is no longer a priority and, as a result, French pensions after 1999 will be indexed to cost of living and not to salaries.

We are all pro-business now. But is this so new? In power all social democrats had to look after their own capitalism, the goose that lay the golden eggs of full employment and the funds for welfare. The real question is whether one should let business get on with it—the orthodoxy of the right—or control the anarchy of markets by regulatory mechanisms, nationally and internationally.

## Industrial Relations

Where there is a major difference between new Labour and virtually all its continental counterpart is in industrial relations. here some degree of continuity with Thatcherism is manifest. The Labour Party is still the only social-democratic party in Europe which has a direct organisational link with organised labour, yet it is the least favourable to the unions. This is not to say that they have not derived advantages from Labour's victory. By signing up to the Maastricht social protocol, new Labour has granted workers a number of rights they did not have under the Conservatives. There is now a statutory limit to the working week. This parallels the steps towards a decrease in working hours currently being taken in France and Italy. There is also a minimum wage, and this parallels the French increase in their own minimum wage. British trade unions have realised that the few victories they can obtain have all come from the once so despised European Union: equality legislation, right to parental leave, rights for part-time workers, restriction on working hours, paid holidays, recognition rights, minimum wage, consultation rights. Thus the TUC (but many individual unions are dragging their feet) has become one of the most vociferous lobbies in favour of the EU and the Euro.

The Labour Government, however, regards any suggestion of a partnership with the trade unions as belonging to the past, as if it is still necessary to atone for the Winter of Discontent—the real cause of which, ironically, was Labour's decision to stand up to the unions.

Throughout continental Europe, trade unions are regularly consulted on economic policy, pensions and welfare reforms. In the UK, they are virtually excluded from political consultation. At the 1998 TUC congress, Peter Mandelson, then Industry Secretary, declared that 'never again' would the government 'contract out the governance of the UK' to the unions. This, however, was never the issue. The question is whether the trade unions are to be regarded as a mere interest group like many others, or a major economic interlocutor alongside the CBI. As things stand, Labour is certainly pro-business, but is it pro-unions? Britain stands virtually alone against the establishment of Work Councils for domestic industry (firms operating across Europe are required to have them). The redrafting of the *Fairness at Work* White Paper published in May 1998 indicates that Labour's priority is to meet entrepreneurial concerns rather than those of the unions. New Labour appears to want to move closer to the US model of politics, where the unions behave like any other lobby supporting one of two rival pro-business parties.

On the continent trade unions are far more involved in political decision-making. In Italy the centre-left coalition has developed a Social Pact with unions (and employers)—unlike Berlusconi who had sought confrontation (and lost). The French government, though faced with the weakest union movement in Europe (in terms of membership), has actively consulted them. In Germany, the SPD has established at the heart of its employment strategy the so-called Alliance for Work involving both sides of industry. The model for such exercise in consensus-building is Holland where the most successful triangular consultation led to remarkable achievements: unemployment down to 5.3 per cent, half the EU average, a rate of economic growth which, in 1998, has outpaced the rest of Europe for the third year in succession, and a level of wage moderation which has brought about a reduction in direct tax.

Jospin, who, according to the *Financial Times* (14 October 1998) has not put a foot wrong since winning the election, has managed to turn the 35–hours week (decried from all quarters as an absurd concession to the communists) into a pro-business measure, thanks to remarkable financial incentives, and a union agreement to moderate wage demands. Few believe that the measure will create many jobs when it is introduced in 2000, but all agree that there will be gains in productivity.

There is clearly remarkable convergence in economic policy between new Labour and continental social democracy. None of this, however, amounts to some grand new vision for the future. This is not surprising. In politics, such things are not devised in a few days, months, or even years by clever policy wonks beavering away in some backroom. They grow out of concrete circumstances, opportunities created, unforeseen contingent factors; they grow out of history. Social democracy, in spite of its recent victories, is still in crisis, having to cope with new developments in the international organisation of capitalism. After many defeats, it has halted the advance of neo-liberalism and recovered morale.

The string of electoral successes and the remarkable convergence which unites parties once so distant thus provides a unique opportunity. Blair's political courage has been mainly directed towards the transformation of the Labour Party into a powerful electable force, purging it from the remnants of a puerile radicalism. Much of this has required the deliberate occupation of a political space previously occupied by Conservatives. Political innovation has been less evident than on the continent, even though Blair is in a more favourable position: given the size of his majority, the friendly relations with the Liberals, the disarray of the Conservatives, the high probability of winning a second mandate, one expects greater boldness.

## Institutional Reform

Where boldness has been conspicuous is in the field of institutional reforms: Scottish parliament, Welsh Assembly, abolition of the hereditary principles in the Upper Chamber, reform of local government, incorporation of the Convention of Human Rights into the British legal system. To these items we must add the prospect of the introduction of a more proportional electoral system based on the proposals of the Jenkins Commission. What has been achieved so far has already brought about the most important constitutional change since the end of the war. If the impetus for change led to a serious reform of the Lords and a new electoral system, Blair's government would be remembered as a landmark in Britain's constitutional history.

This is all the more remarkable as constitutional engineering has tradition-ally been quite absent from the agenda of the West European Left throughout the post-war period. While the (Leninist) communist tradition decried the liberal bourgeois state as an instrument to be smashed because incompatible with the development of a socialist society, the social democrats went to the other extreme and accepted the existing institutional arrangements *in toto* even when—as in Britain—these were redolent of archaic and feudal features, mostly invented and often ridiculous.

The constitutional part of Blair's 'Project' amounts to a massive redefinition of the powers of the executive, towards a less centralised state. This is all the more startling as the government appears to want to retain control over all forms of devolved power, especially if there is a risk, however minimal, of this falling under the sway of anything smacking of leftism. Yet it is no simple matter to occupy the centre ground while ensuring that there are no opponents on one's left, and to multiply centres of power while keeping control over all of them.

Nevertheless, such constitutional remoulding has required coalition-build-ing skills of which the UK had been hitherto deprived: liberal democrats, Chartists 88, nationalists, libertarians, even 'wet' Conservatives have been harnessed to Blair's institutional revolution to great effect. Here new Labour has been more innovative than continental social democracy, though, of course, the constitutional backwardness of Britain has forced Blair to be more radical. Yet, in this field too, there has been a convergence, especially on the question of devolution of power. This is partly due to the common—if untested—belief that a strongly centralised state may no longer be the best political shell for social democracy, partly due to the strength of regionalist and nationalist movements. These have been evident in Belgium (where regional autonomy appears to have reached a limit beyond which the state itself would implode), Spain (where the successes of the Catalan nationalists have stabilised the regional set-up) and Italy (where the strength of the Northern League has forced the left to enlarge its commitment to devolution).

Not everywhere has decentralisation been popular. For instance, in Portugal the socialist government's plan to divide the country into eight administrative regions which would elect their own assemblies and regional presidents was heavily defeated in the referendum held in November 1998. In France, however, Jospin appears to want to build on the legacy of the first Mitterrand presidency, whose de-centralisation was unparalleled in French history. One of his main priorities, however, is the democratisation of the French Senate. This Gallic equivalent of the House of Lords is indirectly elected for nine years (one-third renewed every three years) by the so-called *grands électeurs* i.e. those elected to public office in local government. As a majority of these are rural municipal councillors, the conservatives have an inbuilt majority. Jospin wants to make the composition of the Senate reflect more closely the composition of the National Assembly. He and Blair thus face a similar problem: how to democratise the Upper Chamber without transforming it into a rival or a mere twin of the lower chamber.

Jospin's proposed constitutional changes also include strengthening the principle of gender parity, thus progressing beyond the more defensive principle of non-discrimination on grounds of sex enshrined in the present constitution. He also wants to grant greater independence to the judiciary (the UK parallel comes from the incorporation of the Human Rights Convention into British law, which gives more powers to the judiciary) and extend legal recognition to non-married people including homosexual couples (the UK parallel is a lowering of the age of consent for homosexuals).

Further major constitutional and legal changes are afoot in the rest of social-democratic Europe. One of the most significant is likely to come from Germany. At present its nationality laws are based on the racist principle of the *jus sanguinis* which grants greater residence rights to people of German origins, including those who do not speak the language and never resided in the country, than to the millions of Kurds, Turks and Arabs who work, live, and pay taxes in the Federal Republic nor to their children even if born in Germany. The Red-Green coalition has promised to revise these laws, incorporating into German law the principle of the *jus solis* (as in France and Britain) whereby citizenship is also granted to those born in the country.

## Conclusion

My contention throughout this essay has been that the degree of unity outweighs the inevitable diversity typical of the West European Left, and that such unity or convergence is unprecedented. This provides the Left with a rare opportunity for reshaping the continent. The stakes are considerable. The Left has now identified itself firmly with the European project. The failure of this project would be far graver than a mere electoral defeat. Such defeats often amount to the ordinary losing of battles, and hence to reversible retreats.

The collapse of the European project, however, would be like losing the war. It would foreshadow the dissolution of the European Left in any recognisable shape. It is unlikely, after all, that the Left could reconstruct itself in any viable form out of the inevitable economic and political dislocation which would occur. With Europe sinking, once again, in regional rivalries, squabbling nationalisms, and narrow politicking, there would be no serious obstacle left to the world-wide hegemony of unfettered market forces.

# European Social Democracy: Convergence, Divisions, and Shared Questions

## FRANK VANDENBROUCKE

TAKING a long-term view of social-democratic history, Donald Sassoon argues, convincingly, that we witness 'an unprecedented, Europe-wide convergence of the parties of the Left'.[1] There seems convergence of a short-term nature too. Read a sample of the European literature on the welfare state published over the last five years by centre-left policy institutes, parties and scholars. In chronological order, you may start with the 1994 report issued by the British Commission on Social Justice, and end by reading the chapters on the German welfare state in the 1998 report published a few months ago by the 'Zukunftskommission' of the social-democratic Friedrich Ebert Stiftung (Zukunftskommission der Friedrich-Ebert-Stiftung, *Wirtschaftliche Leistungsfähigkeit, sozialer Zusammenhalt, ökologische Nachhaltigkeit. Drei Ziele—ein Weg*, Dietz, Bonn,). Despite important national differences, you will be struck by the recurrence of the following fixed points, on which many social democrats seem to agree:

1 Welfare policy cannot be reduced to employment, but employment is the key issue in welfare reform. Moreover, the nature of the employment objective has changed. 'Full employment' as it was conceived in the past in most European countries, underlying traditional concepts of the welfare state, was full employment for *men*. The social challenge today is full employment for men and *women*. This is linked to the transformation of family structures and our conception of women's role in society. It points to the need to rethink both certain aspects of the architecture of the welfare state and the distribution of work over households and individuals as it spontaneously emerges in the labour market.

2 The welfare state should not only cover social risks as we traditionally defined them (unemployment, illness and disability, old age, child benefits). It should also cover new social risks (lack of skills, causing long-term unemployment or poor employment, single parenthood) and new social needs (namely, the need to reconcile work, family life and education, and the need to be able to negotiate changes within both family and workplace, over one's entire life cycle).

3 The 'intelligent welfare state' should respond to those old and new risks and needs in an active and preventive way. The welfare state should not only engage in 'social spending', but also in 'social investment' (e.g. in training and education).[2]

Published by Blackwell Publishers, 108 Cowley Road, Oxford OX4 1JF, UK and 350 Main Street, Malden, MA 02148, USA

4 Active labour market policies should be higher on the agenda and upgraded, both in quantity and in quality, by tailoring them more effectively to individual needs and situations. Active labour market policies presuppose a correct balance between incentives, opportunities and obligations for the people involved;

5 Taxes and benefits must not lead to a situation in which poor individuals (or their families) face very high marginal tax rates when their hours of work or their wages increase, or when they take up a job. Benefit systems that are too selective, are beset by 'poverty traps', as in the UK. 'Unemployment traps'—discouraging mainly low-skilled workers from taking up jobs—characterise not only selective welfare systems, but some other systems as well, in differing degree.

6 It is necessary to subsidise low-skilled labour, by topping up low-skilled workers' pay, or by selectively subsidising employers, combined with decent minimum wages.

7 People who work part-time or in flexible jobs should be adequately integrated in and protected by the social security system.

8 Such an 'intelligent welfare state' needs an economic environment, based upon both a competitive sector, exposed to international competition, and the development of a private service sector, which is not exposed to international competition, and in which low-skilled people find new job-opportunities. Continental Europe typically lags behind in the development of the private service sector. Wage subsidies for low-skilled people can also be instrumental in that respect.

Delors has written an excellent short paper for the Party of European Socialists on a 'new model of development', in which the foregoing points—concerning the family and the distribution of work, wage-subsidies for the low-skilled, development of the service sector, etcetera—fit very well.[3] One finds the same core insight—that tackling unemployment and reforming the welfare state requires a new European social and *economic* model—in many social-democratic documents. The Friedrich Ebert Stiftung's Zukunftskommission proposes a 'new German model' along the same lines, stressing, for instance, the need to create a market for low-skilled labour in services.

The recurrence of these 'fixed points' reflects the potential for a useful convergence of views on the welfare state among European social democrats, at least on the level of general diagnosis and general policy guidelines. I do not suggest that a consensus on such guidelines would lead to close convergence of national social models within the European Union, or to close convergence of practical policy measures. Different political, institutional and cultural backgrounds explain why differences in measures and in models will persist; imposing homogeneity would certainly not be sensible. Nevertheless, indicating such a convergence of general views on employment and employment-centred welfare reform among social democrats is not a theoretical exercise. For instance, without this kind of convergence the political process set in motion by the 1997 Luxemburg Job Summit would have been more difficult. It is one of the reasons why the discussion of the National Action Plans and the elaboration of European Guidelines for Employment Policies turned out to be a substantive exercise—contrary to what sceptics might have feared.[4] More fundamentally, without common vision on the future of the European social model, however diversified, European politics is doomed to stagnate and, finally, to fail.

Of course, establishing the potential for convergence of views on the welfare state entails much more than what I have said so far. A comprehensive approach of welfare reform requires positions on the future of pensions, health care, and the much-debated issue of universality versus selectivity in social security. It is possible to specify 'fixed points' on these issues, similar in terms of generality to the fixed points I deduced concerning employment and employment-centred welfare reform. If formulated on a suitably foundational level, they stand a good chance of representing much of European social-democratic thought and practice today. Consider, for instance, the following statement on universalism, which I would add to my list of fixed points:

9 Neither selectivity of benefits nor universalism are social-democratic dogmas: they are not foundational values, but methods to be judged on the basis of efficiency and stability. These criteria are interconnected: stability depends upon legitimation of welfare state provisions in the eyes of the public at large; efficiency, together with other considerations, supports legitimation. In some sectors universalism can lead to visible 'waste' of money, and so undermine legitimacy. But in other sectors (e.g. health) universalism can be a precondition to sustain a broad base of support for the welfare state, and to create communal experiences in society. Selectivity—in the form of an 'affluence test' rather than a 'poverty test'—can be a condition for efficiency. However, too much selectivity typically catches people in poverty traps and reduces efficiency. In other words, social democrats should find an appropriate, 'broadly based' balance. The foundational value in this endeavour is the idea of a fair distribution of burdens and benefits, and the political challenge is to find majority support for a distribution that is accepted as fair.

Again, it has to be stressed that convergence of view on this level of thinking will not necessarily lead to convergence on practical measures. I advocated somewhat more selectivity in parts of the Belgian welfare state during the eighties, against received wisdom in some quarters of my party, because I considered them at that moment as insufficiently selective. In the UK, on the other hand, it is understandable that reformers on the centre-left stress universalism, against the prevailing British systems of means-testing. To understand each other's practical positions, we should not generalise from our parochial situations, but look for more general principles underpinning our positions.

So, taking Sassoon's long-term view, it is plausible to present recent social-democratic history as one of convergence; taking a short-term view, one can identify points of convergence on subjects such as employment and welfare reform. However, the account of 'fixed points' I have summarily sketched here leaves open some basic normative questions, and it also overlooks or conceals divisions and differences in emphasis within the European centre-left. I will first discuss a division that is, I believe, important for the immediate future. Then I will return to normative questions left open by my scheme.

## Keynesians Versus Supply-siders?

Confronted with my fixed points, many social democrats would add that the emphasis on employment for low-skilled workers must not lead to a one-sided approach. To be successful, they would say—and I would concur with them—targeted employment policies require a sufficient overall pressure of demand for labour. Hence macroeconomic policy is important. More precisely, as the French, German and Italian governments and some others argue: Europe needs macroeconomic policy coordination, *a fortiori* in the context of EMU. They thereby appeal to some basically Keynesian insights.

This appears to be a division between the British Third Way on the one hand and much of continental social democracy on the other. Now, words can exaggerate differences; one might argue that the fiscal stance of the UK government over the next three years is classically counter-cyclical. Moreover, one should not be afraid of some internal division within the centre-left: that is the stuff of politics. Yet, what worries me is that some arguments presented as inspiring the Third Way seem unable to grasp the relevant discussion.

The demise of Keynesianism is essential in Giddens's construal of the *need* for a Third Way, as he explained in *Beyond Left and Right*: 'Keynesianism became ineffective as a result of the twin and interconnected influences of the intensified globalisation and the transformation of everyday life. . . . Keynesianism worked tolerably well in a world of *simple modernisation*; but it could not survive in a world of *reflexive modernisation*—a world of intensified social reflexivity. Reflexive citizens, responding to a new social universe of global uncertainties, become aware of, and may subvert, the economic incentives that are supposed to mobilise their behaviour. Keynesianism, like some forms of policy which helped structure the welfare state, presumes a citizenry with more stable lifestyle habits than are characteristic of a globalised universe of high reflexivity.'[5]

Since we are not given a shred of empirical support for the supposed link between lifestyle instability and the demise of Keynesianism, this remains a rather dogmatic statement. But that is not the main point I want to make here. This way of thinking overlooks the *real* difficulties social democrats have encountered with Keynesian policies in the past, and it makes it hard to engage in an intelligent and productive dialogue with, for instance, the French and the Germans today.

I cannot go through all the arguments here, but let me put it as follows. The identification of 'classical social democracy' with 'effective Keynesianism' relies on hidden assumptions, which are too easily taken for granted. Once, so it is assumed, we lived in a 'golden age' during which, first, the appropriate policy for social democrats confronted with unemployment was *in all circumstances* some mixture of fiscal and monetary demand expansion organised by governments. Keynesianism, so conceived, was essentially unproblematic in less open economies. Neither of these assumptions is true.[6] In his important work, *Crisis and Choice in European Social Democracy*, Scharpf neatly expounds various problem constellations for which fiscal or monetary demand management offers no solution: stagflation, fuelled by cost-push inflation, is one example. Incomes policies were the key additional instrument needed to tackle stagflation. So, close cooperation between governments and unions was necessary.[7] Even when confronted with the usual swings of the business cycle successful economic policy depended on the voluntary cooperation of unions and employers. The policy instruments directly available to governments do not suffice to cope with all problem constellations, not even in a closed economy.

I stress this point, not because external constraints, enhanced by international economic integration, do not exist; they do. I stress it to eliminate the bizarre idea that 'in the golden era'—before globalisation, so to speak—social democracy could always successfully rely on the single track of fiscal and monetary demand management by governments to fight unemployment, whatever the problem constellation causing it. Returning to contemporary discussions, the real issue may be formulated as follows. Successful macroeconomic policies—successful, that is, from the point of view of social democrats—require coordination and mutual trust between at least three actors, or sets of actors: budgetary authorities (governments), monetary authorities (central banks), and employers and trade unions who negotiate wage increases. The requirement facing the latter is, more precisely, the acceptance of some discipline concerning the growth of the average wage level in both slack and tight labour markets. The difficulty of achieving coordination and trust between these actors is exacerbated now on the European level, where we will have layers of governments, layers of employers and trade union organisations, and one monetary authority. Now, the French, following longstanding pleas by Delors, have a project, designed to overcome this difficulty, which they summarise by the idea of *'un gouvernement économique'*—an economic government for Europe. The idea, replicated summarily in Lafontaine's writing,[8] is that, within the Euro-zone, close economic coordination between governments should create *'un pôle économique'*, i.e. a point of reference for the Central Bank, and that this should, ideally, be supplemented by some forms of Europe-wide collective bargaining. This generates a complex agenda, to which specific proposals concerning coordination between the various Councils of Ministers are added.

Space forbids pursuing this in any detail, let alone to discuss the strengths and weaknesses, the opportunities and the risks involved. Here, I only want to stress that a sensible reading of this approach is that it is structural: it intends to create the institutional conditions for a sustainable mix of demand and supply policies, more precisely for the necessary flexibility in monetary management, *à la* Greenspan, the successful president of the American FED. Although the approach relies on Keynesian insights, there is no question of a 'dash for growth', nor of 'Keynesian fine tuning'—these, so we learned, are illusions. Also, demand policy is likely to be most effective when based upon monetary policy; fiscal policy will play a lesser role than the traditional conception of Keynesianism suggests. What we need, institutionally, is the creation of sufficient trust and coordination among the main actors, so that the ECB can confidently relax monetary policy when it is economically indicated. The essential difficulty in this approach is the perception of an irreversible decline in the coherence and cohesion of collective bargaining and corporatist institutions in Europe. The challenge in that respect is to create new forms of successful national corporatism, and to design a European model that can incorporate the variety of national models. Although optimism of the will should, in these matters, be counterbalanced by pessimism of the intellect, all-out pessimism on the future of collective bargaining is not warranted: the Netherlands provides a well-known example of the possibility of successful neo-corporatism.

My concern is this: here we have defining issues for the immediate and longer-term future of European social democracy, and a source of potentially disruptive and destabilising divisions between European governments. The intellectual framework underpinning Giddens's presentation of the Third Way offers no purchase on this debate; in a sense it declares itself un-interested. It claims that the world has changed so dramatically that textbook macroeconomic analysis and steering have become *irrelevant*. I believe that this is not only wrong, but also that it hampers one's capacity to engage in key debates within European social democracy, such as the management of the Euro, the future of European collective bargaining, the future of budgetary politics, the future of the European model *tout court*. The fact that Giddens lists corporatism as one characteristic of social democracy, but defines it as 'state dominates over civil society', reinforces the intellectual difficulty created by his implicit dismissal of textbook macroeconomics. As Colin Crouch has pointed out, this shows little understanding of what neo-corporatist industrial relations meant in those countries where they were most practised.[9] It precludes a useful dialogue on the role of corporatist structures in the renewal of the European model on the continent.

Problems of language and communication play some role, but should not stand in our way. Clearly, *'un gouvernement économique'* sounds *a priori* fine to many French ears, but the French will have to realize that 'an economic government' is not exactly *'un slogan porteur'* for Anglo-Saxons. But, apart from problems of presentation, overcoming this division requires open and undogmatic discussion on the level of empirical theory. The basic fact, from which one should start, is that the European nations are confronted, first and foremost, with a *thorough Europeanisation* of their economies rather than with their globalisation (which is not to deny that globalisation is an issue in its own right). Economic reality dictates European economic governance.

Nearly all continental social democrats add proposals on tax coordination to this agenda of European economic governance. The problems of taxation and the welfare state are interconnected. For instance, gradually introducing new sources of funding for social security, such as taxing the consumption of energy, to diminish taxes on employment and to create more jobs, requires European coordination. If the extreme caution with which new Labour operates in this domain is tactical, the disagreement concerning tax coordination may turn out, in the longer term, to be not fundamental and can be surmounted. If, however, the British aversion to discuss tax coordination is ideologically entrenched, some of my optimism concerning the potential for positive convergence on welfare reform will be seriously dented. In the latter case, it will be very hard, if at all possible, to shape a common European approach to employment and welfare reform beyond what the Luxembourg and Cardiff summits have already achieved.

## Shared Normative Questions

The foregoing discussion calls for careful analysis of changes in our economic and social environment. Scrutiny of the facts often reveals that the real changes are less spectacular; or less decisive, than sweeping generalisations suggest. This *caveat* not only holds for some of the views discussed in the previous section, but also for some of the 'fixed points' mentioned in the first section. (The truth is often complex and unexciting. Balanced reasoning and empirical verification are, sadly, not the stuff of best-sellers.) However, locating the essential discussion about the future of social democracy in changes in the world in which social democracy operates also reflects an *a priori* judgement that may be mistaken. Maybe it is not primarily the world that needs to be reconsidered, but our social-democratic system of values. I, for one, believe that social democrats should be prepared to rethink the way they translate their foundational values— such as 'equal concern for all people'—into normative standards of justice, that is, into conceptions of rights and duties, and into criteria for distributive justice. This goes against the grain of much of our discussion on social democracy or the Third Way. In political discourse 'values' are often defined in very general terms. To say, then, that 'our values are unchanged', but that the world has changed, so that we have to revise the practical implementation of our values, is politically and emotionally comfortable—we do not lift the anchor of our values—yet it does not tell the whole story. However reassuring it may sound, it is not necessarily a true reflection of what is going on in the debates on social democracy and the Third Way. Between foundational values and practical implementation lie standards of justice, that is, normative criteria indicating what is, ideally, to be achieved for a society to be just. It may well be the case that many social democrats are now in the process of reviewing, not their values, but their standards of justice, so conceived. *A priori* I do not consider this a problem. Maybe we *should* revisit and review settled ideas on justice in society. Therefore, I find Tony Blair's insistence on the importance of the discussion of ideas and values most welcome. Although he stresses very much the unchanged character of social-democratic values, he simultaneously and on many occasions has made it clear the discussion is 'about ideas'.

I would like to mention, briefly, some normative questions concealed by my account of the centre-left's fixed points on social policy at the end of this century. But first I should point out that the awareness that full employment can no longer be defined in the traditional 'male' sense (my fixed point 1) has led, in many quarters if not everywhere, to an even more fundamental shift in objectives than the one I specified in the first fixed point. Nowadays it is not so much unemployment figures that exercise policy makers, in their longer term thinking, but labour market *participation rates.* This is quite a different thing, both in a practical and in a more fundamental sense. Characteristically, governments are less and less interested in fiddling with unemployment statistics. They also consider the growing number of people in disability or early retirement schemes to be as problematic as unemployment figures. The drive towards increased participation rates is supported with references to the value, for each citizen, of active participation in society, and/or references to the idea of inclusion. I propose to start from that idea, however vaguely defined.

If we take it that participation is the value underpinning employment policies, we can formulate one cluster of questions, concealed by my fixed points, as follows: *what* is it participation *in, why* is that so important, and how do we want to distribute the *benefits and burdens* of the drive towards participation—if we really mean to achieve an inclusive society, that is a society in which *all* participate?

In practice, references to inclusion and participation focus on a narrow definition of participation, that is, participation in the labour market. Moreover, increasing participation is sometimes seen, essentially, as increasing participation in the private sector of the labour market. This reflects a morality of 'supported self-reliance', i.e. a morality stressing both the importance of self-reliance, and the need for governments to support the individual's effort to achieve it, by means of training, education, etc. The idea of self-reliance has, partly at least, a moralistic (or paternalistic) flavour: paid labour is so central in this approach not only because of the monetary and non-monetary rewards for those who do it—such as self-esteem—but also, I take it, because of the beneficial effects it has on the way people structure their lives and integrate into society. A slight degree of such moralism in political discourse—'the government knows what is good for you'—does not disturb me. More importantly, one should certainly not dismiss the value, for the individual, of non-monetary rewards from labour market participation: it *is* important, and there is nothing paternalistic in recognising *that* fact. (Note, though, that one can construe the argument for taking labour market participation as the central policy objective quite differently. Increasing labour market participation is crucial in an ageing society, if we want to be able to maintain a certain parity between the benefit levels for the inactive and the average wage of the active, an argument used in the Dutch debate. This is a much more down-to-earth justification for increased labour market participation, focussing on the economic viability of a generous welfare state.) Labour market surveys show that many people willingly pay a monetary 'price'—having less overall net income than they would if they were to live on benefits—to obtain the esteem and self-esteem provided by self-reliance. Phelps's argument for a massive programme of employment subsidies to boost the income of people with low economic productivity explicitly refers to the idea that achieving self-esteem in a market economy can be valuable but quite costly for individuals:

The measure of cash reward for the *work* supplied by the disadvantaged to the market economy is only their *earnings*. And the *net* reward from this work is only the *excess* of these earnings over the entitlement benefits for which these workers become ineligible as a result of their wage income. Our self-esteem from being self-supporting, not dependent upon the state or kin, hinges on our sense that what we have provided ourselves and our families is largely due to our own efforts. If the net reward is actually negative and large, those low-wage workers with comparably low private wealth may feel themselves too poor to be able to afford the pecuniary sacrifice necessary to 'buy' the self-esteem of being self-supporting.'[10]

In other words, for a society to be really inclusive, achieving self-esteem via self-reliance must be 'affordable' *for all*.

If we really mean it, the inclusive society is not a cheap option. It requires not only extensive investment in education and training, massive subsidies to increase the net-income of low-productivity people as Phelps proposes, but also, as Solow emphasises, the effective supply of jobs via which people can participate in economic life. According to Solow, the crucial question is who will pay for the achievement of an inclusive society. As for the American welfare debate, Solow concludes: '(W)e have been kidding ourselves. A reasonable end to welfare as we know it—something more than just benign or malign neglect—will be much more costly, in budgetary resources and also in the strain on institutions, than any of the sponsors of welfare reform have been willing to admit. And the reasons are based on normal economics.'[11] Solow's point can be put in yet another way, with reference to some empirical facts. High employment rates are a necessary but not a sufficient condition for fair equality of opportunity in society or social inclusion, as comparative figures on poverty in the working age population show (if we take that as one good yardstick for social exclusion). The relative poverty rate for the working age population in the US is almost twice as high as in Germany or France, and almost four times as high as in Belgium, although a far greater proportion of the working age population has at least one job in the US. Likewise, poverty at working age appears to be more widespread in Australia, Canada and the UK, all of which are countries with much better employment records than most of the Continental European countries.[12] Note that this in no way diminishes the individual and collective value of citizens' participation in the labour market. These figures question whether high employment rates are a sufficient condition to achieve, for the population of working age, the normative value we attach to the idea of participation.

Moreover, if participation is to be a central and overarching value for social democrats, it cannot be limited to participation in the labour market. First, active participation in the community can be pursued by activities outside the labour market—think of the role of parents in local schools. In general, care should be considered as a valuable form of participation in society. A comprehensive view of active participation implies that more be done to allow people to combine work and family life, not only by providing professional childcare, but also by means of flexible systems for short and long-term parental sabbaticals, available to the whole labour force and not only to a lucky minority. Pursuing a comprehensive view of participation suggests even more ambitious propositions. The Dutch social democrats proposed the introduction of an overall 'participation law' in their social security system, covering various activities, going from training, job search, to specified socially useful work outside the market; it seems that the Dutch coalition government now pursues this idea by promising 'framework legislation on care and leave'. Atkinson's participation income is a yet more radical proposal, set in the context of a criticism of means-testing.[13]

## Citizenship and Responsibility

I hope these summary remarks suffice to show that the goals of participation and inclusion inevitably put both the ideals and the practical politics of redistribution high on the agenda. They do so not necessarily because we start from egalitarian convictions (Phelps explicitly says that he is not an egalitarian), but because huge burdens and benefits are to be distributed in the process of achieving participation and inclusion. Social democracy has to define itself both by its ideals of distributive justice and by its pragmatic capacity to build coalitions between 'winners' and 'losers'. Social democracy is a broad church, but it cannot flourish without a recognisable and unifying identity. Standards of distributive justice—motivated by equal concern for all—and democracy are key elements in that respect. However different the national institutional backgrounds, these are questions shared by all parties of the centre-left in Europe. Related to these issues, a further normative query confronts the parties of the centre-left: it concerns our conceptions of citizenship and responsibility. I cannot discuss these complex questions exhaustively here. Plant's interpretation of the British New Deal provides, however, a useful background for some brief points. Plant argues that the New Deal instantiates 'not only (. . .) quite a different view from social democracy, at least in its mid-century UK form, it also implies a role for the state, for bureaucracy and for the purposes of taxation which could not be justified by neo-liberal ideas.' New Labour's welfare reform is a 'genuine alternative' to both the first (neo-liberal) way and to the second (social-democratic) way. What is at play, according to Plant, is something one might call 'supply side citizenship': '(I)n a global market there cannot be a rich and growing form of end status citizenship; that is to say, a bundle of goods which are due to the citizen as a right outside the market. Rather, supply side citizenship stresses that citizenship is an *achievement*, not a *status*, it is available through participating in the labour market and reaping the rewards that accrue from that, and investment in skills is part of equal opportunity as a right of citizenship in this new economic context.' Still, this approach has more in common with social democracy than with neo-liberalism, in Plant's view. But it differs from social democracy in yet another respect: '(T)he question of whether the position of the poorest groups equipped with marketable skills will improve relative to the rich will be, so far as I can see, a matter for the market to determine. Either these skills will allow the poorest groups to improve their position in the market, or they will not. The social democrat, however, wants to see such a policy pursued as a direct aim of government, not as something to be left to the market.'[14]

With reference to Labour's *actual* policies, Plant slightly overplays the last argument, since the transition from the Family Credit to the Working Families Tax Credit will change the results of the market reward structure more or less significantly for nearly one fifth of British families. Moreover, the increased expenditure entailed by the enhanced generosity of the new system for low-income families appears, on closer scrutiny, to be pure 'deadweight' from an economic point of view: the officially planned extra spending concerns expenditure that will not act as an incentive to change behaviour, but will go to people who are expected to continue to do the same jobs with the same earnings as they would have done without the change. In other words, the British government is using the language of incentives to sell a redistributive programme. However, I believe Plant has a point, in that a cluster of ideas is at play, the constitutive elements of which cannot simply be read as classical social democracy and neo-liberalism. Behind the New Deal there is, first and explicitly, the general notion of 'reciprocity', or, 'no rights without responsi-bilities'; secondly, there is, more implicitly, the emphasis on participation in market exchange and market reward as the instrument of reciprocity. In other words, if we disentangle the underlying ideas as Plant presents them, then it can be argued that we have here, first, the introduction of a new, respons-ibility-sensitive conception of social democracy, and, secondly, the narrowing down of the idea of personal responsibility to reaping the rewards generated by market exchange. I believe the first idea is promising, while the second, if pursued without correction, is troublesome.

We have good reasons to develop a more responsibility-sensitive conception of social democracy. Today even more than in the past, social democracy needs a moral programme, if it is not to become hostage to the natural tendency to conservatism of an 'affluent majority' and degenerate to the defence of sectional interests. I believe a coherent moral programme has to be built around an ethic of responsibility. Although personal responsibility regularly surfaced as a theme in social-democratic discourse during this century and sometimes played an important role, it would be disingenuous to claim, now, that it was always prominent in our thinking. Blair is right when he says that in recent decades, responsibility and duty were the preserve of the Right. He thinks it was a mistake for them ever to become so, for they were powerful forces in the growth of the labour movement in Britain and beyond.I think four features distinguish a responsibility-sensitive conception of social democracy from a market-exchange conception of responsibility. First, in a responsibility-sensitive conception of social democracy the government not only levels the playing field and equips and helps people to confront the market, it is also prepared to change the result of the market reward structure in a more egalitarian direction by means of taxes and subsidies, when differential market reward is *not* a true reflection of personal responsibility and effort. Second, in a responsibility-sensitive conception of social democracy the government accepts as part of its responsibility to ensure that sufficient opportunities for participation in the labour market do emerge. Third, a responsibility-sensitive social-democratic government takes it that citizens display social responsibility in various forms of participation, not only in the labour market, but also in caring and other social activities that the market does not remunerate. Fourth, 'the easy rhetoric about the moral responsibilities of the poor and the powerless should be more than matched by a more difficult rhetoric about the social obligations of the rich and powerful'.[15]

Earlier I argued that the goals of participation and inclusion inevitably put both the ideals and the politics of distribution high on the agenda. Distributive justice has to be based on the foundational value of 'equal concern for all'. What standards of justice can now best be thought to realise the value of 'equal concern'? Some abstract problems discussed in the framework of egalitarian philosophy over the last 20 years are highly relevant in this respect, since they provide the possibility to develop a true social-democratic, responsibility-sensitive conception of equality. The reconciliation of appropriate conceptions of equality with appropriate conceptions of personal responsibility has been a focal point of many exchanges in the philosophical domain developed by Rawls, Sen, Dworkin, Cohen, Arneson, Roemer, Kolm, Barry . . . Crucial arguments relate to the difference between 'having a talent' and 'deserving' the compensation for using that talent in the market. At first sight, it might appear as if abstract discussions about 'talents' are far removed from the real world. Many people would object to such theoretical preoccupations that individual talents are not overwhelmingly important in determining income distribution. And from the traditional point of view of the left, with its emphasis on the distribution of material means of production, such a focus on human capital is a radical change of perspective. I believe, however, that these reflections on the meaning and normative consequences of differences in human capital are crucially important. They can be connected with what many modern social democrats consider a key social issue in actual societies.

Julian Le Grand captures a core idea of modern egalitarian philosophy as follows: '(O)ur judgements concerning the degree of inequity inherent in a given distribution depend on the extent to which we see that distribution as the outcome of individual choice. If one individual receives less than another owing to her own choice, then the disparity is not considered inequitable; if it arises for reasons beyond her control, then it is inequitable.'[16] Equality, so conceived, is *not* uniformity, for instance uniformity of income, independent of people's personal choices and personal effort (for the simple reason that this would constitute *in*equality in social advantage). It is however more demanding than 'equality of opportunity' as the latter is conventionally used: individuals' choice sets, Le Grand goes on to say, are determined not only by the social and individual barriers they face but by their initial resources or endowments, which include their natural abilities and the resources that they acquire through inheritance, gifts, family background, education prior to the age of majority, etc. Equalisation of choice sets thus may require judicious manipulation of economic and other barriers in order to advantage the less well endowed. Or it may require compensating those with little natural ability by other resources, such as education, so as to bring their range of choices as close as possible to those naturally endowed. One may add to the last example the possibility that people who perform poorly on the labour market, independent of their will, have to be compensated financially via redistributive taxation, wage subsidies or mechanisms like the Working Families Tax Credit. Personal responsibility, based upon choice, is thus a key concept in modern egalitarian philosophy.

Personal skills are the combined result of individual talents and effort to develop those talents. Hence, the market value of your skills is the combined result of luck and choice:

1 *luck*, first with regard to your original talents, as determined by the genetic endowments with which you are born and your early education, during which you did not make choices yourself; and secondly, luck with regard to the market for your skills, i.e. the interaction between the demand for your skills, which is influenced by other people's preferences, and the competing supply of the same skills by other workers;
2 *personal choice*, regarding the kind of skills you choose to develop on the basis of your talents, and the effort you put into it.

This is the domain characteristic of modern egalitarian philosophy. That these issues are intrinsically difficult does not mean that they can be assumed away.

Political discussions about the relevance of personal skills and about the extent to which individuals are responsible for the skills they develop and for the position they consequently have on the labour market, presuppose the fundamental ethical discussion about talent, choice and just desert lying at the heart of modern egalitarian justice.

## Poverty of Theory?

Social-democratic action needs a moral programme nourished by empirical theory. Having painted the long-term picture of social-democratic convergence, Donald Sassoon concludes (op. cit.) on some pessimistic notes, one of which he labels 'the poverty of theory': 'A further negative aspect of convergence is the practical end of an intellectual framework able to guide or inspire the parties of the Left. The European Left can no longer rely on theoretical instruments—such as Marxism or Keynesianism—to find a way out of the present impasse. Here the fault lies not with the politicians but with the intelligentsia'. Obviously, Sassoon does not argue for a return to Marxism or Keynesianism. Still, I doubt whether references to Marxism and Keynesianism constitute the best way to illustrate the contemporary intellectual challenge. True, once the idea prevailed that social-democratic action could and should rely on a self-contained body of scientific theory, clearly separated from 'bourgeois' thinking. And it may be the case that after Marxism, some social democrats have embraced Keynesianism as if it were the new social-democratic *passe-partout*, to the effect that any criticism or nuance vis-à-vis traditional Keynesianism came to be seen as 'neo-liberal'. If so, that was simply a mistake. Does the demise of the belief in a separate, self-contained domain of socialist theory mean that, today, we lack intellectual resources? Not at all. The intellectual resources required to develop both the moral programme and the empirical theory, which social democrats need, are available in contemporary political philosophy and in social, economic and political theory. They are not available as a neat, unified programme. Connecting with them requires grasping complex and conflicting arguments and empirical evidence. Building bridges between practice and theory is a painstaking exercise. The endeavour is not well served by sweeping generalisations which all too often prevail in our discussions, by the 'glib rhetoric that appeals to those who want to sound sophisticated without engaging in hard thinking'.[18] The intellectual challenge, nowadays, is to confront rhetoric—on a variety of subjects such as 'globalisation', 'the end of Keynesianism', 'the end of welfare as we know it', or 'the coming crisis of capitalism'—with clear thinking and hard facts. The challenge is also to revisit, critically and constructively, our own core ideas. The intellectual resources required to do that are abundantly available. Social democrats are not in want of intellectual resources, even less are they in want of political power today. Two conditions might hamper our common action: lack of open-minded communication across national borders, and reluctance to engage in a thorough debate on ideas. We have never had fewer excuses for failure, on any of these accounts.

## Acknowledgements

I am grateful to P. Robinson, J. de Beus, A. Chipp, G. A. Cohen, C. Crouch, D. Miliband, D. Sassoon, A. B. Atkinson, B. Tuyttens and W. Merkel for generous comments and criticism (some of which they will, no doubt, maintain).

## Notes

1 D. Sassoon, 'Fin-de-Siècle Socialism: The United, Modest Left', *New Left Review*, No. 227, January/February 1998, p. 92

2 I should emphasize that the relation between social investment and social spending is not 'either-or'. The distinction highlights a pragmatic trade-off between two tracks of redistribution in society, which are both necessary, and we should avoid creating false dichotomies. The idea that the 'social investment state' might *replace* much of the traditional welfare state is unreal, given that we live in an ageing society. This is an issue which different parties may give a rather different gloss, but I cannot pursue this here.

3 J. Delors, *Réflexions et propositions pour un nouveau modèle de développement*, Party of European Socialists, mimeo, May 1997.

4 Cf. the assessment of the French Employment Minister, M. Aubry, in Action pour le Renouveau Socialiste, *Quelle gauche pour le XXIe siècle?*, October 1998, Paris, pp. 48–49. See also the interesting and remarkably non-complacent account by the European Commission (Commission Européenne, Direction générale 'Emploi, relations industrielles et affaires sociales'', Direction V/A, *Des lignes directrices à l'action concrète: les plans d'action nationaux pour l'emploi*, May 1998, Luxemburg).

5 A. Giddens, *Beyond Left and Right. The Future of Radical Politics*, Polity Press, Cambridge, 1994, p. 42.

6 This may sound like a rather bold statement. I elaborate on this (and on Giddens's account) in F. Vandenbroucke, *Globalisation, Inequality, and Social Democracy*, London, IPPR, 1998.

7 F. Scharpf, *Crisis and Choice in European Social Democracy*, Cornell University Press, Ithaca, 1991, pp. 25–37.

8 O. Lafontaine and Chr. Müller, *Keine Angst vor der Globalisierung. Wohlstand und Arbeit für alle*, Dietz, Bonn, 1998, p. 105.

9 C. Crouch, *A Third Way in Industrial Relations?*, paper presented at the conference 'Labour in Government: the Third Way and the Future of Social Democracy', Minda de Gunzburg Center for European Studies, Harvard University, 13–15 November 1998. See A. Giddens, 'After the left's paralysis', *New Statesman*, 1 May 1998, pp. 18–21.

10 E. S. Phelps, *Rewarding Work. How to Restore Participation and Self-Support to Free Enterprise*, Harvard University Press, Cambridge Mass., 1997, pp. 21–22.

11 R. M. Solow, 'Guess Who Pays for Workfare?', *New York Review of Books*, 5 November 1998, p. 27.

12 I. Marx and G. Verbist, *Low-paid work, the household income package and poverty*,

paper presented at the LOWER Conference, London, 12–13 December 1997, p. 5; Fig. 2 and Table 1.

13 A. B. Atkinson, *Incomes and the Welfare State*, Cambridge University Press, Cambridge, 1995, pp. 301–303.

14 R. Plant, *The Third Way*, Friedrich-Ebert-Stiftung Working Papers 5/ 98, September. 1998, pp. 9–10.

15 T. Wright, *Socialisms. Old and New*, Routledge, London, 1996, p. 147. For a formal examination of the nexus 'responsibility, equality, incentives' see F. Vandenbroucke, *Social Justice and Individual Ethics in an Open Society. Equality, Responsibility, and Incentives*, D.Phil. thesis, Oxford, 1999.

16 J. Le Grand, *Equity and Choice. An Essay in Economics and Applied Philosophy*, Harper Collins Academic, London, 1991, p. 87.

17 Cf. G.A. Cohen, 'On the Currency of Egalitarian Justice', *Ethics* 99, 1989, pp. 912–944; and S. White, 'Interpreting the 'third way'. Not one road, but many', *Renewal*, Vol. 6, No 2, Spring 1998, pp. 25–26.

18 P. Krugman, *Pop Internationalism*, MIT Press, Cambridge Mass. 1996, p. ix.

# Ownership and Social Democracy

## GERALD HOLTHAM

THE neo-liberal political wave of the 1980s and 1990s privatised utilities, swept away state planning or corporatist structures and cured inflation by the expedient of accepting unemployment more than double 1970s rates. It also switched from direct to indirect taxes and reversed a century-long tendency to income equality.

An intellectual legacy of this period is the acceptance that commercial motives are uniquely effective in mobilising large organisations. Nothing can be done or organised with any expectation of efficiency unless someone stands to make money out of it. The church, the state, the army are all organisations with no commercial purpose, but that just makes us uncomfortable. At the very least, all their ancillary operations must be contracted out for someone to undertake for profit. No other activity can be undertaken except within the framework of a commercial organisation and preferably a PLC.

The evidence that this is sensible has always been thin. But politicians are, rightly perhaps, not interested in arguments about history. Labour needed to change its image in the minds of aspiring people and lose its identification with a traditional working class. The argument therefore went by default. Moreover, it is now asserted that whatever the rights and wrongs of the 1980s, subsequent economic development—globalisation, the information revolution and all that—have irrevocably under-written the superiority of the neo-liberal way.

Yet the evident reservation of left-leaning intellectuals about the Blair Government, in spite of its notable achievements and its recurrent tendency to be inconspicuously redistributive, stems from its refusal to engage in intellectual debate about where we have come. In fear of looking unfashionable or pointlessly re-opening old wounds, it is content to rest on the orthodoxies of its predecessors so far as economic and social policy are concerned. Within the confines of these orthodoxies—interpreted as the constraints of reality itself—it wishes to be fair, efficient, meritocratic and to make more than mere gestures towards equality of opportunity. Yet there is nothing distinctively social-democratic in any of that. It is quite consistent with Christian Democracy. It leaves Tony Blair becalmed to the right of Harold Macmillan.

This essay considers the issue of ownership and the role of public ownership in a modernised social democracy; but we must put such issues in a context. How should a social democratic vision of society differ from contemporary reality or from text-book versions of how capitalism is supposed to be?

© The Political Quarterly Publishing Co. Ltd. 1999
Published by Blackwell Publishers, 108 Cowley Road, Oxford OX4 1JF, UK and 350 Main Street, Malden, MA 02148, USA

# Core Values of Social Democracy

Traditional social democracy sought to combine political freedom and economic equality, thereby distinguishing itself from both totalitarian communism and liberalism. Equality was not seen as a precise, far less an absolute, goal, but the distribution of wealth, income and opportunity generally was so unequal in modern societies that it was possible to favour greater equality without getting into nice philosophical arguments about exactly what equality meant or how much was enough.

Long before the collapse of communism, an attachment to what used to be called bourgeois democracy had become entirely uncontroversial in the West; certainly it does not distinguish social democrats from the new Right. Attitudes to equality therefore remain the touchstone for distinguishing social democrats from liberals or conservatives. The meanings of equality and attitudes towards it are worthy of a book in themselves and a full discussion is beyond the scope of this paper.[1] Leading figures in new Labour have repudiated any commitment to equality of outcomes in favour of equality of opportunity. This is less of a departure than it appears. Although few would oppose equality of opportunity in principle, whatever their political persuasion, it is the Left which favours extensive collective or state action to bring it about. Attempts to secure equality of opportunity by such means inevitably conflict with the interests and, arguably, the freedoms of the relatively well to do. While favouring equality of opportunity in principle, the Right will generally give precedence to some other value like personal freedom, or freedom of choice, whenever there is any conflict.

It is not different values that underlie political positions in a society at peace so much as a different ranking of a common set of values. At one level, equality of opportunity seems a rather bland aspiration. But given that true equality of opportunity would require everyone to start with similar prospects, even a rough approximation to it is impossible if people's circumstances are too unequal in key respects. Equality of opportunity, given inequality of people's endowments of talent, will result in unequal outcomes. Yet those unequal outcomes will need to be restrained, at least in certain areas, if equality of opportunity is to be preserved in successive generations. A practical commitment to equality of opportunity is, therefore, sufficient to distinguish a social democrat. Social liberals have a visibly more tepid commitment to the ideal, while the new Right will generally oppose any practical, collective measure to promote it.

An alternative but complementary description of key social democratic values turns on the notion of economic and social rights as corollaries of citizenship. Many on the Left would reason as follows. If a certain level of income, access to education and health care and adequate housing are necessary for full participation in society, including competing in a basically capitalist economy on remotely equal terms, then surely those things are rights of citizenship in any society wealthy enough to be able to assure them for everyone. Economic, social or welfare rights do not entail equality, but they aim at what Frank Vandenbroucke describes as a 'threshold version of equality';[2] they are a precondition for equality of opportunity and have been embraced by new Labour under the slogan of the 'inclusive society' or combating social exclusion. The idea of such economic rights, as opposed to civil and political rights, is anathema to the new Right which has criticised it as nonsensical.

Raymond Plant has conveniently summarised the debate and what follows draws on his formulations.[3] One of the key criticisms of the new Right has struck a chord with public opinion and hence with new Labour politicians. It holds that rights for some entail obligations for others. Civil and political rights, to things like freedom of speech and association, entail only the obligations on others not to obstruct. The obligations can always be discharged, therefore, and the right can be enforced. Social and economic rights, in contrast, involve access to resources so there is an obligation on others to provide those resources. But what if they cannot? In that case, the right cannot be enforced. The Right also objects that there is no obvious limit to these social and economic rights—unlike civil rights, which are defined permissively—so in practice they are likely to be inflated by interest-group politics.

Plant, however, points out that even rights that are not *ipso facto* claims on resources must be enforceable. And the means to enforce them, more often than not, cost money. Police and courts represent claims on resources in the same way as social welfare. Everyone would agree that a citizen has the 'right' to own property secure from plunder. In practice to secure that right is expensive, so expensive indeed that the right is not in fact fully secured; crime exists and is quite common in some areas. The issue of how much money to spend on police, prisons, rehabilitation services etc. in order to protect property rights and how to deploy those resources, comes down to a political decision. Trades-off are involved; if we spent more, potential victims of crime would be better off at the expense of tax payers. If political decisions are feasible and permissible about the extent of collective responsibility to provide police protection for citizens, they are equally feasible and permissible about a collective responsibility to provide social welfare.

Plant summarises as follows. (I give an extended quote since it contains a number of themes to be pursued):

The idea of welfare rights, contrary to some of the basic ideological assumptions of laissez-faire capitalism, confers an economic and social status outside the market; it involves the idea of a just distribution of resources and, therefore, a correction of market outcomes. It also entails the idea that citizens' obligations do not stop at mutual non-interference, for citizens have positive obligations to provide resources for welfare that can be collected coercively through the tax system. Additionally it implies some limit to commodification and commercialisation, in the sense that the basic welfare goods to which individuals have rights are not ultimately to be subject to the market mechanism, since the market cannot guarantee the provision of these goods, as of right, on a fair basis to all citizens. These social rights of citizenship are also to be ascribed independently of any character assessment of the individual bearer of social rights. They are unconditional, based upon the status of citizenship alone and not on whether the individual lives the kind of life that others in society would wish. In this respect, too, social rights are on a par with civil and political rights. Civil and political rights are not dependent on living a virtuous life; nor does one have to be a member of the deserving poor to qualify for social rights.[4]

While this defence of social rights by Plant seems robust enough, new Labour has been sufficiently uneasy about criticism of it to emphasise the fact that rights entail obligations. However, they have not chosen to emphasise the obligation to pay taxes, which is a clear counterpart to welfare rights. Instead, they have emphasised duties on the part of those receiving certain welfare payments. Unemployment benefits, for example, is a right but it entails a duty to look for work. While education and health rights remain unconditional, if ill-defined, the right to income support is conditional and citizenship is a necessary but not sufficient condition for it. There is no doubt that this approach conforms with the views of many voters in the UK and is therefore electorally shrewd.

The intellectual justification rests on some notion of desert. People should be allowed to retain as much as possible of 'their' earnings, and income support should be restricted to people who really need or deserve it as a matter of principle. This is a view which accords with much 'common sense', but the more it is examined, the more problematical it appears. Everyone wishes to retain a notion of personal responsibility when thinking about society, so some idea of desert is indispensable. But the real issues are quantitative. Given that everyone's income is the result of their training and education as well as social and physical infrastructure and their co-operation with other people, the idea of desert does not get us very far in determining what are appropriate rates of taxation. That point is strengthened by the fact that in even the best-performing capitalist systems, the existence of monopoly and other unequal power relations means that income is not always proportional to contribution. The view that taxes should always be as low as possible (if it means more than that tax revenues should not be wasted) is essentially a conservative one, adopted by many *soi-distant* social democrats on the basis of electoral calculation.

Other practical objections to universalism also hinge on electoral calculation. Provision of universal services and an unconditional income guarantee are apparently expensive in that they entail high tax rates. The expense is apparent, because if the services are in fact to be enjoyed they must be paid for, if not by taxes than by user charges. Nonetheless taxes appear more ineluctable than insurance premia and the link with the service is less evident, so the provision of universal services runs into tax resistance. Another practical argument is that unconditional services and income support with the tax rates they entail would significantly affect incentives to work, save and invest. Fears about the effect on investment have increased with the growing international mobility of capital in recent decades.

# Merit Goods and Public Provision

These arguments have been sufficient to convert many social democrats to the view that unconditional income support is not possible. Existing universal benefits such as the old age pension or child benefit have been allowed to wither by the Labour Government or threatened with taxation.[5] New or enhanced schemes of income support have generally been conditional on certain sorts of behaviour or have entailed means-testing. Whereas in the early 1990s, many social democrats saw the ideal development of welfare systems as tending towards a 'citizen income', Labour in government has moved in a different direction, while attempting quietly to increase the extent of redistribution in an *ad hoc* manner.

The support for certain universal public services, notably health and education, however, has remained stronger and more general, while the existence of a police service free at the point of delivery is taken for granted. (Oddly enough, this does not extend to the judiciary. That legal services should be equally available to all citizens seems an inescapable social democratic principle, but neither old nor new Labour has ever attempted to deliver on it.)

The irreducible commitment to some form of equality of opportunity comes down, therefore, to, in effect, declaring that a range of particular goods and services are 'merit goods'. That is to say we believe that minimal access to them is a prerequisite for everyone and there is a collective responsibility to ensure that access. Furthermore, we are more concerned about equality of access to this particular range of goods and services than we are about equality in general. We accept that the rich person will holiday in the Bahamas while the poor person will stay at home, that one will wear Armani while the other favours second-hand from Oxfam, but we wish to limit the inequality in their access to merit goods, like critical health care.

Not all matters of public policy concern take this form. The state is concerned with pensions, but its concern is purely to ensure adequacy, not any form of equality. People should not be destitute in old age and we must collectively ensure they are not, in a way that does least damage to individual incentives to work and save. But if we are content that people's income is unequal in their working lives, it is irrational to seek a greater degree of equality in retirement. Redistribution is required only to the extent necessary to finance the minimum provision for all, not as an end in itself.

Yet that is not true of real merit goods—those we wish to apportion on the basis of need or ability to derive benefit from them, not on the ability to pay. We want to withdraw those from the money nexus, in Plant's phrase to limit commodification and commercialisation. What makes something suitable to be a merit good? In some cases, the ideal of equality of opportunity suggests immediately that something should be a merit good; primary education is an obvious example. Health is generally so regarded. This seems to reflect the fact that most people do not like money to be the main arbiter in matters of life and death. 'Women and children first' was regarded as an acceptable way to ration places on the lifeboats of the Titanic. Auctioning places for money would widely be regarded as despicable—though it may have happened. This instinct must be respected if the belief in the moral equivalence of human individuals is to be preserved. I do not think it can be denied that there is, though, an arbitrary, historical element in the list of merit goods in any society. In the UK, primary and secondary education and critical health care enjoy a place; housing, public transport and a postal service were hybrids, subject to subsidisation and/or price control.

The state at one time took responsibility for providing other things like water, electricity and gas without their being merit goods in quite the same way. There was some attempt to maintain a uniform tariff, irrespective of the marginal costs of supply, respecting some notion that citizens were to have access on equal terms, whatever their situation. But this was not followed rigorously. Devices like peak load pricing showed some readiness to relate price to cost, and it was always the case that the service was purchased by individuals to the extent they could afford it.

A merit good is one where there is a collective decision to make it available to everyone on identical terms, usually on subsidised terms, sometimes free. If it is free or heavily subsidised, no market exists in the good and access is determined on some other basis. The decision about on what scale to supply is political, and if supply is less than potential demand, some rationing scheme is involved. That is unlikely to be ideal, but is considered preferable in these particular cases to 'rationing by price'.

One of the strongest modern orthodoxies is that there are advantages to separating consideration of entitlement from considerations of means of supply. To say that people should be entitled to income support, education or whatever, whether up to a threshold or whether on the basis of more general entitlement, implies nothing about how those things should be supplied. Even within public services we can have a 'purchaser provider split' where some public authority takes responsibility for organising access on behalf of the public but where the organisation of production is in other hands and is procured by contract. Various phrases such as 'steering not rowing' are used for this general approach.

This essay accepts the force of that analytical distinction. We can and should talk separately of issues of desert and entitlement. Most of the remaining ideological debates on the left have focused on the demand side of the pair, on entitlement, the role of equality, what the state should try to achieve and on whose behalf. A similar debate has not occurred recently about means and, in particular, the role of public provision and of public ownership of the means of provision. While there is a measure of consensus that means are a matter for pragmatic decision rather than a matter of principle, there is very little discussion of what should guide the pragmatic decision. Nor does a pragmatic decision ever seem to be taken on the merits of an individual case. The symbolism of the decision and what it says about the style and political positioning of the government has generally been regarded as more important. And where it has not, financial considerations, shaped by the conventions of public accounting have been the main factor driving the decision.

To move the debate along we need some taxonomy. I distinguish four cases.

- Case one is where goods and services are both produced and consumed individually. Private producers turn out things they think the consumer wants or can be induced to buy; the consumer chooses via a market mechanism. Goods and services change hands for money and money is earned in exchange for labour. Most goods and services in our society are covered by case one.
- Case two is where consumption is collectivised, leaving production in private hands. We can withdraw, say, health from the market, finance a certain scale of provision through taxation and allocate it on the basis of need, clinically determined by professionals. Yet the doctors, hospitals etc. could all be in private hands competing for the state's money and patronage.
- Case three is where the state nationalises the production of a good or service and simply sells the product in the market at a price that covers cost, acting much like a private producer. In the past utilities were operated partly in this way.
- Case four is where we collectivise both demand and supply. We establish universal entitlement and equip and operate the whole infrastructure of supply. This applies in practice to education. Although the state has no legal monopoly of supply, for most of the population state schooling is the only sort to which they have access.

Cases two, three and four involve public participation. But only cases three and four, on the face of it, involve public ownership of the means of production. Three has become entirely unfashionable and four is under pressure, with this Government, like the last, showing a strong preference for replacing it with case two.

The argument for doing so sometimes entails the assertion that ownership is not required for control. Control may be desirable, but it can be obtained via contract and by regulation of the suppliers. This regulation seeks to align the interests of the public with the mercenary interests of the producers so that their pursuit of profit ensures the efficiency of provision. Public ownership cannot harness the profit motive and is therefore on its last legs.

## Three Justifications for Public Ownership

So much for context. I argue now that public ownership is a protean notion that can embrace very different arrangements. The arguments for considering it take three quite different forms that are independent of each other.

First, if universal entitlement to merit goods is to survive, even if provision takes the case-two form, a wholly new type of public ownership is required. The only true solution to the problem of outgoings that rise faster than GDP is an income source that rises faster than GDP. That entails some collective ownership of capital, as President Clinton realised when he proposed investing US state pension funds in the equity market.

Secondly, there are arguments for case three and four forms of public or co-operative ownership in restricted circumstances, even on a fundamentally liberal view of society. These arguments are reviewed.

But, thirdly, the liberal framework is too restrictive for proper consideration of all relevant issues. The linchpin of new Right views of the economy is the idea of consumer sovereignty. That individuals are more than mere consumers is generally conceded. 'Citizens not consumers' is a slogan often repeated when people are arguing for resource allocation to be controlled by political, and putative democratic, means rather than by commercial means. This may have implications for ownership forms.

I now consider each of these three arguments in turn.

## Social Democracy and the Claim on Resources

The first argument for public ownership has nothing whatever to do with control of any economic activity. It is indirectly related to the commitment to provide merit goods, but does not depend on any particular scheme for their supply. The argument quite simply is that since we wish to organise some of society's consumption collectively; we need a collective claim on some of society's wealth.

One of the central difficulties of social democracy is that some of the merit goods, notably education and health care, are things whose costs tend to rise disproportionately quickly, or the demands for which tend to grow disproportionately quickly, or both. The cost of providing these services therefore tends to rise relative to income in general. If the services are being provided free and financed from general taxation, the share of tax in GDP must rise over time. That is politically difficult to sustain. Most of the strategies for dealing with this problem amount to surrendering the basic principle of ensuring equality of access to the merit goods in question; they imply that the state assures a bare minimum of provision, which diminishes in importance for most people, and above that it's everyone for herself.

Real GDP has grown at just over 2 per cent a year in the United Kingdom since the Second World War. Expenditure on health has increased rather faster and yet there is now widespread recognition that the share of GDP the UK expends on health is low by international comparisons and is inadequate to meet legitimate demands. It must grow in future by at least 3 per cent a year, which appears to entail a rising tax burden. Yet since the 1950s, the real return to an investment in ordinary shares has averaged 6 per cent a year.

Indeed, since the 1970s the return has been at an unsustainable rate above 10 per cent, and in recent years even higher.

With annual health expenditures near £40 billion, imagine the consequences of having a national patrimony of, say, £50 billion invested in equities. A rate of return of 6 per cent would allow 3 per cent each year to be devoted to health expenditure, some £1.5 billion initially, while the fund continued to grow at 3 per cent. This would relieve the pressure on taxation of labour income.

The idea of a community fund has often been advanced in discussions of the state's 'liability' to provide pensions. And it was advanced more generally by James Meade, among others, as a means of providing a general Citizens Income.[6] It seems most appropriate to use the device, not for a general Citizens income, for which there is currently little support, nor yet for pensions, where privately-earmarked pension funds may have advantages, but for those elements of public expenditure where no private property claim is appropriate and where the claims of collective consumption are least disputed.

It is not argued that such a device could fund all or even the major part of state spending on things like health and education. But it could go a long way to financing the necessary increments to that spending. That is particularly so in a period like the present one when the share of profits in national income has been rising. Attempting to increase the tax burden on wage income in those circumstances is particularly difficult. Of course, the future may be different. Although it currently seems improbable, we may well enter a period where the wage share of national income rises and the rate of return on equities falls back. In that case nothing is lost; the state retains the power to tax and more of incremental expenditure would come from tax income, at a time when it was presumably easier to collect. The proposal for a community fund simply expands the revenue sources available.

The objections to this suggestion are essentially those that the Chairman of the Federal Reserve, Alan Greenspan, advanced when President Clinton proposed to invest US state pension funds in equities; namely that politicians would inevitably meddle with the companies in which there was a public stake. It is elementary to address this issue. The total capital value of shares on the London Stock Exchange is approaching £1000 billion so that the public stake we are discussing would represent a small minority interest and would not overwhelm the market. Clearly everything depends on the institutional arrangements for administering the fund and the conventions that grow up surrounding its management. All that is required is that a board of trustees be appointed from outside politics to supervise the fund and that they delegate its management to commercial fund managers. Government ministers would be at two removes from investment decisions. The role of the state would simply be that of passive rentier.

The larger question raised by this proposal is where would the patrimony come from? A sum of £50 billion cannot be raised rapidly. The government could plan, however, to trim some current expenditures relevant to existing plans and hypothecate certain tax revenues to the fund. The obvious revenues to hypothecate are those derived from taxes on capital. Proceeds from inheritance tax, for example, could be expanded by the closure of notorious loopholes and the revenues hypothecated. Similarly capital gains tax receipts, which are very small, could be hypothecated. Companies should have the option of paying taxes by issurance of scrip, which would dilute the holdings of existing shareholders but not affect cash flow. By these means sums of several billion pound a year could be hypothecated to the Community Fund, and in about a decade a sum of £50 billion could be raised. The growth of the fund could be accelerated by taking advantage of the equity premium—the extent to which returns on equities exceed that on government bonds. At the present time, with the British government running a current budget surplus, there is excess demand for government bonds on the part of private financial institutions, reflected in extremely low yields at the long end of the maturity spectrum. British government 30 year bonds currently yield less than those in Germany, whereas British ten-year bonds yield significantly more than their German equivalent. The British government could issue enough 30 year bonds to satisfy private savers' demand, driving the yield at least to the German rate, and invest the proceeds in a Community Fund.

This is a long-term solution to be sure. But the problem is itself a long-term one. Given political will, a government can respond to the demands of the electorate by raising taxes to increase spending on merit goods. What is in doubt is its ability to do so indefinitely.

## Public Ownership of Utilities and Public Services

The second set of arguments are utterly different in context and nature. We now consider when it is appropriate to keep activities in the public sector, whether they involve the production of marketed output or non-marketed public services—situations corresponding to cases three and four.

There are certain situations where, even within the corpus of neo-liberal belief, a solid argument for collective ownership can be made on economic grounds. The two forms of collective ownership which are widespread in the capitalist countries are state or public ownership and the co-operative; the latter can be further subdivided into the producer co-op and the consumer co-op or mutual. The fact that these forms are widespread and that they tend to occur in many countries in the same sectors of the economy should alert us to the possibility of a functional explanation rather than mere historical accident. Current fashion is to forget or downplay the reasons why activity in some sectors has tended to be organised collectively.

In fact, the historical distribution of collective ownership across sectors accords rather well with the predictions of economic theory as to when such ownership is likely to be relatively efficient. The conditions under which public ownership of utilities will have advantages were set out by Mayer and discussed at some length in Holtham.[7]

Public ownership can be viewed, in neo-liberal terms, as a restriction on the shareholding of the enterprise in question. That can be justified if three conditions are met. First, the market in question should be characterised by a high degree of concentration, with monopoly or oligopoly. Furthermore this market characteristic should not be accidental, but justified by the characteristics of supply and demand conditions such as large economies of scale or scope that make many producers uneconomic. Secondly, complete contracts must be infeasible or costly, with the consequence that the government cannot grant a concession or a franchise to a private monopolist, the terms of which are sufficiently comprehensive to cover all eventualities and avoid the risk of unforeseen abuse. Thirdly, future flexibility must be more important than current commitment in a particular sense to be explained: sometimes a contract with a private supplier provides others with a commitment that facilitates raising capital and making complementary investments; on the other hand it generally leads to a loss of policy flexibility in responding to shifts in consumer needs during the course of the contract. Where the loss of flexibility is great the public can be 'locked in' to an extent that outweighs the initial advantages of the contract.

In practice, these three conditions are most frequently met in the case of large 'network' services, where scale economies dictate a monopoly producer, and where consumption has significant externalities in the sense that it benefits other people than the direct consumer. Urban transport, for example, benefits employers of commuting workers as well as the workers themselves. And water consumption on baths and showers brings benefits to the fellow-commuters of the bathers, not to mention its public health implications.

These conditions are most closely met in practice with undertakings like the railways or the London underground and with water utilities. The privatisation of water and railways has not had the evident advantages associated with privatisation of telecommunications, for example. There, technical advance eroded a natural monopoly and made competitive private supply the obvious structure. No technical advance has eroded the natural monopoly of water and railways and their privatisation remains unpopular with the general public, which perceives no or few improvements in service and an increase in price.

The main argument for privatisation of these services and the proposed privatisation of air traffic control services is held to be financial, that in the public sector they are subject to a borrowing restriction and therefore cannot invest adequately. To say that this argument has no merit is to be guilty of exaggerated understatement. The argument is both a nonsense and an insult to public intelligence. It is ironic that the railways were originally nationalised, because it was held that rates of private return were inadequate to secure enough investment. Having been nationalised to cure underinvestment, the railways are now privatised to cure underinvestment, with rates of return being supported by public subsidy.

The fact is that the return on capital required by private shareholders is considerably higher than the cost of capital to the government. In a capital- and infrastructure-intensive industry like water or railways, capital costs dominate all others. It is highly unlikely that private owners can wring out enough efficiencies to compensate users for the higher cost of capital. Consequently the price of the service rises without adequate benefit to the consumer. That is currently true of many rail and water franchises.

The capital constraint in the public sector is an artefact deriving from accounting conventions that are not only illogical but unique to the UK. Other countries, for example, distinguish between borrowing by the state that must be serviced from taxation and borrowing for public enterprises that generate revenue and can consequently service their own debt. Other countries appropriately impose borrowing restraints on the latter that are different from those on government borrowing for general expenditure. The restraints depend on the balance sheet and prudent gearing of the enterprise itself, not on macroeconomic considerations. A rational control regime is set out by Radcliffe.[8] The risk the state incurs by allowing borrowing of its enterprises against their own balance sheets is generally small and is simply not worth the cost of passing to the private sector, which will wish to be compensated for the risk at excessive (to the government) rates. It is generally better for the state to bear the risk itself or to charge it to the users of the utilities. In other words, the Treasury charges utilities an actuarially sound fee for guaranteeing the debt. Generally this charge will be enormously less than private share-holders would demand—very much to the benefit of users.

In the case of public services that are not marketed, existing macroeconomic controls on borrowing are appropriate. Evading them by signing contracts with private suppliers who are then left to make the investments—as in the Private Finance Initiative—is very risky. The state changes the form of its liabilities, from bonds to contracts, but does not reduce them. To the extent that it pays a higher cost of capital, its net liabilities may increase (depending on what economies the private supplier can generate). And it certainly loses flexibility in being tied in by long-term contracts. The charm of this device for a centre-left government is mysterious.

## Diverse Objectives

The third set of arguments are more diffuse. We have noted the central role of consumer sovereignty in the liberal world view and the wish of many on the left to assert that a citizen is more than a consumer. Evidently, people are also producers. In fact they achieve much of their sense of meaning from their work and for a significant minority of people it is their main source of happiness and satisfaction. So what is wrong with producer sovereignty? Why should not the economy operate so as to give everyone the best chance of interesting and fulfilling work rather than maximise the goods and services they can consume in their leisure time?

These propositions and questions strike many modern social democrats, particularly in the UK, as highly subversive. There are strong historical reasons for this. Since World War Two, the UK has declined as an economic power and in terms of its ranking in income per head relative to many other countries. Labour was the first political party to draw attention to this and to use it for political purposes, but a general sense of failure pervades the British intelligentsia when considering economic and commercial matters. Consequently, the usual symptom of an inferiority complex is evident: namely an aggressive attempt at compensation. Mrs Thatcher embodied this most clearly with a series of 'more commercial than thou' policies. And it was continued by her successors to the accompaniment of plangent boasting about being the 'enterprise capital of Europe'. The modern Labour Party inherits this attitude. It is reinforced in the Party by its own electoral failure after 1979. The failure was largely the result of the electorate coming to believe that the Conservatives were more efficient managers of a capitalist economy than Labour— partly because Labour was in power for much of the period of high inflation in the 1970s and partly because of a reflex anticommercialism on the Labour Left which continued to doubt the legitimacy of capitalism, though having nothing plausible with which to replace it. The Conservatives managed eventually to dissipate their advantage without much assistance, but Labour leaders still feel impelled to prove they can be trusted with managing a capitalist economy by manifesting the same single-minded, not to say one-track, commercialism as Mrs Thatcher.

While this leaves many social democrats uneasy, they have generally not clearly articulated the problem or its solution. Let us try and take a more balanced view. We have four quite different requirements of the economy: that it should produce as many material goods and as much wealth as possible; that the output should be distributed in a fair and just way or should, at least, permit redistribution to achieve that; that it should afford as much interesting, meaningful and fulfilling work as people wish to do with as little unattractive drudgery and personal insecurity as possible; that it should be in broad essentials susceptible to democratic control so that its operation does not conflict with a sense of freedom and autonomy among citizens. These desiderata could be accepted by social democrats and liberals alike, but it is important to recognise that there are likely to be trade-offs among the objectives. Democracy can have costs, for example, both because voting systems can be inefficient ways of allocating resources, and because the business of sharing information and reaching a consensus may be a slow and laborious way of reaching decisions. A conflict between efficiency and distributional objectives is frequently asserted, indeed exaggerated given that excessive inequality too has economic costs.[9] It is also evident that people's interests as consumers and producers may well collide, though it is not always so.

The recognition of trade-offs protects us from wishful thinking or the belief in free lunches. Of course, we cannot subject every economic decision to democratic review, we cannot redistribute income in any way that we wish, and we cannot guarantee everyone exactly the kind of work they wish for the hours they wish to work. At least, we cannot necessarily do so without serious consequences for the sum total of output. But that does not mean we must ignore or downgrade three of our legitimate objectives in favour of churning out the maximum output. In the past, the socialist Left denied the existence of trade-offs and appeared to hold that any degree of democratisation, redistribution and protection of worker interests was compatible with an efficient economy. That was not true, but somehow we have slipped past thinking about trade-offs and come to talk as if the maximisation of production via profit was the only legitimate objective. Sometimes this is buttressed by assertions that 'globalisation' has made the world economy so ruthlessly competitive that we must maximise output and profit or starve! We have gone from asserting you can have it all to asserting you can have only one thing. Both propositions are false.

The mature approach is to acknowledge all the legitimate objectives, but accept that there will be trade-offs that will sometimes be unquantifiable. Judgments must be made. Once we accept the possibility of trade-offs, it becomes evident that the parameters of those trade-offs are unlikely to be the same in difference economies or in different sectors of the same economy, since they will vary with technical, technological and cultural factors. Different solutions or compromises will be appropriate at different times and places. That in turn could lead to a variety of different management or control regimes and of different ownership structures. In itself, that is likely to be a good thing. The principle of necessary impurity or requisite variety, long established in cybernetics, holds that variety in a system is necessary for robustness in the face of shocks or unforeseen developments.

Perhaps these rather abstract statements require an example. It is a matter of common observation that commercial broadcasting has not in the past led to variety, but to an homogenisation of output that tends to avoid the difficult or challenging. This may change as digital technology reduces the costs of transmission, but up to now the most successful solution has been a publicly-financed broadcaster competing with the commercial stations for customers, but not primarily driven by a profit motive. This has been far from a perfect device, but it has provided a space for minority productions. Contrary to the fears of Mr Greenspan, the public ownership of a broadcaster has not, at least in some countries, made it more susceptible to government propaganda than commercial stations.

If organisations like the BBC can be criticised, it is not because they are publicly owned, but because their governance and accountability structures are primitive. Since they represent the assertion of a public interest principle distinct from commercial concerns, they should be more democratically accountable than they are. To resist the government of the day and maintain the degree of independence often indispensable to discharge its duties properly, a public corporation requires its own separate democratic legitimacy. For this reason there is a case for having direct election to the board of governors. The BBC and future public corporations should perhaps have the structure of a new form of mutual organisation in which users (licence-holders) have a right to vote. Public ownership thereby has a role in enlarging and diversifying our democracy.

## Conclusion

This essay has argued that in the light of the continuing values that underlie social democracy, there are three types of argument for considering public ownership of productive assets. The arguments are quite distinct and cover: the means of financing near-universal public services at an adequate level; the efficient organisation of monopoly activities of social importance, and the claims of democracy and the need to promote other interests than commercial ones in many areas of society's life.

None of the arguments holds that public ownership is a principle in its own right; all accept that the question of ownership should be determined in the light of other objectives, and the decision in any case requires empirical judgment. In certain situations, however, the case for public ownership can be strong. This needs to be asserted at the present time when the intellectual climate, reinforced by political calculation, leads any public ownership to be regarded as an embarrassing hangover from the past or an opportunity to raise quick funds via a sale of assets.

## Notes

1 Jane Franklin, ed., *Equality*, London, IPPR, 1997.
2 Frank Vandenbroucke, *'Globalisation, Inequality and Social Democracy'*, London, IPPR, 1998.
3 Raymond Plant, 'Citizenship, Rights, Welfare' in *Social Policy and Social Justice, The IPPR Reader*, ed., Jane Franklin, Polity Press, 1998.
4 Plant, *op. cit.*, p. 58.
5 Child benefit partly replaced an earlier children's tax allowance. It was, in effect, the cashing out of the allowance. Making tax allowances into cash payments with the same cost to the government is generally progressive, since as tax allowances they are worth more to those on higher marginal rates of tax while the cash payment is the same to all recipients. To tax such payments bring the notion of cashing out tax allowances into disrepute.
6 James Meade, *Agathotopia*
7 C. P. Mayer, 'Public Ownership: Concepts and Applications' in D. R. Helm, ed., *The Economic Borders of the State*, Oxford, OUP, 1989; and Gerald Holtham, *'Freedom with Responsibility: Can we unshackle public enterprise?'*, London, IPPR, 1998, esp. ch. 1.
8 Rosemary Radcliffe, 'Public vs Private Enterprise: Is there a third way? in Holtham, *op. cit.*, ch. 2.

9 Glyn Andrew and David Miliband, eds., *Paying for Inequality: The economic cost of social justice*, London, IPPR, 1994.

# The Parabola of Working-Class Politics

COLIN CROUCH

BRITISH politics since the general election of May 1997 presents two central puzzles. How did it come about that such an enormous shift of electoral opinion resulted—with the major exception of policies for constitutional reform—in such extensive continuity of policy between the outgoing Conservative and incoming Labour governments? Why is it that, despite new Labour's intense identification with modernisation and change, politics at the end of the 20th century appears uncannily similar to the end of the 19th? The answer to both questions is to be found in an understanding of the current state of class politics. This in turn has major implications for the future course of social democracy.

It is extraordinary how many of the distinctive policy discoveries of the 20th century are being unthought at the century's end, returning us to the thoughtways of the 19th. Deficit public spending is again seen as profligacy, not as a useful means of easing recession. Social welfare is a residual expression of compassion for the deserving poor, not a universal citizenship right. Workers' rights are a drag on entrepreneurial freedom, or inconvenient sops offered to keep trade unions quiet, not extensions of citizenship to the workplace which are quite likely also to improve employees' contribution to efficiency. International market forces are as ineluctable as the weather, not capable of being shaped or moderated by creative policy-making.

New Labour shares much of this change in thinking, and differentiates itself from the Conservative Party rather as did the Liberal Party of the last 20 years of the 19th century, in a radical constitutional reform agenda. Colin Matthew[1] has described how Tony Blair has here resumed—with far greater success—much of the unfinished business of W. E. Gladstone in the 1880s, especially in Ireland and in Scottish and Welsh devolution. New Labour's reform list is in fact considerably longer than Gladstone's, and includes the House of Lords (not picked up by Liberals until 1910), and relations with the European Union. The latter was of course not available in the 1880s, but new Labour's position on European integration well demonstrates the essentially constitutional and liberal rather than social democratic nature of its radicalism. The government has waived the opt-out from the employment policies emanating from the then Social Protocol of the Treaty of Maastricht insisted upon by its predecessor, but it seeks a minimalist interpretation of the already limited rights being secured by those policies. For example, in accepting the working time directive it took maximum advantage of all possible exceptions and dilutions; and it has lobbied actively to prevent any extension of employee consultation rights under any future directives. The government has waived the opt-out because it wishes to be a constitutionally normal

Published by Blackwell Publishers, 108 Cowley Road, Oxford OX4 1JF, UK and 350 Main Street, Malden, MA 02148, USA

member of the Union, not because it shares the desire of some other European social democratic parties to use a strengthened Union to extend the international rights of labour as a counter to the pressures of global capitalism.

There is not really a simple return to the 19th century, as though the ideas and experiences of the 20th never existed. The state welfare budget remains in all advanced countries except the USA higher than it was in the so-called golden age of Keynesianism in the 1960s and 1970s. The universal welfare state exists and is popular, and those who seek to privatise or residualise it have far to go before they have realised their goal. Rather than a straight line of policy positions running between the 19th and 20th centuries, we need to think in terms of a parabola, with time as one of its axes and policy as the other. Even where a new Labour politician or thinker seems to have a similar policy position to a late 19th century Liberal, he or she necessarily stands in a different point in relation to the accumulation of the 20th century's social democratic inheritance—and also faces a different direction in relation to that inheritance, coming away from rather than moving towards it.

The combined similarities and differences of new Labour in relation to late 19th century Liberalism can be best seen in the New Deal at Work policy.[2] This shares much of the approach of classic Scandinavian social democracy in the imaginative assistance it offers the work force to adjust to global markets; but the overall approach of public policy is further to deregulate those markets. New Labour aims to make the population fit for global capital; there are no equivalent plans to make capital adapt to the needs of the population.

If we are to interpret the 1997 election in the light of these policy consequences, we have to believe that there was a strong desire in the electorate for constitutional changes, while there was broad satisfaction with the main outlines of Conservative economic and social policy. This is not however what a reading of opinion polls at the time would suggest. An alternative possibility is that voters wanted Conservative policies, but believed the Conservatives themselves to be incompetent and corrupt, and wanted different people to implement the same policies. In other words, new Labour are Thatcher's well behaved step-children, her own direct progeny having behaved badly. This is more plausible than the former explanation, but it is difficult to believe that this was enough to account for the landslide.

A third possibility remains open: that many voters did not like what was happening under the Conservatives, but their discontents were inchoate and poorly expressed; no-one articulated them. The early 1980s, leftist Labour Party had been interested only in those concerns that suited its existing prejudices. In the mid 1990s new Labour did listen to the concerns emerging from the electorate and fashioned a response to them, but in the way that a firm surveys consumers before modifying a product. It responded to what its research found in an individualised and passive public; it was not interested in shaping those concerns into autonomously organised political demands.

But if this is so, how did it come about that a sophisticated electorate in a politically mature country could be left with only inchoate expressions of dissatisfaction, incapable of making a political demand beyond hoping that a fresh set of leaders might make things better? Addressing this question brings us to our central theme: the fate of class in British politics, and in particular the parabola of class politics during the course of the 20th century, which parallels and is a major cause of the parabola of policy.

I am here using classes in the sense understood by political sociology: broad groups, identified by their economic relationship to each other, which, under certain circumstances, acquire a sufficient sense of collective identity to define their shared interests and find means of expressing them politically. A class can exist passively, in the sense that an outside observer can see that a group might potentially articulate shared interests, but it only exists actively if it actually does so. Only a small minority of members of a class will participate in this process of organisation and expression, but if they do their work skilfully they will win the passive support of the majority, at least in the sense that no other group will rival them in presenting an alternative agenda of the class's needs.

Now, it is a central mantra of the contemporary political elite that class no longer exists. Some would contest my analysis by arguing that the confrontation between left and right, between capital and labour has now been transcended, and that the new politics needs to move beyond these terms (see for example Anthony Giddens's recent contributions to the debate).[3] I fully agree that there are new issues on the political agenda which do not immediately concern that confrontation—those of ethnicity and gender for example. But this must not be exaggerated. Several of the issues that Giddens states as being beyond capitalism—such as environmental damage and so-called natural disasters—are often the direct consequence of deregulated global capitalism, a fundamental class question.

An alternative form of the end of class argument is that the problems of working life which were central to class politics are no longer important; people nowadays see themselves as consumers, not workers. This very common assertion also sees in the general growth of prosperity and individual opportunity, and in the decline of manual work, evidence that class problems requiring the attention of a social democratic state have today been resolved. However, we have enough evidence from the past 20 years of British and American neo-liberal politics to know that in the more purely market-oriented societies to which we have moved, income inequality, relative and even absolute poverty increase sharply. The new flexible labour markets make life very insecure for at least the bottom third of the working population; it is particularly puzzling that removal of the state welfare cushion is felt to be justified at precisely a moment when the market economy is less able to guarantee secure jobs than it was during the Keynesian period.

Talk of the delayered, non-hierarchical modern corporation—which is held to render trade unionism unnecessary and to have made managerial authority employee-friendly—is similarly misguided. In only a minority of workplaces have these changes been associated with a democratisation of work organisation. In many others the reduction of hierarchies has occurred only because advanced technology makes it possible for senior management to control directly and without going through an intermediate hierarchy of middle management. This can make access to decision-making levels of a firm more remote and difficult for ordinary employees, not less. Alternatively, informality and delayering has taken the form of putting former employees into the position of self-employed sub-contractors, but working for a single firm. While this is often interpreted as a growth of entrepreneurship, in reality it does not reduce dependency on an employing organisation by these so-called self-employed, but simply removes them from the social security and labour protection laws designed to look after employees as such. Further still, while the decline of manual work in manufacturing industry and coal-mining has reduced the proportion of work which is dirty and dangerous, much of the new service sector employment brings its own degradations. In particular, work in the rapidly growing personal services sector frequently involves a subordination of the person to employers and customers that has reintroduced many humiliating features of the old world of domestic service. Shoeshine boys and baggage carriers are back on the streets—back to the 19th century indeed.

But modern work problems are not just confined to the bottom third. Throughout the occupational structure people are finding that their jobs are taking up more and more of their lives and bringing them unreasonable stress. The down-sizing processes engaged in by most public and private sector organisations in recent years to cut staff costs have produced excessive work loads at many levels. In the UK and USA, after a century of gradual reductions, working hours are now lengthening—the parabola again. Since both men and women now work within the formal economy, there is less overall time for leisure and family life. This is happening in an age when parents need to devote increasing energy to steering their sons and daughters through an increasingly difficult childhood: pressures from various forms of deviance, and growing pressures from those areas of capitalism which have discovered that children are exceptionally soft touches as customers, compete with an increasingly frenzied need to do well educationally in order to keep one's nose in front of an occupational race which is constantly increasing both its rewards to winners and its punishments to losers.

Politicians might argue that it has become increasingly difficult for the state to meet needs for protection from the market's vagaries (citing globalisation and other vaguely defined excuses). But to argue that objectively these needs no longer exist is quite specious. Needs for means to restrain the pressures of the market, including those of work, remain high on any objective political agenda, at least for any party stemming from the left. All that might have diminished is the capacity of those worried about such questions to place them on the political agenda. This is where an analysis of the way in which class operates in contemporary politics becomes relevant. It also brings us to the strongest element in the argument that class has become irrelevant: it is increasingly difficult to perceive classes as clearly defined social groups. To examine this fully is complex: here there is space to do so only with reference to three crudely identified class groups.

## The Decline of the Manual Working Class

It is the experience of the traditional manual working class which primarily forms the parabola. At the end of the 19th century many skilled and some unskilled manual working groups had successfully organised themselves into trade unions. In Britain there was no once and for all struggle for the suffrage as there had been in a number of continental European countries, the right to vote being very gradually extended to include growing numbers of male manual workers between 1868 and 1918. There was however considerable experience of political exclusion as newly enfranchised working-class interests tried to find those in the existing system willing to represent their interests. There was also a strong sense of social exclusion, most non-manual groups of the period regarding even skilled manual workers as unfit to be suitable social companions. These factors were reinforced by patterns of residential segregation that produced single-class communities within neighbourhoods in most industrial towns.

The divisions were never clear-cut, and other cleavages often proved more important: that between Anglicans and non-conformists, for example, or between English natives and Irish immigrants. However, there was enough class-related political activity to make an impact. The working class's relative social exclusion meant that its discontent was constantly feared, and the poverty of parts of it made it a worrying social problem. From the end of the 19th century through to the third quarter of the 20th, finding ways of coping with the political existence of this class was the major preoccupation of domestic politics. For most of this time the class was growing in numbers, and eventually also in income, so that it began to have an effect on consumer markets as well as on policy for industrial relations and social welfare. It could plausibly be presented as the class of the future, and politicians of nearly all parties knew that their own futures depended partly on their ability to respond to its demands. Further, it was only when economies were reshaped to make possible working-class prosperity—through various combinations of Fordist production methods, Keynesian demand management, neo-corporatist industrial relations, and the welfare state—that the dynamism of mid 20th century mass-production capitalism took off. Improving the quality of capitalism might not have been what Marx envisaged by the power of the proletariat, but it was in part the form that it took.

Then, in the mid-1960s, the relative size of the manual working class began to decline. Increased productivity and automation reduced the numbers of production workers needed for a given unit of output, while employment in administrative support activities, as well as in the various services sectors (especially those associated with the welfare state) were growing steadily in size.[4] The collapse of British manufacturing in the 1980s and new waves of technological change in the 1990s eroded direct industrial employment even further. While large numbers of people, especially men, continued to be manual workers, the class was no longer the class of the future.

By the end of the 20th century large parts of it were engaged in defensive, protectionist battles only, in the UK more than in most other advanced societies. The early stages of the decline had been marked by an industrial militancy that veered between mere defence and the construction of new strategic possibilities, though in Britain the former usually predominated. In the 1980s the final ferocious battle of organised labour, the miners' strike of 1984–85, was one of hopeless last-ditch defence alone.

At the political level the Labour Party had been responding to the relative decline of the manual working class since at least the 1960s with some attempts to add various growing new non-manual groups to its coalition. The desperate leftward lurch of the party in the early 1980s however led it to forget its historical future-oriented role, and to attempt to forge coalitions of out-groups. In the deindustrialising north, in Liverpool, the party was forced back into a defiant proletarian redoubt—a strategy first and disastrously pursued by the French Communist Party. In the new cosmopolitan, post-modern south, in London, there were attempts to forge a non-class rainbow coalition of the excluded, bringing together ethnic minorities and various interests primarily concerned with sexual orientation; a path also followed at the time by the US Democratic Party. Both were destined to fail.

The manual working class had begun the century as the future battering on the door, representing the collective interest in an age damaged by individualism: it brought the message of universal citizenship, and the possibilities of mass consumption in a society that knew only luxury goods for the rich and subsistence for the poor. By the end it represented history's losers: advocacy of the welfare state began to take the form of appeals for compassion, not demands for citizenship. The parabola had been described across the century.

## The Resurgence of the Capitalist Class

The parabola of capital is the inverse of that of the manual working class. Fully ascendant in the late 19th century, capital then underwent some very uneasy decades. Concern that the unremitting pursuit of private profit neglected collective goods and public welfare and threatened social cohesion led all kinds of political forces to advocate controls and limits on that pursuit. The Russian Revolution brought both the reality of revolt by suppressed classes whose interests were neglected and, until some time in the 1960s, the apparent possibility of an alternative to capitalism as an economically successful regime. Especially in the decades after World War II, capitalist interests accepted more and more constraints: nationalisation, progressive taxation, the regulation of labour standards, the dynamic growth of a welfare state which virtually excluded such major potential consumption areas as health, education and social insurance from the reach of profit-making. However, the fact that one describes the retreat of capital as paralleling the rise of labour does not mean that there was always a zero-sum relation between the two classes. As already noted, capitalism in fact made great gains from the mass consumption released by workers' rising incomes and security. It also gained from the social infrastructure established under the impulse of Fabian and other social democratic ideas. Workers similarly benefited from the growth of wages and consumption opportunities of capitalist innovation—far more than did their counterparts in the rigid economies of the communist world.

The subsequent numerical and political decline of the working class nevertheless brought advantages to capital and management, especially as it coincided with other significant changes. Technical innovations, particularly in communications technology, made possible a globalisation of activities by large firms. Alongside that went a deregulation of financial markets which massively increased the flexibility and mobility of capital as opposed to that of labour. Simultaneously, management techniques were advancing in sophistication and capability, particularly those for the management of personnel. The distinction between capitalists and managers, once seen as a major domestication of the force of capital, again became obscured as senior managers were given stock options in their companies. Also, with finance deregulated and new means of off-loading and sharing risks being developed by the financial markets, while the economic prospects of companies fluctuated more than during the post-war decades, equities markets acquired a new general economic importance. Maximising shareholder value became the sole indicator of corporate performance.

Coinciding with these changes was a decline in self-confidence among government elites. The collapse of the Keynesian paradigm in the 1970s inflation crises, and the inability of routine bureaucracy to deal flexibly with the constantly changing tasks of a rapidly shifting economy and society led to a crisis of government style. At another time, government might have remodelled itself, learning lessons from other institutions but retaining a clear view of its *sui generis* role as the force sustaining public and collective interests. During the 1980s and 1990s, however, the triumphant resurgence of private capital and management produced an orthodoxy that whatever methods the private sector used were bound to be superior to those of the public. Government organisations were required to behave as though they were firms, a process rapidly extended to universities, schools, hospitals, charities and virtually all other non-capitalist institutions. Analogues of profits have to be found to provide goals; analogues of money to be the forms taken by exchange; analogues of customers to deal with everything from students to prisoners.

As the virtuosi in the ways of the capitalist enterprise, private-sector managers and the consultants who advise them therefore become major repositories of wisdom on how to run the state. Persons from profit-making businesses are appointed to preside over public organisations, further increasing their already disproportionate access to government and policy-makers. Public-sector and charitable organisations also turn increasingly to business for sponsorship, which involves becoming attractive to the priorities and preferences of businessmen. Government encourages this process by making its own allocations dependent on ability to attract private sponsor-ship, in effect enabling business donors to determine how government spends public money. Something very similar occurs when donations are tax deductible. In this way capitalists acquire many bites at the cherry of political power.

Further still, the market model being generally deemed superior, and governments generally wanting to reduce their debts, large parts of the public sector have been sold to private capital in privatisation exercises.[5] This has further increased government and public dependence on decision-making by the holders of private capital. It is a central claim of neo-classical economics that in a market economy the accumulation of capital presents no problems of social or political power, because capital operates as a mass of unco-ordinated, anonymous players in the market, subject to its rules and not actually capable of using power strategically. (Organised labour's power on the other hand is dangerous, because it requires an interference with, a disruption of, markets.) However, this is true only in the text-book case of pure, perfectly competitive markets. Many privatisations have been shared out among small numbers of very large oligopolistic companies, who are sold the privatised industry or service after a far from anonymous political bargaining and lobbying process.

At the end of a century during the course of which much political energy was spent taming capital, that force has now acquired a new power and prominence, and is defining its class interests more sharply than at any time since at least the Second World War.

## The Incoherence of Other Classes

It is more difficult to tell the class story of the rest—today the clear majority—of the population: the diverse and heterogeneous groups of professionals, administrators, clerical and sales workers, employees of financial institutions, of public bureaucracies and of welfare state organisations. Defined histori-cally by education standards, incomes and working conditions superior to those of manual workers, most of these groups have often been reluctant to ally themselves to the class interests and organisations of the working class. Most have however failed to generate much autonomous political profile at all. Occupational organisations are usually (with some very important exceptions among the professions and public service employees) weak;

voting behaviour is very mixed, lacking the clear biases of manual and true bourgeois classes. This does not mean that people in these groups are apathetic about public life. On the contrary, they are the most likely to be found as active members of interest organisations and cause groups. But they are spread across a wide political spectrum of these, and therefore do not confront the political system with a clear agenda of demands—as does the resurgent capitalist class and once did the manual working class. They are often seen as politically closer to capital, in that in two-party systems they have tended historically to vote more for anti-socialist than for labour-based parties. But their position is more complex than that; they are for example strong supporters of the citizenship welfare state, especially services for health, education and pensions.

Closer inspection enables us to see more definite patterns within this middle mass. There is often a public/private division, the former far more likely to be unionised and—rather obviously—to be involved in organisations and lobbies for the protection of public services. The privatisation of much of the public sector had an important electoral logic in the 1980s, when the Conservative Party was becoming one opposed to public employees and therefore sought to reduce their numbers.

There are also major hierarchical divisions. Little or nothing connects routine office workers to senior managers, both the incomes and educational levels of the former often being considerably lower than those of skilled manual workers. It is essential to recognise the role of gender here. In general, and of course with exceptions, the lower down a hierarchy, the lower the pay, and the lower the educational level that a non-manual worker attains, the more likely she is to be female.[6] The gender divide provides at least as sharp a cultural cleavage within the non-manual hierarchy of the office or shop as the manual/non-manual one within the factory.

If one assumes that senior managerial and professional workers have good reasons to associate themselves with the political interests of capital—unless they work in the welfare state—the question why the lower ranks of the white-collar hierarchy have not developed a distinctive politics of their own becomes almost equivalent to the question: why have women not articulated an autonomous politics of the junior non-manual classes, in the way that men did for the skilled manual working class?

The puzzle can be easily answered. First, women, as guardians of the family, the non-work sphere, were less inclined than men to shape their political outlook with reference to the workplace. They participated less in organisations of all kinds, except the church. For complex reasons that need not concern us here, it has been conservative parties which have stood for these domestic and religious interests. Although large numbers of women have joined the work force during the past 30 years, the majority have done so part-time, so their particular connection to the domestic sphere—if no longer to the religious in a society as secularised as England—has only been partly attenuated.

Secondly, while men, as the gender active in public life as a matter of course, could set up unions and movements without anyone at the time regarding their male character as embodying some kind of attack on the female sex, for women the situation is very different. To articulate a feminine vision is to criticise a masculine one. Given that the majority of people relate to their wider society through their families, it is difficult for women to develop the specific interests of their distinctive occupational groups without causing domestic tension and with little hope of forming communities. It is no coincidence that specifically feminist organisations usually articulate the concerns of single women more effectively than they do those of married ones.

However, major changes have been occurring. Partly because of secularisation (though also the changed political position of the church), far more importantly because so many women work in the largely public community and social services sector, and perhaps because of the sheer increase in female employment even if it is often part-time, the development of a women's political agenda has been the most important single innovation in anti-establishment politics of the past 20 years. Its only rival in this has been the ecology movement. In response, new Labour's policy agenda is feminist in a number of areas. In this part of the middle England electorate, where some autonomous organisation and interest articulation have taken place, the political system has responded in its time-honoured way. The 1997 general election was the first occasion that a majority of British women who voted did so for the Labour Party. Curiously, therefore, at the very moment that the Labour Party was dropping its class perspective, it was in fact gaining from a major adjustment in the class structure, as women's voting began to fall into line more with their class position as primarily lower-level employees. It is unlikely that the Labour Party of the 1980s could have brought off this achievement.

Beyond the gender area, however, non-managerial, non-manual workers still exercise little autonomy in clearly defining and articulating and pressing their interests.[7] Indeed, in many employment disputes, an employee can only articulate a grievance over the exercise of managerial authority if she can demonstrate gender or ethnicity aspects in the case.

It might be objected to this account of the weakness of middle-Britain interests that if anything politicians are obsessed with this group and with responding to its concerns. However, these concerns are processed by the political system in a manner which defines them as entirely at one with those of capital. This is what Conservatives have been doing for more than a century. If new Labour is successfully rivalling them in its appeal to middle Britain, it is simply because it has started doing the same, not because it is articulating the wider concerns of these groups. They are represented as having no discontents except with the quality of public services—which is increasingly taken to mean that they want these privatised. They are encouraged to seek no means of social improvement other than for themselves and their children obediently to climb the career ladders established by business elites.

For new Labour to claim, as Mr Blair did in a speech to the Institute of Public Policy Research in January 1999, that the social mobility involved in the latter is part of its radicalism is unconvincing for a number of reasons. First, it is dishonest to promise equality of opportunity and at the same time to renounce the social-democratic critique of inequality of initial conditions, for without a reduction in these there can be no equality of opportunity. Second, general upward mobility requires very little political action and represents no great social change in a society where the number of managerial and professional jobs expands faster than could possibly be filled by the offspring of existing incumbents given normal birth rates. Finally, to claim that the old establishment is being made to make way for a new is specious if no policies are developed for reducing the position of that old establishment. These would require major taxes on inherited wealth and action against public schools. In the absence of any move for these, new Labour can only promise a new establishment that it will join the old one, not replace it.

## The Problem of New Labour

Overall, therefore, the configuration of class political power at the end of the 20th century comprises the reverse parabolæ of the manual working class and capital, with those non-manual groups potentially likely to align with interests critical of the capitalist resurgence remaining slow to define their own interests, despite the fact that they constitute the main growth points of the contemporary occupational structure. The position of new Labour can easily be understood from this perspective. Its party's former social base had become associated with defensive decline and defeat, and no longer provided a viable launching pad for accessing the future in either the electorate or substantive issues. The organisations which were supposed to ground the politicians in the concerns of the people—the Party itself and its associated trade unions—became increasingly detached from an electorate that no longer conformed to the Party's view of what it ought to look like, and gave completely misleading signals.

The achievement of new Labour was to shake off the impediment of this organisational albatross, but—with the very important exception of feminism—this has left it as a party with relatively little in terms of distinctive social interests. This leaves it free to be a party for all. But outside the electoral arena itself, in the crucial battles of day-to-day politics, to have no particular interests is to exist in a vacuum. That is something which political nature abhors, and the newly strident capitalist interests have rushed to fill it. This explains the paradox of new Labour, which has puzzled its sister parties throughout western Europe. Here was a new, refreshing, modernising force, more oriented to the future than any of the others; but as its social and

economic policy agenda emerged, it has seemed increasingly to be a con-
tinuation of the preceding 18 Conservative years.

That new Labour is moving beyond the rapprochement and co-operation
with business interests which is essential to all social democratic parties to
becoming simply a business party is evident at a number of points, not least
the unusual relationships that came to light during 1998, linking many
ministers, their advisors, firms of professional lobbyists who charge companies for access to ministers, and companies themselves. To the extent that
some of these activities are concerned with finding sources of party funds
from the business world to replace trade-union funding, they relate very
directly to Labour's dilemma of seeking an alternative social base to the
working class. The consequences are emerging at a number of points.
Employer interests have been able to secure a considerably greater influence
than labour ones over new Labour's responses to European industrial
relations policy and its own trade union legislation. The private pensions
industry is more deeply engaged in the government's pensions reform than
any organisations representing pensioners. The new firms established to sell
services to the state education system have acquired considerably greater
access to education policy formulation than have teachers' unions or local
education authorities—even Labour ones.

There is no space here to discuss all these cases in detail, but just one
illustration from education will demonstrate the general point. The government wishes to involve private business in the running of the state education
system. Official announcements stresses the value to vocational education of
involving local employers, but firms of a very particular kind are really at
stake. There is a growing number of new education enterprises, specialised
firms seeking the privatisation of parts of the state education system as a
source of profitable business. Beginning under the Conservatives by buying
parts of the privatised careers advice service, they have moved on to carry out
many of the school inspections undertaken on behalf of the Office of Standards
in Training and Education (Ofsted).[8] These firms are anxious to extend their
role. The government is developing a rhetoric of the failure of local education
authorities (LEAs), and ministers wonder aloud whether it might not be better
for private firms to run parts of educational administration. But the rhetoric of
LEA failure started early in the government's life, while LEAs were still
limited in their possible actions by the considerable reduction in their
authority over schools which had been introduced by the Conservatives.[9]

The government is giving these enterprises a leading role over LEAs in
several of the Education Action Zones that it is establishing in deprived areas,
and it has floated the idea that in general parts of a service which are not
performing well might be sold off to private firms. Ministers are careful to talk
about co-operatives and other alternatives to LEAs too, but the experience of
the privatised careers service shows that, while in the initial years some of
these may flourish, after a while a small number of profit-making concerns
cleans up the market.

It is important to see what is happening here. In the difficult world of entrepreneurship a firm's life can be made a lot easier if consumption of the product is compulsory, and just has to be sold to one central purchasing authority which is available for lobbying, rather than the anonymous business of selling in the true market. Providing services in the compulsory education system to government departments is a perfect example of such a solution. Another one is the national pensions system; while still in opposition Mr Blair praised the Singapore model of compulsory private pensions. Widely regarded as the trusted guardian of the welfare state, anxious to be rid of its own inherited lobbies and pressure groups, eager to be loved by business, fully converted to the doctrine that the capitalist enterprise provides the best available model of human organisation, new Labour is the obvious political vehicle for moves of this kind. In his January 1999 IPPR lecture, Mr Blair offered reassurance that he does not regard education, health and welfare as appropriate areas for the market. But it is not the market, as an arena of anonymous competition, which is at stake here, but privatisation and contracting-out of compulsory public services, as well as public-private partnerships, following a process of lobbying by a small number of firms with privileged political access. My theme of a return to the 19th century here breaks down; this is the economics of the 16th and 17th centuries.

Mr Blair and his colleagues are by no means the first Labour politicians to seek and receive the attentions of millionaires; they are however the first to do so with virtually no pressures from other social interests within their party to balance their influence.

In these circumstances it is not realistic to expect the Labour Party to be a force mobilising and expressing the discontents emerging from the new population. At the best of times, parties moving into government have little interest in articulating new discontents, as this only makes their own lives difficult. Parties which respond to the anxieties of new social interests are usually invaders of the political scene: the labour movement in its time, regionalist movements, green activists, and—one has to admit—racist groups. Political groupings which are new but formed from among existing parliamentary elites—like the short-lived *soi-disant* Social Democratic Party of the 1980s, or new Labour—are unlikely to play the same role. The Labour Party leadership and its circles of advisors and lobbyists have become what French and Italian socialist parties so often were: groups within the political elite who establish a certain rapport with social movements of the left, but do not really stem from those movements.

Social democrats must get used to the idea that the Party can no longer be the vehicle for reinventing social democracy. This is something that must be done through unions, movements, think tanks developing, publicising and lobbying on their own, neither constantly looking over their shoulders to ensure they have not embarrassed ministers, nor expecting the Labour Party to be the natural channel for their demands. Where the Party as a local government force, watching the privatisation of many of its activities, will stand in relation to this process it is at present difficult to see. Possibly it will become a further autonomous force, as is occurring with the movement of mayors in Italy.

In some ways this will be a less claustrophobic form of politics than we have had in Britain, where the leadership's disciplinary hold over a party prevents the latter from working independently on the interests which it seeks to represent. At the other extreme is the USA, where the absence of any national party system leaves groups of all kinds free to try to mould a party's concerns. Closer to the UK, but more relaxed, are most continental European cases, where frequent coalition government requires a separate sense of the party (which must continue to develop its own priorities) and the government (which must reach accommodations with other parties). Within limits, this can happen without immediately imparting an air of crisis and schism. A move to proportional representation might gradually bring something of this kind to the UK, but meanwhile the Party as such is likely to remain either an instrument of the leadership or something in self-destructive opposition to it. This imposes a need to look to other organisations to develop new ideas—not in opposition to new Labour, but separately from it.

One interestingly paradoxical implication of this observation is that those who fear the implications for social democracy of current political changes should not focus their anxiety on protecting the existing electoral system and opposing relations between the Labour and Liberal Democratic parties. Traditional Labour activists have usually liked the first-past-the-post system because it seems to reproduce a two-class model of society. This has always been partly illusory, in that Labour has not had a strong record of winning majorities under this system, nor has it benefited from the divorce with the Liberals which it implies. Today however when there is not even a semblance of an established two-class politics, all the model does is either to induce a hopeless nostalgia for the days of the majority manual working class, or to impose an artificially narrow discipline of two-party organisation which, given the current predispositions of the Labour leadership, cannot be used to articulate new class concerns.

British politics needs a new openness and fluidity if emerging social forces are to find their own expression. The tasks at stake in the reinvention of social democracy are extensive. To take just a few examples: Trade union concerns must evolve so that they embrace the needs of modern employees—which means both representing those in new precarious forms of employment (which will continue to grow), as well as being able to provide serious professional advice to employees whose firms genuinely involve them. The concerns of public employees must be more successfully tied to their professional role as skilled practitioners within their services, rather than as job protection. Work must be reshaped so that it both enables families to provide stable lives for their children and permits committed labour-market participation by fathers and mothers. More generally, international solutions must be sought to the insecurity being produced by unregulated capitalism—as a number of continental social democratic parties are now seeking to do. If new Labour's constitutional reform agenda provides increased political space within which these projects can be launched, that is as much of a contribution from it as can be expected.

## Notes

1 H. C. G. Matthew, 'Learning from Gladstone', *Prospect*, August/September 1998.
2 I have discussed this in more detail in 'A Third Way in Industrial Relations?', paper presented at a conference on 'Labour in Government: The "Third Way" and the Future of Social Democracy', Center for European Studies, Harvard University, 13–15 November 1998.
3 A. Giddens, *Beyond Left and Right: The Future of Radical Politics*, Cambridge, Polity, 1994; *The Third Way: The Renewal of Social Democracy*, Cambridge, Polity, 1998.
4 For a fuller analysis see C. Crouch, *Social Change in Western Europe*, Oxford, Oxford University Press, 1999, Part I.
5 It is notable that governments are permitted to regard the sale of industries or services as net increases in their assets. Strictly speaking there is no increase in assets at all, merely a change to a more liquid form. However, this accounting fiction has been permitted throughout the world because of a general ideological consensus that privatisation should be encouraged.
6 For a fuller discussion, see Crouch 1999. *op. cit.*, chs 4 and 5.
7 A specific articulation of public-service employee interests as a kind of class interest has been more sharply significant politically—and it overlaps to some extent with gender questions, such a high proportion of these workers being women. However, this can be problematic. Especially in a period of public-service retrenchment, the representation of public-service employee interests can lead to the interpretation of public service as being primarily about their jobs—rather than services for citizens and their quality. This was one of the distortions of early 1980s socialism, one consequence of which has been new Labour's distancing itself from these interests.
8 This is in itself interesting; usually privatisation involves putting a service in the market sector, but regulated by a public agency. In the UK today schools remain in the public sector, while much of the task of regulating them is given to private firms.
9 Labour's School Standards and Framework Act 1998 had already redesignated local authority schools as 'community schools'.

# Has Globalisation Killed Social Democracy?

PAUL HIRST

IT has been fashionable to portray social democracy as finished. It is widely held that social democracy depended for the effectiveness of its economic and welfare policies on the temporary mid-century hegemony of the nation state. Now, however, only some form of economic liberalism is compatible with the new global economy dominated by international market forces. The nation state can no longer govern processes that are supra-national, chief of which are the world financial markets. The only remaining issue, if it is true, is whether it is possible to have economic liberalism with a human face, or just rampant and ruthless *laissez faire*. This is the rational core of the current debate about the Third Way, once one discounts the media hype.

In a world of growing inequality within and between nations, the *issues* that social democracy attempted to address are still there. The questions are whether there is a viable politics to articulate them and whether there are effective means to deal with them. Resolving these questions depends on the two others addressed in this article. Whether globalisation exists in the way that is frequently claimed, as the dominance of national economies by uncontrollable world market forces? Whether social democratic politics can redefine itself, outside of the institutions that prevailed in post-1945 Europe, and preserve the welfare state?

## How 'Global' is the World Economy?

The state of the world economy is hotly debated. The evidence for and against globalisation is complex and its significance tends to depend on which of the competing hypotheses one inclines toward. However, there seem to be good grounds to dispute the thesis that there has been a rapid and recent process of economic globalisation. In *Globalisation in Question*, Grahame Thompson and I have argued against the notion of a truly global economy driven by supra-national market forces and dominated by trans-national corporations.[1] Rather, we claim that there is still an inter-national economy, based on flows of trade and investment (that are modest relative to GDP) between the three main economic blocs of North America, Japan and Europe. This we call the Triad. At the core of the Triad are two nation states, the USA and Japan, and the EU, an association of states that pool sovereignty for certain common purposes. Nation states are thus not declining in power per se. States now have radically different governance capacities and face different constraints. Small well governed states outside the Triad do have options for

Published by Blackwell Publishers, 108 Cowley Road, Oxford OX4 1JF, UK and 350 Main Street, Malden, MA 02148, USA

autonomous action, as the very different macro-economic policies of Singapore and Taiwan show. Both have either ridden-out or avoided the worst of the Asian crisis. The EU has not stripped its member states of sovereignty, rather it has enhanced their overall capacities by governing and stabilising key economic variables, and in particular by promoting co-ordinated action in external economic policy, giving most of the states an influence in international negotiations they would otherwise lack.

It is only possible to present the evidence against the extreme globalisation thesis here in summary form as follows.

- With the exception of the USA—where the ratio almost doubled from 10.5 per cent to 19 per cent between 1973 and 1995—for most major advanced economies the ratio of merchandise trade to GDP at current prices is only marginally higher or actually lower than it was in 1913— Germany had a ratio of exports and imports to GDP of 35.1 per cent in 1913 and 38.7 per cent in 1995 and the UK 44.7 per cent in 1913 and 42.6 per cent in 1994. This is hardly a revolution in international exposure.
- It is often argued that these figures are misleading. With widespread capital mobility, foreign direct investment (FDI) has become a major substitute for trade. Yet the figures show that the main flows of FDI are between members of the Triad and between them and a small number of newly industrialising countries. In 1981–1990 75 per cent of flows were between members of the Triad. In 1991–96 the Triad plus the ten most important developing country recipients of FDI (China being defined as the coastal provinces plus Beijing), some 30 per cent of the world's population, accounted for 84 per cent of FDI flows. The developed world is not being stripped of its capital.
- Whilst the stock of inward FDI as a percentage of GDP more than doubled in the developed economies between 1980 and 1995, nevertheless, the overall stock of FDI remains modest for most major countries: in 1980 the figure for Japan was 0.3 per cent of GDP and it was the same in 1995; for the USA it was 7.7 per cent in 1995 (up from 3.1 per cent) and for Germany 6.9 per cent (up from 4.5 per cent). The share of FDI in gross fixed capital formation confirms this. In Japan it was a negligible 0.1 per cent in 1994, in the USA it was 5.9 per cent in 1995 (comparable to the average for 1985–90), and in Germany it was 1.7 per cent in 1995 (again comparable to the 1985–90 average of 1.6 per cent). The vast bulk of investment is still domestically owned and there is little tendency toward escalating capital mobility, certainly not on a scale that would alter domestic capital markets.
- Most companies are multi-national rather than truly trans-national, that is, they produce and trade from a base in one of the Triad countries. Thus German multi-national manufacturing firms concentrated 75 per cent of their sales in the home region in 1992–3 (up from 72 per cent in 1987). The comparable figures for Japan and the USA being 75 per cent and 67 per cent respectively. In the case of assets, Japanese manufacturing firms had 98 per cent of their assets in their home/country region in 1992–3, and US

multinationals 73 per cent. This concentration of multi-nationals in their home bases is confirmed by the low share of the output of affiliates in GDP. On a world scale this rose from 5.2 per cent in 1982 to 6.7 per cent in 1990 before falling back to 6.0 per cent in 1994. For the European Union the share rose from 5.7 per cent to 8.6 per cent in 1990 before falling to 7.7 per cent in 1994. For North America, affiliates accounted for 5.1 per cent of GDP in 1982, rising to 7.0 per cent in 1990 and then falling to 5.2 per cent in 1994. The share of affiliates shows how much of the output of multi-nationals is produced by them outside of their main location. The figures hardly demonstrate a vast growing trend toward the internationalisation of production.

- Lastly, there is the issue of the internationalisation of financial trading. Much is made of the huge volumes of daily trading in the financial markets (about $1.3 trillion). This ignores the fact that a great deal of this is 'churning' the same stock of capital. Moreover, the role of these flows in the distinct national capital markets is still relatively minor. Thus foreign holdings of equity in major economies are quite low: 5 per cent in the USA, 11 per cent in Japan, 9 per cent in both Germany and the UK, all at the end of 1996. The degree to which pension funds invest in foreign assets varies enormously from 4 per cent in the USA, 3 per cent in Germany, 14 per cent in Japan, to 60 per cent in Hong Kong in 1993. The foreign assets and liabilities of commercial banks also vary greatly, from low figures like 2.6 per cent of assets and 8.2 per cent of liabilities in the USA in 1996, to very high levels like 47 per cent of assets and 48.8 per cent of liabilities in the United Kingdom. The figures for pension funds and banks reflect different institutional and regulatory structures. Policy has some real influence here. For example, Singapore's main compulsory pension fund is required to invest in domestic financial assets and its foreign holdings are, at least formally, zero.

Enough evidence has been presented to show a world in which trade and investment are still highly concentrated among the major developed countries, in which the major multi-national companies are still closely tied to their home bases in Triad countries, and in which, despite rapidly growing volumes of international financial trading, distinct national capital markets persist. World market forces have by no means erased national economies. If that is so, then the issue of the scope and objectives of national economic policy and of supra-national economic governance is at least open to debate rather than being foreclosed in favour of further global de-regulation.

## What is Social Democracy?

Social democracy is generally presented by its critics and advocates of the new Third Way in the form of caricature. The caricature presents social democracy as statist and bureaucratic, as tied to an obsolete class system, as corporatist and dependent on a national economic sovereignty that has passed away in the era of open economies. Yet if we strip away this caricature and the historically contingent features, then social democracy can itself be seen as the original third way between *laissez-faire* capitalism and state socialism. Its aim was and is to stabilise and humanise capitalism, containing the scope of market forces. Three elements are essential and enduring in the social democratic project. First, that it attempts to minimise the cost of capitalism for individuals, either through growth and employment enhancing policies, and/or, through welfare state provision for the contingencies of unemployment, ill-health and old age. Secondly, and this distinguishes it from social market versions of the welfare state, that it attempts to tackle and reduce major unjustifiable inequalities in power and wealth. Thirdly, that it accomplish these objectives within the limits set by parliamentary democracy on the one hand, and private property and the market economy on the other.

These goals certainly require the exercise of the public power, but not rigid statism. It is debatable whether they require capital controls, or whether the economic sovereignty of the Bretton Woods states was as real as is now believed. Welfare provision certainly does not require top-down bureaucracy, and services can be provided to a substantial degree through the third sector, through publicly-funded citizens' organisations in civil society. Social democracy does not need to be conceived in class terms, it was always seen in the general interest of the mass of the population. As we shall see, traditional corporatist institutions may have declined, but negotiated social governance is alive and well across Europe. Business elites in much of Europe still see the need to co-operate with other social interests in order to maintain economic performance. It is interesting to note that even a confirmed moderniser like Anthony Giddens in *The Third Way*, though he sees the need to adapt to changed conditions, also sees that a radical centre worthy of the name can only be a revitalised social democracy.[2]

The question is whether these enduring tasks of social democracy can be accomplished in a new context. The key threat contained in the rhetoric of globalisation is capital mobility. Fritz Scharpf perceptively set the terms of the problem in *Crisis and Choice in European Social Democracy* in the late 1980s: mobile capital and immobile labour change the terms of the bargaining, capital can threaten to defect and is thus able to sanction policies and levels of tax to which it objects.[3] If policy is set by business interests and capital markets rather than the state, then democracy is irrelevant—the people can vote for what they like, business elites will decide what they get. The limits of the market system are then so severe that no worthwhile radical policy can be accomplished within them. John Gray argues in *False Dawn* that the 'social democratic regime presupposed a closed economy' (p. 88).[4] Such regimes will be threatened by downwards harmonisation as they 'progressively dismantle themselves, so that they can compete on more equal terms with economies in which environmental social and labour costs are lowest' (p. 92).

It is more difficult now to present the Asian economies as offering a fundamental challenge to the Triad as destined to grow uninterruptedly until they supersede the established economies. However, the real threat of capital mobility does not involve relocation to Indonesia: rather the options in Europe are more likely to be the Czech Republic or Portugal. Is the Czech Republic an Indonesia on Germany's doorstep? Hardly, it is more likely to be another Spain in which multi-nationals established branch plants and which grew dramatically on entry to the EU, but not at the expense of its neighbours.

The key question, not asked in the purely abstract account of the liberalisation of national capital accounts, is what 'capital' is? First it is firms, and, as we have seen, even most large multi-nationals have been reluctant to re-locate their core production facilities away from their main markets. Secondly, it is the funds mobilised by financial institutions, but these are in the main the savings, pensions and life insurance of the broad middle class of the advanced industrial countries. Capital is the financial assets not only of plutocrats, but of a large part of the household sector. This does not prevent the managers of financial institutions from making bad investment decisions in Latin America or Asia, nor from growing wealthy at the investors' expense, but it does show capital has to flow from and to the household sector. In the end those flows can be directed and controlled to some degree by public policy if need be. Singapore has done this with its pensions system. Capital is mobile, but it has sources and destinations that limit the scale of its migration. Domestic capital markets still provide 90 per cent of national investment. Modern economies are increasingly dominated by services, in the USA this sector now accounts for some 80 per cent of GDP. Although there is a growing trend toward the tradability of services, the vast bulk of this sector will continue to be domestically sourced, thus reinforcing the tendency toward localisation.

Thus the logic of modern economies tells against the international technocracy and many national business elites, whose current rhetoric centres on the inevitability of globalisation. It is the old lesson, clear from the 1930s, that the main job of social democracy is to rescue capitalism from the stupidity of its own leaders. Indeed, those elites in the UK and USA have become so insulated from democratic pressures or countervailing powers that they listen only to themselves. Thus the reform of corporate governance has to be central to the new social democratic agenda. Managerial power needs to be curbed, and mainly in the interests of economic efficiency through greater accountability. This is a million miles from most of the current platitudes of the Third Way. The fear of globalised capital has been central in promoting the retreat of labour parties from confronting the issues of wealth and power. This is clear in the UK, which has no shortage of capital and is a substantial net capital exporter. Yet British politicians behave as if the UK is absolutely dependent on foreign direct investment.

## Can the Welfare State Survive in a Globalised Economy?

Social democracy should have a fourfold agenda. Tackling the international financial markets and monetary system. Promoting growth and employment.

Re-regulating to promote democratic accountability of companies. Maintaining and promoting welfare and public services. I shall concentrate on the issue of welfare here, since space prevents covering the other issues properly. The growing flows of international capital raise the issues of the international re-regulation of markets to prevent destabilising crises like that of 1997–8 and also the containment of volatility in exchange rates. This task is beyond the scope of single national governments, but it always has been, and it is not beyond the scope of co-ordined action by major states and international institutions. Attitudes on these issues are changing rapidly, even among elites. It is unlikely that radical action will happen quickly, although further international de-regulation is now likely to be shelved and some measure of co-ordinated action to prevent financial crises getting out of hand has already begun. The real obstacle to co-operation and especially to a new exchange rate regime is not global markets, but the diverging interests of the major states, especially Japan and the USA.

The scope for macro-economic policies to promote growth and employment is currently unclear. It appears that changes in economic structure have made it difficult to reduce the levels of high unemployment in Europe by classic Keynesian stimuli. Beyond a certain modest boost to demand, investment is needed to create jobs and, therefore, there is a time-lag during which demand is likely to be met by foreign competitors, especially in manufacturing. External pressures will then force a change of policy. This raises the prospect of the co-ordination of national policies to stimulate demand. Yet none of the members of the Triad is well placed for this: the USA at the moment does not need it, it has been booming; Japan's government seems unable to find stimuli sufficient to persuade consumers to spend (in a context of great uncertainty and without a welfare state to cover risks, they play safe and save, thus perpetuating the crisis); and the EU is locked into a low inflation regime to secure the birth of the Euro. At present, then, the scope for co-ordinated macro-economic action beyond that to reassure financial markets seems small.

The re-organisation of domestic financial institutions for the greater protection of investors and of corporate governance in the interests of greater external accountability are also issues central to the behaviour of managers and, therefore, of capital markets. Policy change is unlikely here until radical opinion becomes less cowed about tackling business elites head on. For the remainder of this discussion I shall concentrate on the welfare state. Its survival is central to the core social democratic goals outlined above. Welfare is the non-optional element in the project, and if it is destined to be cut back to Poor Law standards under international competitive pressures, then the wider agenda of social democratic reform is stalled and the only hope is a dogged defence of what entitlements can be salvaged.

In a sense, the question posed in the heading above is a foolish one, for clearly many welfare states have done just that. In the post-1945 period, a high degree of internationalisation has been typical of smaller advanced industrial countries like the Netherlands or Sweden, whereas countries like Japan and the USA have had much lower trade to GDP ratios. Thus the apparent paradox that the smaller more exposed countries have had extensive welfare states, and the larger, more insulated countries either very incomplete systems as in the USA, or, almost none at all as in Japan. The paradox is explained by the fact that small countries are not cushioned against the shocks transmitted by the international economy, and thus have had to adapt directly to them. Part of that adaptation was the widespread adoption of active industrial policies, and the corporatist co-ordination of economic actors, in order to enhance overall economic performance. Also crucial is an extensive welfare state that enabled individuals to bear the costs of economic dislocation whilst active policy measures were taking effect. Corporatist co-operation and high welfare spending have gone together. Thus wage restraint, tax levels and welfare provision were closely linked in unions' bargaining strategies.

Dani Rodrik in a valuable discussion, *Has Globalisation Gone Too Far?*, endorses this view of the past experience of small internationalised economies, but also argues like Scharpf that capital mobility has changed the terms of the bargain between labour and capital decisively in favour of the latter.[5] Yet if such strategies are so ineffective, why are they persisted in and why do they seem generally to lead to favourable outcomes in economic performance? In a period when British politicians assume corporatism is dead, it is interesting to note that social pacts have re-emerged as a major tool of economic management in several European countries in the late 1980s and early 1990s—in Finland, Ireland, Norway, Portugal and Spain.[6] Negotiated social governance is an asset that at least some national business elites are willing to accept in order to achieve economic stabilisation in an open economy. Capital is not threatening to defect or refusing to bargain in a wide range of small highly internationalised economies.

Sweden has been taken as the paradigmatic example of social democratic failure. John Gray argues that Sweden's difficulties have 'implications for social market economies everywhere' (1998: p. 82). A public sector that consumed 68 per cent of GDP, that had set a high floor for wages, and that had acted to maintain full employment as an employer of last resort had rendered Sweden internationally uncompetitive. These policies finally led to the widespread threat of business to defect abroad and the refusal of the employers to co-operate in the corporatist system: in 1990 the SAF withdrew from centralised wage bargaining and in 1991 from all corporatist forums. But Sweden is *not* a paradigmatic case of social democratic failure. Its policies were always highly distinctive and the crisis of the early 1990s had important conjunctural causes. Sweden's troubles followed on a series of major macroeconomic policy mistakes, such as the credit-fuelled and inflationary consumer boom that followed the precipitate loosening of credit controls in the mid-1980s. This negated the benefits of the earlier major devaluation of the Krona and forced policy back toward an explicit target against the Deutschmark. Also crucial to business threats in the early 1990s was uncertainty as to whether Sweden would join the European Union, a vital concern in such a highly export-oriented economy.

Sweden was not alone in making major policy errors. Thatcherite Britain had a similar experience with the dismantling of credit controls and the reckless 1988 budget, followed by the debacle of ERM entry in a period of rapidly accelerating inflation. Sweden is also unusual in having one of the most concentrated industrial structures in the world. It is dominated by a few large multi-national firms, heavily export-oriented and controlled by a tiny wealthy elite. Post-war social democratic policies boosted the export competitiveness and profitability of those firms, whilst leaving their management and ownership unchallenged. Only too late did social democratic strategists, like Rudolf Meidner, see that the effect of their wages solidarity policies had been to create super profits. The government's introduction of wage-earner funds to receive a share of equity came too little too late. By then the major firms had so much control over the Swedish economy that they could dictate the policies of the country. Thus did the Swedish social democrats pay for their arm's-length indulgence of the power to manage in the 1950s and 1960s.[7]

One has only to make a short ferry trip to see that Sweden is by no means typical of Scandinavia, let alone of social democracy in general. Moreover, Sweden is slowly recovering economically. It has been forced to accept unemployment, but it has not dismantled its welfare state. If high levels of public expenditure inevitably crippled economic performance and led to capital flight, then Denmark ought to be finished. In 1993 public expenditure was 63.8 per cent of GDP and taxes were 51.6 per cent of GDP in 1995, the highest in the EU. Yet, after a poor performance in the 1980s, Denmark has recovered well in the 1990s, with growth above the EU average, falling unemployment, and a positive balance of payments. Denmark's welfare state still enjoys majority public support and there has been little effective agitation against it from business. The reason is that Denmark has a very diverse industrial structure, heavily dependent on small- and medium-sized firms. Denmark also has a relatively weakly-regulated labour market, and whilst the rules for dismissal are highly favourable to employers, benefits have been readily available. The welfare state is funded mainly from general income taxes and VAT at 25 per cent: corporate taxes and employers' contributions to social security benefits are low. Thus, providing the general population is willing to pay for it, the welfare state imposes few direct costs on businesses. This is also a service-centred rather than a benefits-centred system. Most families benefit from good public services, like readily-available day-care for children. Hence there is a public perception that all benefit from the welfare regime. Denmark has one of the most egalitarian distributions of income in the world, with collectively funded services as an important part of the standard of living. The society is not divided into insiders and outsiders, with a distinct 'welfare class' that the employed pay for but do not identify with. Only 3 per cent of households in which the principal wage earner was unemployed were below the poverty line in 1988 compared to nearly 50 per cent in the UK.[8]

Denmark can be seen as exceptional, but other examples show that European welfare states can reform and adapt, boosting economic performance whilst maintaining levels of welfare that are high by comparison with other industrial countries. In the late 1980s the Netherlands appeared to be a failing economy and a clear demonstration of the employment-restricting effects of continental-style welfare systems, with high social insurance costs borne by employers. Firms adapted by boosting productivity and shedding labour. They were able to do so by using the pension system to fund early retirements and by using disability benefits to get rid of marginal workers. In 1983 the employment/population ratio was 52 per cent—the lowest in the OECD. In 1989 in a population of 15 million there were 1 million on disability benefits, and unemployment was still approaching 10 per cent.

As Jelle Visser and Anton Hemerijck show in their perceptive study 'A Dutch Miracle': Job Growth, Welfare Reform and Corporatism in the Netherlands, the 1990s have seen a dramatic turnaround. Unemployment had fallen to 6.5 per cent in 1996, employment growth has been above the EU average at 1.5 per cent, and inflation remains low at 2.5 per cent.[9] These outcomes have been achieved by corporatist negotiation over wages and employment conditions, and vigorous government action to restrict access to benefits and promote employment. Whatever one's stance on economic theory, the Netherlands was carrying an unsustainable burden of those able to work living on permanent welfare. The employers and unions together used the consociational machinery to dump problems on the welfare state. Reform has been successful, even if cuts in access to benefits and benefit levels were very unpopular. Both coalition partners, Christian Democrats and Social Democrats, lost heavily in the 1994 elections amidst widespread protests. The social democratic response, however, must be that welfare is intended to protect individuals from contingencies, not to offer an unconditional alternative to work, or to employers an easy excuse to sack workers.

Disability benefits had become a problem that had to be tackled even if Holland had been an autarchic economy. The same can be said of the Italian state pensions system. The retreat here is not from 'globalisation', but from the cumulative effects of attempts by previous governments to buy industrial peace at the expense of mortgaging the future. In the early 1990s Italy was faced by the twin pressures of recession and the conditions of European Monetary Union. Italy had to contain the galloping growth of pensions expenditure and also cut public borrowing. Servicing the public debt had begun to consume some 10 per cent of GDP and was crippling expenditure on current services. Italy does not have an over-extensive welfare state by EU standards, public expenditure on social protection stood at the relatively low figure of 24.5 per cent of GDP in 1990. The pensions system imposed escalating costs, was unsustainable in terms of Italy's demographics, consumed an excessive part of the welfare budget, and was also chaotic and unfair in the entitlements it gave to different groups of workers.

Berlusconi's attempt to impose reform by fiat collapsed in 1994 in the face of mass mobilisation by the unions and the threatened defection of coalition partners. Thereafter, the centre-left governments were able to mobilise both unions and employers for a successful national dialogue on reform. The unions participated actively and secured a national majority of workers in favour of reform. This reform was partial, but did reduce costs and also achieved greater fairness between different schemes. Italy is not a small state, and it shows that national corporatist dialogue can still work in the larger economies if the conditions are right.[10]

The point of these examples is to suggest that welfare states can adapt despite intensified international competition: there is no inevitable 'race to the bottom'. Several lessons can be drawn from these examples. First, that welfare state crises are frequently the legacy of accumulated specific features and of past macro-economic policy failure and concessions. They have specific national and institutional causes and are not mere examples of a generalised crisis of the welfare state brought on by globalisation. Secondly, that reform need not be mere retrenchment, it can contribute to enhancing economic performance, as in the Netherlands, or to ensure sustainability and fairness, as in Italy. Thirdly, the scope for negotiated social governance remains substantial and the demise of traditional corporatist institutions has been prematurely announced, even if they are less representative and are playing new roles. Even in countries with difficult and antagonistic political and industrial relations systems, like Italy, negotiated reform and dialogue are possible. Fourthly, welfare systems that rely on general taxation and universal provision are more flexible in responding to changing economic circumstances and less likely to excite employer opposition than ones which rely on corporate taxation and employer-specific contributions.

## The EU—Globalisation in One Trade Bloc?

The response to the foregoing might be to argue that European welfare states are not threatened by an abstract process of globalisation, but by the successful creation within the EU of the Single Market and the advent of Monetary Union. Capital is not forced to fly outside the trade bloc, it can still maximise its leverage by bargaining about its location in a continental-scale economic space. Fritz Scharpf has focussed on this problem in a series of seminal articles on the consequences of the further integration of the EU.[11] He argues that the EU has a chronic mismatch between its high level of economic integration and the weakness of governmental institutions at Union level, whilst national states no longer have the power to cope with the consequences of a continental-scale economy. This ushers in the prospect of regulatory competition, where national states seek economic advantage by cutting taxes and labour market regulations to attract capital. In a way this has already been happening, with the UK deliberately seeking to attract inward invest-ment through low wages and poor employment protection, or with the Netherlands using wage restraint to boost its international competitiveness. Thus Martin Rhodes contends that many of the new social pacts across Europe are examples of 'competitive corporatism', oriented toward control-ling costs and securing industrial peace but without the redistributive dimensions of traditional social democracy.[12]

Scharpf's point is that such a process of regulatory competition is above all a threat to democracy. French voters may have deliberately chosen to preserve their existing welfare entitlements, but the socialist government may be unable to secure them and at the same time meet the conditions for EMU. This sober analysis shows how naïve were the assumptions of many social democrats, especially the British Labour Party, in the late 1980s and early 1990s in expecting the EU to act as a bulwark against international competitive pressures. It was assumed that the EU would develop continent-wide welfare rights and be strong enough to prevent 'social dumping' from Asia. But the threat now seems to be less Asia than the neighbours next door. Large-scale welfare harmonisation, involving redistribution from north to south in Europe, is politically out of the question. Equally, Europe's welfare states and the entitlements they offer are so different, that real harmonisation on the model of the Single Market would involve comprehensive institutional reform across Europe and a reduction in benefits to the lowest common denominator.

Scharpf makes it clear that there are options both for national policy and at the Union level that could mitigate tendencies toward regulatory competition. A limited degree of tax and social welfare expenditure harmonisation between comparable countries like Germany and the Netherlands, rather than the impossible convergence of, say, Portugal and Denmark, would limit the scope of regulatory competition. Likewise states should shift toward forms of financing and delivery of benefits that do not provide disincentives for either employers or the unemployed. The point is that Scharpf's analysis is a worst case derived from rational choice assumptions. Even within it, there are clear options to contain capital flight. Yet most firms have other reasons for choosing to stay in a particular location. Capital markets are still stubbornly national and national business systems, including systems of industrial relations and skills formation, still offer real advantages. Thus there is another and more positive side to the fact that Europe has created a single market, but has not harmonised the institutions within which markets are embedded. Firms are insiders in one national context, and outsiders in another, with all the costs of learning and difficulties of adaptation.

Moreover, if there is a lesson from regulatory competition so far it is that it is by no means obviously a good bargain. Britain has not been more successful at attracting investment than has Ireland, in proportion to GDP, despite the latter's stronger union rights and active corporatist governance. The UK has followed the strategy of exporting capital to earn higher returns and relying on foreign firms to do its industrial investment. The effect has been to convert the UK into a branch plant economy, and major firms like LG or Siemens have withdrawn to their national productive core in times of crisis. The UK has a weak core of nationally-owned and managed firms in manufacturing. Its example shows that internationalised production and capital mobility have real limits in a world characterised mainly by nationally-based firms and distinct national production systems. The UK is an over-internationalised country in an under-globalised world.

'Globalisation' has become a key term in a minatory rhetoric aimed at silencing voices that are in favour of regulating markets rather than regulating for greater market freedom. If world free markets really prevailed and were ungovernable then national public policy would be irrelevant, and the voices that demand adaptation to global competitive pressures would be silent. There is still a clear choice in national and EU public policy between the goals of social democracy or the social market and state sponsored and subsidised *laissez faire*. This is most obvious in the Nordic countries, where there is still a vigorous advocacy of social democratic policies. It is also clear that the *laissez faire* globalist case is by no means victorious in France and Germany. It is quite possible that the EU, whilst unable to achieve welfare harmonisation, may be able to adopt policies that contain competitive pressures. The success of the Euro, a modest measure of tax harmonisation, and the capping of 'sweeteners' by local and national government in attracting inward investment would go a long way toward limiting the effects of financial market turbulence and the pressures of firms who threaten to move. Enlargement will increase the scope of such measures. In this respect the UK is once again the odd country out in both ideology and institutions. If social democracy does win the battle of ideas in Europe, then the UK will have to choose what content it will give to the Third Way.

## Notes

1 Cambridge, Polity Press, 1996; 2nd completely revised edition 1999.
2 Cambridge, Polity Press, 1998—all data cited below are from these two sources.
3 Ithaca NY, Cornell University Press, 1991—originally published in German in 1987.
4 London, Granta, 1998.
5 Washington DC, Institute of International Economics, 1997.
6 See G. Fajertag and P. Pochet, eds., *Social Pacts in Europe*, Brussels: European Trade Union Institute/Observatoire Social European
7 On Sweden see A Martin, 'The Swedish Model: Demise or Reconfiguration' in R. Locke, T. Kochan & M. Piore, eds., *Employment Relations in a Changing World*, Cambridge MA, MIT Press, 1995; and J. Pontusson and P. Svenson, 'Labour Markets, Production Strategies and Wage Bargaining Institutions: the Swedish Employer Offensive in Comparative Perspective', *Comparative Political Studies*, Vol. 29, 1996, pp. 223–50.
8 On Denmark see J. Goul Anderson, 'The Scandinavian Welfare Model in Crisis?

Achievements and Problems of the Danish Welfare State in an Age of Unemployment and Low Growth', *Scandinavian Political Studies*, Vol. 20, No. 1, 1997, pp. 1–31; and E. Oddvar Eriksen & J. Loftager, eds., *The Rationality of the Welfare State*, Oslo, Scandinavian University Press, 1997.

9 Amsterdam, Amsterdam University Press, 1997; see also J. P. van der Toren, 'A "tripartite consensus economy": the Dutch variant of a social pact', in Fajertag and Pochet, eds., *op. cit.*, pp. 181–93; and the 1998 OECD report on the Netherlands which broadly confirms Visser and Hemerijck's findings.

10 On Italy see L. Baccaro & R. Locke, 'Public Sector Reform and Union Participation: The Case of Italian Pension Reform'; and M. Regini and I. Regalia, 'Employers, Unions and the State: The Resurgence of Concertation in Italy', *West European Politics*, Vol. 20, No. 1, 1997, pp. 210–30.

11 F. Scharpf 'Negative and Positive Integration in the Political Economy of European Welfare States' in G. Marks et. al., eds., *Governance in the European Union*, London, Sage, 1996; and F. Scharpf, 'Economic Integration, Democracy and the Welfare State', *European Journal of Public Policy*, Vol. 4, No. 1, 1997, pp.18–36.

12 M. Rhodes, 'Globalisation, Labour Markets and Welfare States: A Future Competitive Corporatism', Florence,, EUI Working Paper RSR No.97/36 1997.

# New Keynesianism and New Labour

## WILL HUTTON

SOCIALISTS may be unwilling to concede it, but socialism, at least as conceived by its founding fathers, is in its death throes. Its ethical values remain as alive as ever, and it has solid and irreversible social achievements to its name, but its statist economic programme and the feebleness of the protections it offered individualism and personal freedom have overwhelmed it. At the end of the twentieth century, socialism is only alive to the extent it has adopted the softer, pluralist and more capitalist-friendly values of its near sibling—social democracy. The vitality of liberal capitalism, globalisation, consumerism, the new individualism, the decline of working class solidarity and, paradoxically, the right's acceptance of the need for public health, education and some form of welfare protection have fatally undermined it. But the open question is whether the same forces that are destroying socialism are about to upend social democracy.

The distinction between the two traditions may be fine, but exist none-theless. Social democracy incorporates the same commitment to economic and social justice as socialism, but it attempts to reconcile that commitment with a parallel commitment to individual liberty. It is prepared to make greater compromises with the political centre in order to win political power, and above all it is prepared to be reformist about capitalism rather than attempting to challenge and replace it. Instead of aiming to construct a new economic and social order in which planning and collective ownership play a central role—although most socialists also see such socialist initiatives as coexisting with the market and private ownership in some way—it aims rather to regulate, manage and govern capitalism. Social democrats want to deploy the state to serve their ends, but do not see the state as so embodying those ends that it can replace the private sector; private ownership and the profit motive remain key components of a social democratic universe in a way they cannot in a socialist world. The project is the governance of capitalism, not its substitution.

Beneath these differences lie a number of underlying assumptions that are rarely explicitly stated. Social democrats, while keenly aware of the inequal-ities and oscillations of capitalism and sympathetic to the Keynesian eco-nomic tradition which sees them as inherent to its operation, do not believe the capitalist system is condemned to destroy itself through its own contra-dictions and amorality. It can be managed successfully to generate less inequality; and social institutions, notably public health and education systems, incorporating socialist values can be sustained by a cross-party coalition accepting the validity of progressive taxation to pay for them. Redistribution of income can alleviate the condition of the poorest. For

Published by Blackwell Publishers, 108 Cowley Road, Oxford OX4 1JF, UK and 350 Main Street, Malden, MA 02148, USA

social democrats the political task is to find an accommodation between current capitalism and socialist values and build a political alliance with the centre that can prosecute the consequent economic and social programme.

This will plainly change as capitalism changes, but capitalism's latest mutation, as it severs its national boundaries and goes global, is thought by some on the left to offer as fatal a challenge to social democracy as it has to socialism. Two great trends are undermining the social democratic position. The first is that its former social base on the left is in decline; the shrinking of working class institutions, notably trade unions, is reducing an important source of collectivist and altruistic values. The second is that the state is increasingly circumscribed in its options. It is losing its freedom to spend, tax, borrow and act as autonomously as it used to; moreover, state intervention is seen in practical terms as second-rate and clumsy, while the intellectual crusade by the right that public action is definitionally self-defeating has become the new common sense. Social democracy's tool, the state, is thus diminished; the reliable source of its values, working class solidarity, is under assault; and the capitalism it seeks to manage has grown immeasurably more powerful as it moves offshore. Social democracy, too, looks as though it might be heading for the ideological knackers yard.

The Third Way is new Labour's response to these trends. The argument is that the progressive force in British politics must recreate itself without any of the old socialist component and with a wholesale redefinition of social democracy; it must form an intellectual accommodation and political alliance with liberalism to form a stronger counterbalance to contemporary conservatism. Social democratic concerns to redistribute income, to manage and regulate capitalism and to sustain a universal welfare state are regarded as 'old Labour' and part of the exploded philosophy of tax and spend associated with post-war Keynesianism; indeed, apart from a generalised commitment to public education and public health, and to promote employability, the social democratic element in new Labour thinking is greatly scaled back. Rather, the conception is to counterbalance the rights accorded under the welfare state with a tougher obligation to find work, and in general to promote individual opportunity while leaving the structure of capitalism to develop largely as it chooses. Education and training become the new touchstones of policy, but within a greatly constrained growth of public spending.

This position has attracted fierce criticism from left and right alike for being all things to all men, but as an electoral proposition it has worked extraordinarily well. It has allowed the Labour Party to create a new coalition extending from the professions and enlightened big business through to moderate trade unions; it has spiked the guns of a powerful right-wing press; and it has offered a platform at least to ameliorate the rate of decline of public health and education. It is another variant on the long-standing liberal ambition to build capitalism with a human face.

The difficulty, however, is that the Third Way is driven almost wholly by defining what a progressive party is not, and in the process accepting that the basis framework of capitalism—as interpreted by the conservative right—is not in dispute. In other words, it operates within the same political economy as the right; free market capitalism works. It offers no critique of the capitalist system; no systemic programme of reform and no strengthening of those forces, whether public institutions or those in civil society, that might offer countervailing power. To build up trade unions, for example, threatens the flexibility of the labour market. To raise corporate taxes or higher rates of income tax to fund increased public spending might deter initiative and provoke a migration of capital. There is no confidence in public initiative or enterprise whatsoever: failing schools or overcrowded prisons, for example, are best solved by introducing private business or simulating its approach rather than reforming the public sector. The private corporation and its values are seen as embodying all that is best; the public sector all that is worst. There is a strong case for enlisting the private sector to serve the public interest in public private partnerships, but that presumes a capacity to define the public interest sufficiently robustly to resist private interests' natural desire to redefine it so that it might maximise their profits and advantage.

New Labour's Achilles heel is that, because it has no economic theory which is critical of capitalism, it is wide open to simple business definitions of the public interest because it has no other reference point. The private finance initiative in the NHS, competition policy, or the reform of corporate law are all, for example, cast in terms of what business wants: there is no intellectual framework that can offer any contrary ballast. The great advantage Keynesian economic theory offered social democrats was that it provided a non-Marxist critique of capitalism along with a workable economic and social programme, and allowed them to conceive the public interest as rather more than the interplay of private interests in a free market. Keynesian axioms defined the post-war common sense, and gave the left then as strong a position as the right today. It was incontestable that there was a structural mismatch between the motivations of savers and investors, which self-evidently the price mechanism alone could not solve—and this was the proximate reason for capitalism swinging between boom and bust. The issue was what the state should do to solve this embedded problem, and so legitimised government action. The way forward, to manipulate the budget deficit so that it compensated for shortfalls and excesses of demand, also allowed higher public spending and taxation—and thus gave the wherewithal to finance ambitious social programmes. Tony Crosland could argue that Keynesianism solved the growth issue and gave the state a growth dividend simultaneously; social democrats could pursue their social goals without socialising the means of production. Even the Conservative Party became part of this new social democrat consensus.

But new Labour has felt compelled to junk Keynes wholesale, and accept the new right consensus that budget deficit manipulation only disturbs the natural rhythms of the economy, and because all government debt eventually becomes monetised, is necessarily inflationary. High public spending and high taxation crowd out private spending and place an illegitimate burden on companies and individuals alike; there is some natural limit, around forty per cent of GDP, which should be the cap to the public sector's role. Even the welfare state and universal social insurance have proved counterproductive, changing individuals' natural proclivity to work and instead offering an incentive to idleness and the refusal of work opportunities. Government action should be avoided if at all possible.

The 'Third Way' has been cast within these assumptions. But all are contestable. Keynesian theory has moved on as well, and 'New Keynesianism', retaining core Keynesian insights, offers as vigorous a criticism of the dynamics of the market economy as it did fifty years ago. In the last five years of his life Keynes became increasingly preoccupied with the inter-relationship between the international trade and financial system and their impact on the policy options of any one national economy. He saw the structure of the international financial system, with its bias towards over-rewarding surplus countries and over-penalising deficit countries that inevitably accompanies the short-termism of financial markets, as a locus of economic instability in its own right. Deficit countries were forced into excessive economic retrenchment, while surplus countries could indefinitely avoid the inflation in their price level that might help deficit countries to regain competitiveness. The task was to inbuild automatic stabilisers into the international system, so that deficit countries could ameliorate the vortex of self-reinforcing downward ratchets in demand and surplus countries were forced into recycling their surpluses.

The launch of the Bretton Woods system of fixed but adjustable exchange rates along with the IMF and World Bank were a tribute to his thinking—and it is that tradition that New Keynesians are increasingly revisiting. There has also been a resurgence in interest in how, even supposing complete rationality by economic agents, there are inevitable proclivities for market systems to malfunction because prices do not convey enough information to do otherwise. For example conservative advocates of free market economics suppose that prices are necessarily flexible as buyers and sellers haggle, and that it is only interventions by governments, monopolists and trade unions that cause inflexibility. However, New Keynesians like Greg Mankiw have demonstrated that it is perfectly rational for buyers and sellers to change their prices infrequently, and that if the speed of price change varies between markets, then that alone can be a cause of economic instability. Equally, buyers and sellers may be perfectly rational, but simply have differential access to information—and that can change their bargaining strategies.

A new generation of Keynesian theorists use game theory to demonstrate how strategies by market actors are interdependent with the strategies of those with whom they bargain as they try to gain advantage. In *Just Playing*, Professor Ken Binmore argues that the gains from co-operation between market actors, in all imaginable variants of game strategy, are so overwhelming that he claims to have found a new justification of John Rawls' famous advocacy of the social contract as reflecting basic human instincts for fairness. And, lastly, there is a new interest in growth theory. Free market economists are forced to argue that if markets are efficient then growth emerges as a by-product of factors that are exogenous to the market system—the rate of population growth, for example, or the rate of technological change. New Keynesian economists such as David Romer are not prepared to treat growth as exogenous to the market system, and have made great strides in showing how public investment in education, training, transport and science can have extraordinary spillover effects on productivity growth. Endogenous growth theory, much pilloried after its brief advocacy by Gordon Brown when in opposition, is a New Keynesian advocacy of the power of public initiative in pump-priming productivity growth.

This body of theory is the political economy that must underpin any reconceptualising of social democracy. Four clear inter-related themes emerge. The first is that the first condition for any successful social democratic regime is an international economic architecture that permits countries to forge and sustain their own unique social contracts. After the financial mayhem on the periphery of the world economy over the last eighteen months, and the threat it poses to the prosperity of the western heartlands, this has never been more self-evident. Market systems do not create their own stable architecture; they ricochet from hope to despair. Although there is now a new consensus that fixed exchange rate regimes, whether in Asia or Latin America, have to be abandoned for floating rates, little is solved thereby. Countries adopted fixed exchange rates to attract inward direct investment flows, the accompanying technologies and to achieve low inflation: without them they may be less prone to financial panics and sudden withdrawals of capital, but they will find that the pace of sound economic development sharply slows as inward flows of capital and technology decelerate. The Keynesian anxiety to design an international financial system which allows a fair distribution of global economic growth is never more urgent.

Secondly a much more subtle critique of capitalism is opened up along with a redefined role for the state. If prices are inevitably sticky, information held differentially and there is a tendency for market valuations, especially those in the financial system to overshoot, then the regulatory task is to construct mechanisms of information diffusion and accountability that support and supplement the price mechanism. The issue becomes building a legal and financial constitution in which capitalism can be saved from its own tendency to create monopolies in which markets are cornered, where there is excessive short-termism and incredible rewards to insiders in the know. This is the justification for economic stakeholding; embedding in the warp and weft of capitalism incentives to behave fairly and honourably towards workers, customers, suppliers and investors alike—and where such behaviour is reciprocated.

Thirdly there is a key role for the state in trying to lift the growth of productivity by doing the job the markets do not do spontaneously themselves—addressing externalities and creating public goods. This is the argument for increasing investment, for example, in education where the social rates of return are high, and even to a degree in training where if the returns are lower and more questionable they clearly exist. Public investment in transport, science, research and development and even health brings high economic and social returns as well. The public sector's role is to lead and finance this investment itself; the use of private finance and public/private partnerships of necessity has to be sparing. After all, the private sector neglects these areas precisely because the financial returns are so diffuse and it is hard for the private sector to capture them.

And lastly there is the Keynesian case for setting out and specifying the social contract. The vague formulation of the third way—rights should be matched by obligations—needs to be more tightly drawn into a framework in which collaboration by all parties produces a better outcome than individual decision-making. If there is an obligation to search for work and undertake training, for example, that should accompany social security entitlements, then it needs to be clear what responsibility falls to the state to make sure that work is findable. In other words, if there is a case for weak and powerless individuals to take a greater responsibility for their own circumstances, then the state has to take a greater responsibility for ensuring that they have a greater chance of success than at present.

As it stands, the Third Way has become a de facto means of the state reducing its obligations and shifting the burden of risk onto those least able to bear it, while only offering limited help in compensation. This may be a legitimate position for the right, but it is no part of any conceivable social contract. The social contract approach should be generalised across the gamut—from pensions to education.

Apologists for new Labour will argue that there are traces of all these themes in its thinking, and so there are, but they are not built into a coherent political story. New Labour does not argue for membership of the euro as part of a new international financial architecture; does not portray welfare reform as part of a new and humane social contract; does not argue that the state should take a lead role in financing public investment because it raises growth; and does not take a determined position in refashioning corporate law or the banking system to make good embedded shortcomings in the price mechanism. It cannot, because it distrusts the New Keynesian political economy that underlies such an array of propositions, preferring instead to trust the conservative political economy of its opponents. In the short run this has been successful; but in the long run there is no future in creating a progressive coalition that is not progressive. And there is no liberal social democratic position possible that does not incorporate the political economy of Keynes: a truth that new Labour is set to discover the hard way.

# Response to Will Hutton

RUTH KELLY

HUTTON's analysis is powerful, but ultimately unpersuasive. He appears to have five main concerns about new Labour and the Third Way. First that it offers 'no critique of the capitalist system'. Second, he believes that new . Labour offers no systematic programme of reviving public institutions or institutions of civil society that might offer a countervailing force against the power of capital. Third, he argues that new Labour has no confidence in public initiative. Fourth, he thinks welfare is seen as bad. And fifth, he believes that new Labour has lost Keynes' insight that the international financial system is a locus of instability.

Perhaps the most fundamental concern is the first one. Does new Labour offer any fundamental critique of the capitalist system? I think it does. The Treasury's core economic insight is that Britain has suffered years of under-investment and under-performance resulting from deregulated market forces and that this has resulted in a significant 'productivity gap' between ourselves and our nearest major competitors, Germany, France, the US and Japan. And not only has Brown set about challenging the conventional orthodoxy that the underlying British growth rate cannot be raised by increasing public invest-ment, he has set about doing just that. As Hutton has indeed argued elsewhere, Labour has embraced New Keynesian growth theory—a theory which states that investment in vital public services such as education and transport can raise the underlying growth rate of the economy. Public investment over the next five years is planned to be larger and more sustained than at any time since the 1940s. The departments which won cash in the July 1998 Budget were the only ones likely to contribute to begin to lift the British growth rate and move more people into work—education, health, transport; the losers, those departments least likely to contribute to growth—agriculture, defence, the Foreign Office, the Home Office. At the same time as investing in infrastructure and in the workforce, Labour has had a systematic programme of making work pay, drawing people back into the workforce and tapping their potential: the minimum wage underpins the Working Families Tax Credit; the tax on the privatised utilities (which made excessive profits under capitalism) has been used to fund the New Deal. There has also been significant redistribution—with the minimum income guarantee for pensioners, the increase in child benefit and the help for working parents.

Second, does new Labour have a programme to reinvigorate civil society? Yes, it does. The Fairness at Work Bill will give huge new incentives to unions to enrol members in order to reach the 50 per cent membership threshold which grants automatic recognition in the workplace. Nor have other institutions of civil society been ignored—the voluntary sector, the family.

© The Political Quarterly Publishing Co. Ltd. 1999
Published by Blackwell Publishers, 108 Cowley Road, Oxford OX4 1JF, UK and 350 Main Street, Malden, MA 02148, USA 103

As Tony Blair has written in the opening chapter to his Fabian pamphlet on the Third Way, 'A key challenge of progressive politics is to use the state as an enabling force, protecting effective communities and voluntary organisations and encouraging their growth to tackle new needs, in partnership as appropriate'. The social exclusion unit has as its remit the task of including every citizen in a common and social and economic project, reintegrating them into society and tackling there all sources of the alienation.

Third, Labour does have confidence in public initiative—hence the extra £40 billion announced for health and education over the next three years, an enormous boost for public services. But, I agree, the state is (rightly) not seen as an end in itself, merely as the tool to achieve our goals.

Fourth, welfare. Before the last general election, the Labour Party committed itself to reduce the costs of economic failure. But it is a foolhardy person who would describe new Labour as slashing all state support—the Working Families Tax Credit is an extension of state support, making work pay for millions of families. The challenge for new Labour is to ween people who can contribute to society off benefits and find them new opportunities in the labour market: help for those who can, security for those who cannot. Individuals are no longer seen as atomistic, floating detached in a world to which they have no obligations. Instead, they are seen as participative citizens in society, capable of exercising responsibilities as well as claiming rights.

Fifth, the international financial system. Yes, the international financial system is a locus of instability, and has been responsible for much of the present crisis in the world economy. But Gordon Brown has been at the forefront of attempts to rethink the world's financial architecture, leading the G7 towards some important improvements in co-ordination of information and regulation.

Hutton has argued that 'apologists for new Labour will argue that there are traces of all these themes in its thinking—as so there are, but they are not built into a coherent political story'. If that is the extent of the problem, then the record is not a bad one.

# Environmental Democracy

MICHAEL JACOBS

RAYMOND Williams once described ecological concern as 'a hesitation before socialism'. That of course was in the days when socialism was the love that dared speak its name and the only things before it were hesitations. But Williams' characteristically expressive remark captured the uneasy relationship between the political ideologies of the left and the greens.

Environmentalism was never properly incorporated into either the socialist or social democratic traditions. There was evident congruence of analysis. Those on the left saw the social damage wrought by market capitalism: exploitation, unemployment, inequality. Greens saw its environmental consequences—pollution, resource depletion, extinction of species. Both wanted to control it through various forms of regulated or socialised production under democratic intervention. But these fundamental commonalities failed to bridge a huge gulf between world views.

This was expressed most obviously in the battle over economic growth. For post-war social democrats and socialists, economic growth was the engine bringing to modern society, not just prosperity, but greater equality. For greens it was on an inevitable collision course with the finite capacities of the natural world. This conflict in turn had its social expression. To many on the left the environmental movement looked too much like a case of the middle classes pulling up the ladder behind them, denying higher levels of consumption to the poor and seeking to destroy jobs and raise prices through punitive environmental regulation. But the deeper divergence was cultural. For the left, industrial society itself was not in question. Throughout the twentieth century both socialist and social democratic thought were dominated by the assumptions of modernism. In technological advance they saw the liberation of humankind from natural constraints; in mass consumer society the inclusion at last of the majority in the common wealth.

By contrast, until recently, the dominant strands of environmentalism were anti-modernist in form. Greens objected not simply to the particular environmental impacts of industrial production. Based on a reductionist science which divided humankind from its place in the natural world, they saw modern technology as intrinsically exploitative, of both people and nature. Consumer society was not merely physically unsustainable; its materialist ethic, demanding the creation and satisfaction of insatiable wants, failed profoundly to meet human needs.

If socialists were contemptuous of the environmental movement's bourgeois basis, greens were therefore equally scornful of the left's labourism. To them post-war social democracy represented the co-option of the working class into capitalism, a shadow not an opponent of the right. Green politics

© The Political Quarterly Publishing Co. Ltd. 1999
Published by Blackwell Publishers, 108 Cowley Road, Oxford OX4 1JF, UK and 350 Main Street, Malden, MA 02148, USA

represented a new ideological direction altogether: 'neither left nor right,' as die Grünen in Germany put it, 'but forward'. Of course, this mutual antipathy did not prevent Labour and social democratic parties from the 1960s onwards adopting environmental policies and enacting legislation. The growing pressures of particular environmental problems—notably air and water pollution—made this imperative. But until the early 1990s this was studiously unaccompanied by any kind of ideological concession. Environmental policy, insisted the social democrats, was merely an extension of the left's long-standing tradition of public health reform. There was no deeper 'ecological' motivation. The greens readily agreed. Neither side saw gains to be made from bridging the ideological gap.

Over the past ten years, however, all this has begun to change. Today the gap is closing, and advance units from both camps are putting exploratory planks across it. The ground shifts have occurred on each side. The profound rethink forced upon the left by the neo-liberal hegemony of the 1980s has been paralleled by an equally searching reappraisal of traditional positions within the environmental movement. These processes have been different, and undertaken almost entirely separately. They are not yet complete, but they have so far led in surprisingly similar directions. In this chapter I want to explore the forces which have pushed the left and the greens towards one another in this way, and suggest how further convergence might be possible. My argument is not simply that there has been an autonomous exchange of values, though there has been some of this. It is that social democrats and environmentalists are being driven onto the same territory by common economic and cultural changes in the world they confront. Much of it is new territory for both of them.

## The New Economic Arguments

During the 1980s and 1990s two developments have done most to bring the environmental and social democratic traditions together. The first has been the increasingly inescapable facts of environmental crisis. Twenty years ago the green movement's claims were widely dismissed in mainstream politics as scare-mongering. Most people, on the left as well as on the right, regarded environmental problems as relatively insignificant and the projection of their trends as hyperbole. Today this position has become untenable. Global warming, transport congestion, urban air pollution, deforestation, depletion of ocean fish stocks: the evidence of widespread and serious damage has forced all mainstream political parties to adopt at least rhetorical environmental commitments. In this sense the argument has shifted decisively greenward.

But it has been matched by an equally significant movement in the other direction. In the mid-1980s environmentalism underwent a dramatic conversion. Adoption of the discourse of 'sustainable development', popularised by the Brundtland Report[1] in 1987, brought to an end the implacable

opposition of environmentalists to economic growth. Sustainable development focuses attention on the quality of growth, on its environmental impacts
and contribution to the quality of life, rather than its mere fact. This has
enabled at least parts of the green movement to acknowledge the possibility
that, in fact, growth and environmental protection might be compatible after
all. Where before it had been a matter almost of faith for greens to reject the
claim that industrial production could be made more sustainable by technological fixes, now technological innovation is acknowledged as a necessary
(though not sufficient) condition of progress.

The key to this is the concept of environmental productivity or 'eco-
efficiency'. Current production and consumption patterns are fundamentally inefficient, using energy and materials profligately and generating
unnecessary waste and pollution. By improving resource productivity (for
example through so-called 'clean' technologies), substituting away from
damaging inputs (such as by replacing fossil with renewable energy), and
changing the composition of output (from material-intensive goods to
labour- or information-intensive services), the economy can be made to
produce more with much less. The cost savings available may even make
this process profitable.

Acceptance of these arguments—at least rhetorically—by important elements of the business community has done a great deal to legitimate them.
Indeed, the remarkable trick conjured by the concept of sustainable development has been to bring together in a single 'discourse coalition' those
erstwhile enemies, large business and the environmental lobby groups. As
the latter are no longer committed to a simple anti-growth, anti-business
position, so the former have been enabled to recognise a moderate environmental agenda. This is not to say there is unanimity of view—environmentalists naturally want much faster progress and much stricter regulation—and
of course by no means all of the green movement has accepted the change of
position; but the discourse of sustainable development has unquestionably
brought the environment in from the political cold.

The new environmental facts and the (at least partial) reconciliation of
economic and environmental interests provide the essential platform for the
convergence of social democratic and environmental thought. But the interesting developments are still to come.

One of the most striking features of the eco-efficiency agenda is how similar
it is to the debate about the future of industrial production in Europe which
has preoccupied social democrats in recent years. This is particularly true in
Britain, where the so-called 'productivity gap' between the UK and leading
industrial economies (Germany, France, the US) has become widely discussed. The core objective in these debates is an improvement in productivity
through raising investment levels. But this is exactly what the arguments for
eco-efficiency demand. To increase resource efficiency is to improve productivity. This almost always requires investment in new technologies and new
systems. Indeed, the evidence suggests that the same technologies which can

deliver environmental improvements often also generate wider productivity gains. Clean is also lean.

For social democrats confronting the new global economy, where industrialised countries face fierce competition from the emerging low-wage economies, it has become clear that economic prosperity demands the continuous development of the most advanced high-technology sectors. But this is also the requirement of the environmental agenda. The common analysis and prescription here applies both at the micro level of the investment strategies of individual firms, and at the macro level of the structure of the economy as a whole. Talk of a developing 'weightless' economy as the information-based and service sectors expand is exaggerated: there is still plenty of material weight being generated and causing environmental damage. But the trend towards lower material intensity is certainly evident, and is the inevitable future for advanced economies. The congruence between these new economic forces and the need for 'environmental restructuring' is marked.

But the critical factor here which brings the left and the environmentalists together is that this will not just happen on its own. Government is needed, in three important areas. The first is fiscal policy. Greens have been advocating environmental taxes for several years, arguing that financial incentives can often be the most efficient and effective way of stimulating behavioural change. Taxing energy consumption, charging for pollution, levying tolls for road use: such measures can generally be expected to lead to reduced environmental damage. But they also generate revenue, and this has not been lost on Europe's Finance Ministries, including the UK Treasury. Environmental taxes of various kinds have now been introduced or are under investigation by every government in the EU. The UK has a landfill tax and petrol duty escalator introduced by the Conservative Government, has announced the levying of an energy tax on businesses, is examining water pollution and quarrying charges, and is to allow local authorities to introduce road charging mechanisms.

For today's social democrats, confronted with the awkward gap between the public's desire for better public services and its apparent resistance to paying higher direct taxes, environmental taxation has obvious attractions. The fact that such taxes penalise damaging activity gives them a political justification and legitimacy which more conventional taxes may lack, particularly if the burden falls primarily (as for example with the industrial energy tax shortly to be introduced by the UK Government) on business. If raising revenues from such taxes allows other taxes to be reduced, such as labour taxes or VAT, the evidence suggests that a 'double dividend' might even be achievable, in which lower environmental damage is complemented by higher employment. (More jobs are created by reduced costs in labour intensive sectors than are shed in pollution intensive sectors.) It is little wonder that the social democratic and green agendas are converging here.

The second field is industrial policy. The empirical evidence on environmental innovation in industry suggests that there are considerable barriers to the take-up of clean technologies and systems. Lack of information, shortage of managerial capacity, unavailablity of financial capital and risk averse managerial cultures are compounded by the problem of technological 'lock-in'. Firms become trapped in existing technological and production systems with which they are familiar and to which associated processes and systems have become adapted. New technologies need to be proven before they will be introduced, but without being introduced they cannot be proven.

But all this is entirely familiar from the experience of industrial innovation in general. It suggests what some have already begun to conclude from the debate about raising productivity and investment. The left needs to return to an agenda of active industrial policy. There needs to be greater support for research and development into environmentally benign technologies, a process to which some countries (such as Japan) have given far more resources than others (such as the UK). The regulatory and business support systems need to be brought together, perhaps at a regional level, so that small and medium sized firms can be given hands-on assistance in responding to environmental standards. Reforms need to be made in the banking system and in corporate governance structures to encourage longer-term and more innovatory investment (the familiar complaint of the left about the City of London's short-termism has environmental as well as economic impacts). Tax structures need to be reformed to give greater incentives to investment. And most of all financial resources need to be applied to key firms and sectors to encourage leading-edge technological investment which can provide demonstration models for others.

Industrial policy, broadly understood in these ways, has been one of the casualties of the British left's accommodation to the neo-liberal years. There has been a fear of heavy-handed interventionism, of the past failures in 'picking winners'. But the productivity gap is a symptom of continuing weaknesses in the British industrial economy. Low investment rates are cultural and structural, not simply responses to macro-economic conditions. There is ample scope here to incorporate the new environmental agenda into a wider reassessment of social democratic political economy.

The same is true in the third field of policy, namely international economic management. Environmentalists have for some time been concerned with the structures of the international economic system. Trade and finance liberalisation have been seen as direct causes of environmental degradation, as Third World countries are forced to compete on increasingly difficult terms for export earnings, and environmental and social protection are undermined by free trade rules and the desperate desire to attract foreign investment. For many years their critique had little impact on mainstream politics, including that of centre-left parties, whose international economic policies remained remarkably *laissez faire*.

But again this situation is changing. The global financial turmoil of the late

1990s, in which currency speculation and banking failure sparked collapse in a succession of emerging economies in Asia and elsewhere, has forced attention on the architecture of the new global economic system. Led by the British Labour Government, the advanced G7 countries have begun to make reforms. Initially this has focused on financial stability. But the forthcoming round of negotiations on trade rules under the World Trade Organisation, and the spotlight which the financial crisis has placed on the treatment of developing countries by the International Monetary Fund and World Bank, will force open the wider questions of social and environmental protection. The two sets of interests are now firmly yoked together. It will be of common concern to social democrats and environmentalists that trade rules and economic support policies do not lead to the lowering either of labour or of environmental standards, and that developing countries are not forced to cut social spending programmes and cut down forests (and so on) to repay international debt. The patenting of seeds grown in Third World countries by biotechnology corporations and the exploitation of child labour by global shoe manufacturers raise common issues of how multinational companies can be regulated on an international scale. Indeed, as the governments of the centre-left begin to flex their majoritarian muscles in the European Union, seeing that institution as a potential regulator of multinational capital rather than merely its acquiescent protector, a more actively social democratic international political economy is likely to emerge. We can expect environmental protection now to be a central objective in the new approach.

## Consumption and The Quality of Life

This convergence of the economic agendas of social democrats and environmentalists is marked, but it should not be over-estimated. Though the more pragmatic elements of the green movement have drastically toned down their anti-growth position, they remain nevertheless fundamentally opposed to the trajectory of industrial societies. The exponential expansion of consumer incomes is still in their view fundamentally unsustainable. Though they are happy to emphasise the capitalist possibilities of greater eco-efficiency now, they do not expect that technological advance will be able to keep the environmental impacts of growth in check forever. What they hope is to buy time—perhaps two decades, in which serious efficiency gains can be made in the industrialised nations and the newly emerging countries begin to approach First World levels of income and environmental impact. During this time they see their task as to address the deeper social and cultural causes of growth.

For the more profound green claim, of course, is that consumer society is bad for us. The competitive materialism that characterises modern life does not make people happier. On the contrary, the 'work and spend' treadmill, on which people are forced to work ever longer and more pressured hours to earn the greater income to keep up with the Joneses (who are doing the same), causes stress, depression, ill-health and family breakdown. It creates a culture of inauthenticity, as human relationships and simple pleasures are replaced by expensively consumed 'leisure' activities. It increases inequality as the poor are left behind, leading to greater unhappiness, the breakdown of community and higher crime. In all these ways—hidden by the misleading statistic of rising Gross National Product, which doesn't record the costs of growth—higher incomes obscure a deep failure to make people actually better off.

This has not been the social democratic view. Most people on the left have regarded consumer society relatively uncritically and income growth as a positive good. Indeed, as we noted earlier, they have tended to see green arguments as essentially middle class, seeking to deny to the poor the pleasures of higher incomes they themselves enjoy. GDP growth is still regarded as the central economic objective. But even here there is convergence in sight. It arises in the first place from an interesting change detectable in the position of the left. GDP growth *is* still the objective. But you rarely find today the gung-ho predictions or boasts about growth that used to characterise Labour and social democratic governments. Today the ambition for growth is to keep it to trend rates (2–2.5 per cent in the UK), not to raise it beyond this. This is partly because keeping inflation low remains important; but it is also because in the new global economy faster growth rates no longer look very achievable. It is the intention to make people richer under Labour; but the emphasis has shifted. In the UK Tony Blair stresses his empathy for the 'aspirations' of ordinary working families. But he expresses this as much—if not more—through education and employment opportunities as through personal consumption. Aspiration is recognised, not to be just about spending more, but about getting on in your career and getting the best education for your children. The left's language has subtly shifted. This is paralled in the environmental movement. The discourse of environmentalism in the area of consumption has changed in recent years. Radical greens still argue for voluntary reductions in personal consumption, seeking to persuade people as individuals to adopt low-impact lifestyles. But the pragmatic wing of the movement has pushed the argument onto social ground. They point out that wellbeing is not just about personal consumption. We are made better (or worse) off as well, they argue, through the social goods we consume. Clean air, uncongested streets, green spaces, unpolluted beaches, unspoilt land-scapes, a secure future for our children—these all make us better off, but cannot be purchased individually. They do not make people richer in a narrow income-based sense; they contribute rather to the *quality of life*.

The concept of quality of life has become a central component of the sustainable development discourse today. It seeks to reinterpret the long-standing green critique of consumption in a more socially and politically acceptable way. But the interesting observation for our purposes here is that in doing so it finds itself in what should be natural social democratic territory.

The notion of social goods and their contribution to the quality of life has applications well beyond the environmental. All public services (those that are free at the point of use) are forms of social good. The state health and education systems, social services, policing and local government services such as street cleaning and refuse collection all contribute to people's wellbeing, but are collectively not privately purchased. For social democrats seeking to defend and expand public services, the concept of quality of life is then useful. It insists that the wellbeing derived from collective goods and services is compared with and measured at the same time as that arising from privately purchased ones. Such an argument acquires special value, of course, in debates over taxation. Where improving public services requires raising taxes, the idea of quality of life gives social democrats new ways of arguing. Higher taxation does not make people worse off, as the right argues; it makes them better off. Today, the left needs to say, well-managed public services contribute more to wellbeing than the equivalent marginal extra private spending. Purchasing social goods collectively through taxes is a more efficient, not to say fairer, way of securing these benefits. Taxes are therefore a positive good, not simply a necessary evil.

In fact, the relevance to social democrats of the new environmentalist discourse goes beyond this. The concept of social goods may help those on the left to defend, not just public services, but a wider notion of the good society as well. Many social goods are individually experienced and contribute directly to personal wellbeing. But many do not. Their contribution rather is to some notion of collective or social wellbeing. This is certainly true of many environmental goods. Except for a small number of botanists, it is difficult to argue that the preservation of rare plant species makes any individual better off. The number of people whose personal lives will be made better by reducing marine and river pollution is rather small. Yet this does not mean that people think these aspects of the environment are unimportant and should not be protected. These goods have what environmental economists call *existence value*: people want them to exist, even though they will not themselves in any personal way benefit from them. Tropical rainforests and sperm whales similarly have existence value: many people in Britain give money to protect them, despite having no direct use for them at all. Goods with existence value are all contributions to a rich and good *society*, creating, not simply richer individuals, but a better world for them to live in.

The idea that there are social goods with collective rather than individual value in this way is an important one for social democrats. It insists that there is such a thing as society, whose wellbeing is not simply defined by the aggregation of the wellbeing of its individual members. In turn it provides a defence of many other social goods which create a better society rather than (many) richer individuals. Quality broadcasting is a social good—only publicly-funded broadcasters will provide the range of programming that creates an intelligent, diverse and creative culture, and the evidence shows that a majority even of people who never watch such programmes want them to be broadcast. Academic research, public libraries, museums, art galleries and subsisided arts all similarly contribute to the shared wealth of society, not simply to the wellbeing of those who use them. Everyone gains from living in a society which is rich in culture and learning—and in nature.

The argument applies even more importantly to the moral goods which social democrats seek to defend. For the majority of people, reducing poverty, eradicating homelessness, tackling institutional racism and treating asylum seekers compassionately cannot be described as contributions to private wellbeing. Rather they are aspects of creating a better society. As for environmentalists, it is crucial for social democrats that they can make this kind of argument. Indeed, this goes to the heart of the social democratic dilemma today. Once upon a time the left's demand for social justice had a majoritarian character. When the majority of the electorate were poor, social democrats had merely to appeal to their direct self-interest—in the terms of the present argument, to their personal wellbeing. But today, victims of the success of their own welfare state, the left's egalitarianism has a narrower direct appeal. A majority is not poor. So the arguments have to be different. In appealing to the relatively affluent, the notion of quality of life, the sense of good which people get from living in a fair society, and the value of the social goods that contribute to it, may help. Certainly they will find environmentalists fighting on the same territory beside them.

It will help in this that the environmentalists are now also concerned about the poor. In another feature of convergence, as the left has had to seek wider middle class support, so the greens have come to recognise the connections between the environment and poverty in the industrialised world. Almost all environmental problems affect the poor more than the rich, from the location of factories to air pollution caused by traffic congestion. Greens have acknowledged that, whatever the rhetoric of environmental problems affecting everyone, the rich can often buy their way out (for example, through housing) in a way that the poor cannot. Many social problems are bound up with environmental ones: damp and cold homes are caused by poor energy efficiency; poor people would benefit most from measures to promote public transport and curb the car. Though still largely middle class in social composition, the environmental movement has begun to think through the social implications of its commitments and to make connections. This can only help any wider political realignment.

## Democracy and Governance

Environmental choices are political choices. Whether it is in economic policy or in public spending and regulation to provide social goods, governments must make hard decisions. They are hard in both senses. They involve genuine conflict between differing interests, with real costs. And they are very difficult to handle. For this reason the environmental field has begun to raise critical questions about the processes of government.

In the UK, at least, the environment has traditionally been treated by government in an essentially technocratic manner. Scientific experts have been assigned to determine standards of environmental protection. Economists have performed cost-benefit analysis to determine the appropriate level. Politicians have deferred to experts, often choosing the path of least resistance to business interests, and have been decisions made with minimal reference to public opinion. But this process has become increasingly fragile. Many environmental decisions get past public opinion without difficulty. But in recent years a whole succession of environmental crises have flared up into public controversy following decisions by government which looked simple enough at the time they were made. Mass campaigns against roadbuilding, the export of live animals and the disposal of the Brent Spar oil platform, and widespread public anxiety about BSE and genetically modified foods, have revealed fundamental flaws in the processes of government. In these cases technocratic modes of decision-making have failed to understand public attitudes and perceptions. They have provoked—or revealed—widespread anxieties about society's relationship with the natural world in general and about the risks of industrialised agriculture in particular.

Controversies of this kind feed on one another: public mistrust of business interests and of governments apparently beholden to them are likely to magnify each new risk in a cumulative fashion. The rapid development of the biotechnology industry and new kinds of genetic modification seem certain to offer plenty of opportunity. This is the 'risk society' of which the German sociologist Ulrich Beck has written,[2] in which rapid technological development, largely under the control of private capital, is creating new hazards—some of them literally incalculable, in the sense of being of unknown size—for which governments have inevitably to take responsibility but over which proactive public decisions are barely being made at all.

Governance in these circumstances will never be easy; but as various environmental writers have argued,[3] the minimum requirement in dealing with questions of public risk and ethical concern is that government is open and transparent. Difficult issues must be debated in public. What creates anxiety and feeds mistrust is secrecy, the sense that experts and politicians are making decisions without public scrutiny, and possibly subject to bias from business lobbying interests. These writers advocate new techniques of public consultation and debate, such as citizens' juries, 'consensus conferences' and deliberative polling, and argue that politicians must become much more sensitive to underlying public anxieties if they are to avoid disasters of governance of the kind witnessed in recent years. Even in fields where risk is not the issue, such as land use planning, the argument is that deep conflicts will only be successfully managed if the processes of government are open and democratic, where differences in values can be argued out and contested in public. Various consultative and deliberative community planning processes are now being attempted in this vein, many of them under the umbrella of the movement for local sustainable development, Local Agenda 21.

All this is relatively new territory to environmentalists. Early greens had little interest in the state, arguing that real social change would come about at the level of the individual and community. But it will ring familiar bells to social democrats. For the left, too, has had to rethink its attitude towards governance. The problem here, of course, was the reverse of that faced by the environmental movement: not a lack of interest in the state, but an attitude of complacency towards it. The state was the instrument through which the old social democrats were confident their ends could be achieved. Elected by popular vote, but governed by Fabian technocrats, the classic tradition of social democracy assumed that the rational state knew best and that society could be run accordingly. The painful realisation for the left that the state could fail just as much as the market, that public services are frequently bureaucratic and unpopular, and that public trust in politicians and political institutions has been in freefall, has forced new thinking upon it. The response has been an emphasis, in the new social democracy, on democratic reform. In the UK this has been manifest partly in the constitutional reform agenda, commitment to which has become one of the defining features of the left. But it has also taken the form of an increasing interest in more participative processes of governance within the state—of precisely the same kinds, in fact, which have been adopted by environmentalists. Local government in particular has been experimenting (with strong encouragement from the Labour Government in Westminster) with a variety of new, more open approaches, such as local referenda, 'people's panels' and citizens' juries. The convergence is hardly coincidental. The hard choices which environmental issues present are mirrored in equally difficult questions over other areas of public policy. The need for politicians and the state to regain public confidence in their capacity to govern runs across all issues.

## Conclusion

We can thus speak of 'environmental democracy' in two different senses. Specifically, it refers to the central importance of democratic renewal to environmental politics. Only a reformed state and vibrant public sphere will be able to handle the difficult processes of technological management and conflict resolution which will inescapably be required in the new world. More generally, it offers a name for the convergence of environmentalism and the social democratic tradition. If social democracy is the democratic regulation of capitalism in pursuit of social goods, environmental democracy is its regulation for environmental goods.

Inevitably, this convergence is taking place at different speeds in different countries. In Germany, governing coalitions at state and now national level between the Social Democrats and Greens have institutionalised the relationship not just between the parties but the ideologies they represent. There are still vehement disagreements—convergence is emphatically not merger, and the 'cultural' differences between greens and social democrats remain strong.

But the very possibility of coalition government shows how far each side has moved. Similar shifts have occurred in the Netherlands and in Scandinavia.

In the UK, however, explicit convergence has been much slower. At the level of policy commitment new Labour's environmental record is quite good, but its political leadership and acknowledgement of public concern have so far been rather weak, and the Labour Party as a whole is still not comfortable with the environmental agenda. In turn the environmental movement has shown little interest in making more philosophical overtures towards it. But in the end there may be more important forces at work anyway. Environmentalism will be forced onto the agenda of social democracy because the issues it raises—food and health, transport, climate change, biotechnology—will push themselves to the front of all governments' agendas. The engagement of the environmental movement in the mainstream political world will inevitably slide it towards more social democratic (rather than utopian) policy approaches. It may not have to be an explicit goal of either side for the new environmental democracy to emerge.

## Notes

1 World Commission on Environment and Development, *Our Common Future*, Oxford, Oxford University Press, 1987. The Commission was chaired by Gro Harlem Brundtland, former Prime Minister of Norway.
2 Ulrich Beck, *Risk Society: Toward a New Modernity*, London, Sage, 1992.
3 See for example Robin Grove-White, 'Environment, Risk and Democracy', in Michael Jacobs, ed., *Greening the Millennium? The New Politics of the Environment*, Oxford, Blackwell, 1997.

# The Helmsman and the Cattle Prod

ANNA COOTE

## Introduction

One of the key features of a modern social democracy is that it has strong social objectives, but a weak set of levers for achieving them. What distinguishes New Labour from both the Conservatives and old Labour is that, unlike the former, it is fiercely committed to building a fairer and more inclusive society and, unlike the latter, it does not believe it can get there by the interventions of a 'nanny state'. It wants social change. Indeed, its identity is pinned to that ambition. But it also wants to keep taxes down, to curb spending and—in theory if not always in practice—to limit the size and scope of public institutions. To a significant degree, new Labour must hope that its defining objective will be delivered through the actions of *other people*: individuals and organisations beyond the immediate control of government.

In this essay I explore the terrain between policy formation and implementation under a government that wants, as the saying goes, to 'steer more and row less'. The quaint metaphor casts government as helmsman of a vessel powered by human energy. But since the slave galleys have passed into history, those wielding the oars cannot be forced to row. They must *want* to. They must feel it is *their* responsibility and *their* project: their oars, their boat, their preferred destination. And they must have confidence in the skills and integrity of the helmsman.

I look at why this arrangement is favoured by new Labour, then consider three ways in which it is manifested—through intersectoral partnerships, public involvement and local action—and explore the implications for a social democratic government as the century turns. I argue, inter alia, that steering-not-rowing is a matter of necessity; and that the more you encourage others to row, the harder it can be to steer.

## The 'Third Way' Imperative

Steering-not-rowing, though not original to new Labour,[1] is characteristic of 'third way' politics. It builds on lessons learned from the post-war welfare state, where state institutions grew fat and unwieldy as monopolist providers, ran up uncontrollable bills, and carved out entrenched patterns of need and dependency. It also builds on lessons learned from Thatcherite neo-liberalism, as it became evident that leaving markets and individuals to help themselves compounded inequalities, deepened divisions in society and eroded the capacity of communities to work together for a shared purpose.

© The Political Quarterly Publishing Co. Ltd. 1999
Published by Blackwell Publishers, 108 Cowley Road, Oxford OX4 1JF, UK and 350 Main Street, Malden, MA 02148, USA    117

It is born of necessity more than ideology. A government which seeks to sustain middle-class appeal while it tackles poverty and inequality cannot afford to keep bumping up taxes. So it has to look beyond the state for resources—human and financial—that will help to achieve its social objectives. A well-educated and diverse electorate whose individualist tendencies have been honed by eighteen years of Conservatism will not tolerate too much uniformity or too many restrictions on personal choice. So strategies which enable individuals—singly or in groups—to take action to improve their own lives may have more chance of success than uniform, top-down solutions imposed by direct government action.

Trust between people and politicians has never been strong, but at the turn of the century it is in steep decline. This is partly due to the unprecedented ways in which mass media create illusions of proximity and accessibility which bear no relation to the vast geographical and hierarchical distances between citizens and their elected representatives. Television and the tabloid press bring the nation's most powerful politicians into the people's living rooms and turn them into soap stars. Politicians assume a license to dissemble and manipulate. Viewers assume a kind of intimacy, which suggests an entitlement to get close, know and judge. Disillusionment easily sets in.

Trust is further undermined by the fact that governments are increasingly unable to protect people from new kinds of risk to their health and security.[2] Many contemporary risks arise from developments in science and industry, which are undertaken in the name of progress, but which have unpredictable outcomes. Science and technology cannot control the events they have set in train. Yet the convention remains that, if citizens cannot be protected against these new 'manmade' hazards, they must be protected from the knowledge that they are at risk and that government cannot shield them. There is a mismatch between citizens' expectations, what politicians and experts claim, and what is actually deliverable: a sure recipe for the erosion of trust. A democratic government with strong social objectives arguably has more need to be trusted than a neo-liberal government trying to 'roll back the state'. Ideally it must be able to effect change in a low-trust environment, in ways which can build mutual confidence with the electorate over time.

New Labour wants to steer, not row, because it really has no alternative. In government, it needs to do more with limited resources, to accommodate changing values and attitudes, and to accept the lessons of the past. So it acknowledges that promoting a fair and inclusive society cannot be left to the government, or the market or the individual alone. Of course, many aspects of new Labour's programme are still implemented by direct government action: changes to the school curriculum, new pension rules, fast track procedures for young offenders, to name but a few. But for a range of other purposes, action is required on many fronts, by many players in many combinations: public and independent bodies at national, regional and local levels, commercial and non-commercial ventures, formal and informal groupings and individuals of all varieties, in all corners of the country.

## Investing in Other People

The capacity to pursue new Labour's objectives is dispersed or shared in a variety of ways, each with its own history, rationale, opportunities and dangers. An obvious example is the devolution of power to elected bodies in Scotland, Wales and Greater London. Others include the Private Finance Initiative and contracted-out service delivery. The momentum towards constitutional devolution predates Labour's 'third way' by years, if not decades; and private finance deals and contracting out were inherited from the Tories. But there is another category of dispersal which, if not invented by new Labour (ultimately all ideas are old ones), may be regarded as especially characteristic of the Blair Government, and—as such—an expression of modern social democracy. This is the host of initiatives concerned with local regeneration and sustainability, tackling inequalities and social exclusion, and promoting better health. All are in pursuit of new Labour's defining objectives. All rely for their effect upon inter-sectoral partnerships, public participation and community-based action.

Tony Blair wrote in a 1998 Fabian pamphlet, *The Third Way*, 'Governments ... now need to learn new skills: working in partnership with the private and voluntary sector; sharing responsibility and devolving power ... answering to a much more demanding public'.[3]

Labour's public health strategy, first set out in the Green Paper, *Our Healthier Nation* in February 1998, embodies this approach: 'Without individuals, families and communities working together, Government achievements will be limited.'[4] The Green Paper articulates a 'contract' between government, communities and individuals, with distinctive responsibilities assigned to each level. Similarly, proposals for a new National Childcare Strategy, declared in May 1998: 'Above all, we want to engage all those concerned with childcare—voluntary and private childcare providers, local authorities, TECs and employers, as well as parents themselves in shaping and delivering the Strategy.'[5]

The White Paper on reforming local government, published in July 1998, refers to 'key challenges' facing modern Britain: 'sustainable development, social exclusion, crime, education and training' and declares that local councils must 'work with government, their communities and the wide range of public, private and voluntary sector bodies who operate at local level and who need to come together if these challenges are to be successfully addressed.'[6]

The New Deal for Communities, set out initially by the Social Exclusion Unit in September 1998, pledges support for 'plans that bring together local people, community and voluntary organisations, public agencies, local authorities and business in an intensive local focus'. The Government hopes, says the SEU, that some of the 'pathfinder' estates chosen to test out the new approach to neighbourhood renewal, will be 'run by bodies who have not traditionally led regeneration programmes . . . And all bids will need to involve and engage the community—they won't work if they don't.'[7]

All this suggests a speculative political investment in the possibility of people and organisations outside government being co-operative and acting effectively to help achieve the government's objectives. Like all speculative ventures, it is risky. There are considerable gains to be made, but there are hazards along the way, and there is always a chance that one could lose one's shirt.

## Inter-sectoral Partnerships

The drive to create partnerships between different arms of government, and between government and non-government bodies has intensified dramatically since new Labour came into power. 'Joined-up' policy has become the new mantra—its first major practical manifestation being the joined-up Department of Transport, Environment and the Regions. The Social Exclusion Unit was set up in the Cabinet Office to pool energies and resources for the fight against entrenched poverty and isolation. The new Health Action Zones and the Sure Start initiative for 0–3 year olds both rely on inter-sectoral partnerships—just two examples from the first two years of the new Labour government.

The partnership approach offers considerable advantages. Most social, economic and environmental problems have more than one cause, and so any effective solution is likely to come from more than one quarter. Two or more government departments working closely together in pursuit of a single objective, pooling ideas and resources, will probably produce results that are more than the sum of the parts. A project that involves non-government organisations may attract a broader base of support than one run by government alone, and will be able to tap into a wider range of experience and resources. New ideas may emerge more readily from a mixed group with different professional backgrounds, skills and organisational cultures. The interests of a single provider organisation or professional group are less likely to predominate, since the dynamics of a partnership arrangement will tend to focus attention on the shared purpose of the project. That way, the client group or service user has a better chance of remaining at the centre.

On the down side, successful partnerships can be hard to create and sustain. Disparate groups have to learn to appreciate each other's strengths and values, to work with different cultures and interests. Some are driven by the profit motive, some by philanthropy, some by a public service ethic: interests as divergent as this may be irreconcilable. Those with a habit of dominance have to learn to share power. If the arrangement is to last, it has to depend on more than the commitment of individuals or on the compatibility of leading personalities. Management systems have to be changed—often radically—to promote lateral as opposed to hierarchical relationships, greater flexibility, and a focus on outcomes rather than process or outputs.

Sometimes partnerships between government departments can only succeed if budgets are pooled; between social services and education for childcare provision, for example, or between health authorities and local government in Health Action Zones. But this pooling can give rise to intense political battles over ownership and control. There may be a fine line to tread between the advantages of pooling resources and the dangers of laying the foundations of a new monolith. When it comes to training and development, different professional groups have to learn to work together in new ways, but without creating another specialism dedicated to promoting its own interests and defending its own boundaries. (Social care, educational and nursery nursing skills are needed for 0–3 year olds in deprived areas, but do we really need a new Sure Start professional?)

Inequalities between partners can inhibit collaboration, especially where government and non-government bodies are trying to work together. How can government ensure that powerful partners, such as large businesses, will not subvert its political objectives, by having too loud a voice or taking over too much of the action? How can small community-based groups which are needed to deliver services as part of a partnership plan (to provide childcare, for example), learn to interpret the obscure language and cope with the daunting procedures common to government institutions? Government must find ways of building capacity in external organisations, and developing appropriate skills within its own ranks, so that unequal partners can work together effectively. This is much harder when, as often happens, there is a heavy residue of commitment to direct government action as an ideological goal.

Even where inequalities and ideological differences are not a problem, and where partners enjoy working together, there is always a danger that the partnership process can become an end in itself. Getting different organisations involved in sustained collaboration is quite costly and time-consuming in the best case. In the worst, more time and resources are devoted to inter-sectoral dialogue than to actions aimed at achieving the original purpose.

The need for accountability can be used as an argument for not sharing powers or functions. Groupings within local government, for example, may resist partnership arrangements on the ground that their prospective partners are unelected and unaccountable, and so they themselves must retain control of everything. On the other hand, where partnerships are formed between different arms of government (such as local and health authorities) or between public and independent bodies, lines of accountability may get lost between them, so that it is no longer clear where the buck stops. No one wants government to behave unaccountably. Systems to ensure that the duties of accountability are properly discharged will have to be reconsidered and redesigned to suit new patterns of inter-sectoral working, and these must be well understood and supported on all sides.

Anna Coote

# Public Involvement

The ubiquitous call for greater public involvement in the development and implementation of policy is not hard to justify. Decisions are likely to be better, and plans more appropriate, if the people whose lives they are likely to affect are involved in shaping them. If citizens are invited to participate in decisions made by public bodies, they may be less inclined to feel alienated from the organisation and more likely to trust the process and the outcome. Policy makers may benefit from the input of experience and ideas which would not otherwise be available to them. Public involvement in planning and executing local programmes can build confidence and capacity. It can enable local people to develop new skills, and help to ensure that there is enough enthusiasm and energy to get things done.

However, the potential benefits are easily matched by opportunities to misfire or make matters worse. It is common for organisations to place responsibility for any 'public involvement' strategy in the hands of their communications, public relations or corporate affairs departments, whose core business is usually to promote a positive message. Improving public relations need not be inconsistent with more open and democratic governance, but it often is.

Public bodies wanting to involve the public must be clear about why they want to do it and how far they want—and are able—to go down this route. Are the public to be informed about a decision that has already been taken and persuaded to approve? Are their views being sought about existing services or plans for the future? Are they being invited to share in a decision-making process or to take a decision directly, or to participate in action to implement policy? Are the public to be involved in their capacity as service users, or as groups or communities with particular interests, or simply as citizens and voters?

How these questions are answered should help to determine what means are employed to involve the public. Options, traditional and innovative, include public meetings, opinion surveys and routine consultation exercises, deliberative workshops and polls, neighbourhood forums, citizens' panels and juries, 'planning for real' and, that recently rehabilitated old chestnut, community development. There is no shortage of activity on this front, with health and local authorities and other public bodies using a wide range of strategies and methods: some following well-trodden paths, others experimenting boldly; some doing as little as they can get away with, while others push out the envelope.[9]

In the worst cases, surveys produce superficial or distorted pictures of public opinion, because respondents have no background information or chance to discuss the issues at stake. And hard-pressed voluntary organisations and community groups are so over-burdened with weighty consultation documents that they cannot do their own job properly.

Tensions often arise between protagonists of traditional representative democracy, where the will of the people is thought to be expressed only through the ballot box, and those who want to involve the public in more diverse and experimental ways. Are citizens' panels or juries, opinion polls or focus groups, just ploys to re-route the decisions of democratically elected local councillors, for example? But how much legitimacy can councillors claim if they are elected on a turn out of less than 30 per cent? Conversely, are public involvement strategies simply a fig leaf, lending respectability and an appearance of legitimacy to quangos such as health authorities, whose members really ought to be elected? Where, in all this, is the 'authentic' public voice?

Genuine efforts to involve the public in decision-making between elections can deepen and enrich the democratic process. On the other hand, an inappropriate strategy is likely to be wasteful and ineffectual, to raise expectations that cannot be satisfied, to generate more cynicism than confidence, and to render decision-making less rather than more accountable. Unless an organisation is prepared to cope with unwelcome or unpredictable results, the exercise will be counter-productive. The 'involved' public may feel they are being manipulated or exploited, or believe that whatever they do or say will make no difference—whatever methods are used to involve them. More important still, those who are severely deprived and marginalised are usually much harder to involve than those who are more resourceful and assertive, and so unless special efforts are made to reach excluded groups, public involvement strategies may compound inequalities and deepen divisions between those with a voice and those without.

So far there have been too few opportunities for organisations to learn from each other, within or between sectors, so that good practice can be developed and disseminated. Very little guidance has been issued from the centre, although, to be fair, this is partly out of reluctance to inhibit creativity or stifle the motivation that comes from a sense of local ownership. But the public are involved far more effectively in some circumstances than in others, and this will continue in the absence of a common framework of principles and shared standards.[10]

## Local Action

Just as modern social democracy or 'third way' politics depends on appropriate and effective partnership arrangements and public involvement strategies, so it depends on community-based action: all those small-scale, autonomous or semi-autonomous projects which are planned and run by groups in and around their neighbourboods. Asian women in Bradford organising a vegetable garden, to give themselves exercise, a social focus and fresh food. Families in Liverpool designing and building their own homes. Single mothers on the outskirts of Sheffield taking over a derelict building and creating a thriving community centre. Residents of a soulless east London estate clearing and renovating a neglected pond area, to give themselves 'somewhere nice to go'.[11] Credit unions, play groups, church-based activities . . . and so on.

Some of these activities are carried out in partnership with local or health authorities, with businesses or large voluntary organisations. Others are free-standing. For the purposes of this discussion, 'local action' includes any activity, which is based in the community, which is run by local people, including volunteers, and which is broadly relevant to the social objectives that define the politics of the Blair Government. Much of it goes on whether or not the government takes any notice. In policy terms, the critical questions are, how far it can be relied upon to do what government wants, and how far government can or should intervene, and to what effect.

Local action is both a means and an end for new Labour. Here are the people, the human resources, required to make things happen, and the people often take it upon themselves to raise the necessary material resources, so that there is little or no call on public funds. Ideas, energy, inventiveness and momentum can flow out of community-based groups, creating oases in deserts of deprivation, turning despair into ambition and achievement, and bringing substantial material and emotional gains to individuals and families. Public authorities may be able to stimulate, encourage and support this kind of development, but they cannot reproduce it themselves. And they can seldom provide an effective substitute. Without community action, some aspects of government policy (such as the New Deal for Communities and promoting healthy living centres) cannot be fully realised.

At the same time, one of the things the Government most wants to achieve is 'strong communities': active rather than inert citizenship and social cohesion. It wants local people with the capacity and confidence to work together to improve their own surroundings, social networks and well being, to maintain social order and to support themselves instead of relying on the state. The call for 'strong communities' has been criticised as part of a social-authoritarian agenda. However, many people, faced with the prospect of living as clients and dependents of the state, oppressed by local conditions they feel they cannot control, would like to feel they belong to a strong community.

Local action is both a building block and an outcome of a strong community. It is a component of many partnership arrangements, and it is an example of what happens at the participative end of the public involvement spectrum, where members of the public take direct action. It offers many of the same benefits. It taps into the resources of civil society, it generates new ideas and projects that are informed and driven by the people they are supposed to help; it encourages commitment and a sense of local ownership; it builds and strengthens social capacity.

It also shares some of the difficulties. Community-based activities are unevenly spread across the country and the effects are patchy. Some neighbourhoods and communities are more active than others—and the more active ones tend to be those with more resources in the first place. Those where action is most needed, for example, where poverty and powerlessness are most deeply entrenched, are often the least likely to take action on their own behalf. They also present the greatest challenge to anyone on the outside who wants to encourage them to act.

Inevitably, local action is hard to direct and control. There are clearly tensions between the Government's desire—and need—to rely on local communities acting for themselves, and its impatience with the anarchic messiness and unpredictability of local action. The travails of political innocents, the reinvention of wheels, the false starts, roundabout routes and bumpy rides of local enthusiasts unschooled in project management . . . all are anathema to the sharp, sophisticated officials and advisers at the centre who want to see 'their' policies put into practice. One senior adviser commented that he favoured the 'cattle prod' approach. (Not much decoding required: that's a long, sharp instrument designed to inflict pain from a distance to stimulate movement by slow, dumb beasts.)

New Labour in government wants movement towards its goals; results it can see, describe and reflect back to the electorate—evidence that it has delivered on its promises. But there are no direct lines of command and control: nothing quite as efficient as a cattle prod is available or acceptable, yet government must, if it is to succeed, be able to apply the right stimuli in the right places. It must find the appropriate mix of inspirational messages, incentives, sanctions and rewards, so that individuals and groups at local level will be spurred into action.

And not just any action will do. If you empower communities to shape their own destinies, how can you be sure they will use their power to do as you wish? A vibrant associational life is a sure sign of a 'strong community', but no guarantee that the Government's policy goals will be faithfully pursued. Indeed, the stronger a community, the more likely it is to have the confidence to think and act for itself, and over time it may not always see things the same way as Number Ten. What is more, a community may accumulate a wealth of 'social capital' and then use it for anti-social, inequitable purposes: for example, to harass members of an ethnic or religious minority, or to stop a social housing scheme, or sheltered accommodation for mental health patients, being developed on its patch.[12]

Evaluation presents a considerable challenge. Many projects have complex outcomes that are realised gradually over lengthy periods and often in unpredictable ways. (Sometimes the fact that isolated individuals get into contact with one another is the biggest success of a project with quite a different stated objective.) It is seldom possible to gather 'hard' evidence, for example from randomised control trials or longitudinal studies. Yet some kind of appraisal is necessary: people directly involved need to learn from their successes and failures; intermediate bodies need to assess whether money is being spent wisely (if public funds are involved); and how far outcomes are consistent with goals set locally. Another problem is that local projects can easily lose momentum and fizzle out before they achieve their own goals, let alone those of government. They need support in order to sustain themselves, but inappropriate support could dull their spirits, destroy their spontaneity and, at worst, reduce them over time to needy client groups.

The role played by local government and other intermediate bodies such as health authorities, is likely to be crucial. They can provide lines of communication, institutional back-up and procedures for monitoring and evaluation. They may be able to spot where local strengths are being used destructively, and intervene to stop 'strong communities' oppressing or excluding others. How well this works will depend on the culture of the organisation, the skills and attitudes of officials working at the interface, and the calibre of relationships that are forged with communities.

It is hard for public institutions to deal with loose, unstructured groups and networks unless there are individuals who can speak for them with some authority. Where are the points at which the intermediate bodies can open up conduits for the exchange of information and transmission of stimuli? Who represents the 'community'? Civic leaders feature strongly on the route map of the 'third way'. The ideal community leader, from government's point of view, is one who is so in tune with the government's mood, culture and politics that he or she will carry everyone along in the desired direction. Does the 'social entrepreneur' fit the bill? This is a quintessentially third-way concept, suggesting a mixture of self-starting inventiveness, assertive opportunism, accumulation and expansion, and all in a good social democratic cause.[13] What a different note it strikes from that old-left idea, the community development worker—the local council employee toiling, craftsman-like, on raw materials found in the community to develop socially useful products! The social entrepreneur appears to be the antithesis of the public servant: an individualist, a local hero, a breaker of rules and conventions. At their best, they inspire and lead their neighbours into transforming victories over bureaucratic inertia and local despondency; they make it possible for whole communities to build and share a new sense of power and to make lasting improvements to their lives.

Of course, the phenomenon goes back a long way before modern politics. Creative, charismatic individuals have operated in various guises over the years, both inside and outside the statutory sector—sometimes even as community development workers. The difference is that now they are being rebadged for the new Labour era: named, acclaimed and even trained by a new school for social entrepreneurs. Perhaps this will have a benign influence, signalling that the Government recognises the value of local catalysts and wants to bring them into the mainstream of the new Labour project. But there may be some adverse side-effects. One danger is that many who do not fit the new mould will be overshadowed and left in the margins. Examples include all those who form and join self-help and mutual aid organisations and other small, often mundane, local groups and associations. They may be doing nothing new (Women's Institutes, tenants' associations, carers' groups, Alcoholics Anonymous). They may deal with unpopular causes (drug abuse, mental health, rehabilitation of offenders). They may not have heroic leaders—though some do—but they can transform the lives of their members, and they help to form the bedrock of communities. Many of these groups are hard-pressed and struggle to survive. Many have accumulations of wisdom and experience that are rarely recognised beyond their own membership. They, too, would benefit from inclusion, encouragement and an appropriate framework of support.[14]

Another, related, danger is that the enthusiasm for novelty that infuses new Labour may lead to more conventional protagonists of local action being undervalued and overlooked. Here, examples include not only the groups mentioned above, but also community development workers, trade unionists and local councillors. In each of these categories, there are some fundamentalists who argue that there is only one true way of doing things, and that's the way it has always been; but there are also many with invaluable experience and a huge amount to offer, who are outward looking and able to move with the times. To get the most out of local action, alliances need to be built between the old and the new. Lionising social entrepreneurs may build up political tensions that make those alliances more difficult to achieve.

By their nature, social entrepreneurs want to steer as well as row. Some are contemptuous of all things to do with government and refuses to build relationships with the statutory sector. The more local activities rely on a single leader; and the more insulated they are from intermediate bodies, the more difficult it can be to sustain them over time. Social entrepreneurs, like any other kind of entrepreneur, have their share of human failings and frailties. At worst, they are erratic, obsessive egotists who believe that they alone know how to solve their neighbours' problems and strut the local stage so forcefully that no-one dares to speak or act without their permission. They end by concentrating power in their own hands, rather than empowering their fellow citizens. And they navigate their own course, which may or may not carry their communities towards social democratic goals.

Whether social entrepreneurs help or hinder local empowerment, there is another difficulty in relying upon local action, which is concerned with class and mobility. When policy makers extol the virtues of 'community', they are not talking about their own communities (the widespread intricate networks of the urban intelligentsia) or the middle-class majority (who tend to be individualistic, socially mobile and linked to friends and family by car and telephone). They are talking about those less fortunate than themselves, whose lives are bounded by their neighbourhoods because they are trapped there by poverty, frailty or other immobilising factors, which might be lone parenthood or a probation order. Policy makers see community spirit and community action as ways of sorting out the problems of social exclusion and disorder. Yet if policies to tackle entrenched poverty are successful, more individuals will become socially mobile, their horizons and aspirations stretching out beyond their neighbourhoods. How can local action be sustained when one sure result is that more people will want to get the hell out of their communities?

## Common Themes

Contemplating the dangers and dilemmas associated with partnerships, public involvement and local action, some common themes emerge. The first is concerned with diversity and equality. The challenge for a modern social democratic government is to sustain the strength and coherence of its social objectives in the context of a fragmented and dispersed delivery system. It is obliged to deal with a vast range of individuals and organisations, all with different interests, cultures and skills, and widely varying strengths and weaknesses. It must be able to welcome and accommodate differences, enable diverse groups to work together towards a shared purpose, and reach out to include and encourage those who are least powerful. It must build alliances with both the weak and the strong, yet at the same time it must ensure that advantages do not accrue to those who start out with more and drain away from those who have less.

The second theme is concerned with effectiveness. Government must develop and manage relationships with a wide range of independent organisations. 'Steering not rowing' involves leading from behind, not by the nose, facilitating activity without inhibiting or controlling, supporting without inducing dependence, listening not just telling, and being prepared to share power. It means thinking laterally, being flexible and opportunistic, making connections outside the organisational box and working creatively with diverse individuals and groups. And because these are new ways of working, capacity must be built up on the inside in order to build capacity on the outside.

Government must be able to distinguish between what works and what does not work. It must account for the actions of others, especially when they are spending public money. That calls for clear agreements, effective appraisal and transparent reporting of results back to the public. There needs to be a consistent framework for appraisal, which can be applied across the spectrum of partnership projects, public involvement exercises and local action. This will have to allow for different categories of evidence, applied to different aspects of activity. Clinical standards of evidence cannot be applied to most local projects, but that does not mean they are worthless. In many cases, it is more important to evaluate process than outcomes, and to enable those directly involved to appraise their own work.[15] The views and concerns of the end-user (or equivalent) should be at the heart of any evaluative exercise. And, especially at local level, appraisal should be collaborative, with all the players contributing. Within the framework, different categories of evidence can be useful, and standards may be set and indicators devised in varying ways to suit different kinds of activity. But the whole process must remain open to scrutiny and change, because the art of appraisal, for most kinds of activity considered here, is new and evolving.[16] The challenge for government is to ensure that lessons can be learned at all levels from diverse and innovative activities, but that appraisal does not inhibit enthusiasm and creativity, or dig procedural ruts, or become an end in itself, serving only those whose jobs depend on it.

The final theme is concerned with power and control. If you are relying on other people to row the boat, they must have the energy and motivation to do so. That implies sharing power between the centre and the periphery, between government and non-government bodies, between the state and the people; it implies sharing a sense of ownership and devolving a fair degree of control—often right down to local levels. Government must be able to maintain clear goals and find ways of steering effectively: by influence and incentive, rather than by dictat or direct intervention. Those at the centre must learn to live with less power and to govern with less certainty about how policy goals will be interpreted and developed in future; to be open and responsive to signals coming from many sources beyond their own control.

The Blair Government has a manifest urge to augment the authority of the centre, to be a strong and purposeful government, with immense power emanating from a highly popular, presidential-style premier. It wants to push through an ambitious programme of social change. It wants to consolidate electoral support behind the premier and the programme. And it wants—indeed, it needs—to share and disperse the capacity to implement its policies. Will 'steering not rowing' enhance and enrich the *democratic* life of the country in a cumulative manner, as more and better bridges are built between the state and civil society, as more citizens find and exercise their voices, as more decisions are taken and acted upon at local levels—so that those who wield the oars really do feel that it is their boat and their destination? Alternatively, will the dispersal of power into a fragmented delivery system undermine the capacity of government to meet its election promises? Or will the democratising tendencies that are part of the new Labour package be overwhelmed as the centre hones its cattle prod, developing new ways of controlling from a distance—through unequal partnerships, for example, or techniques for manipulating public opinion, or newly-bred cadres to manage local action and keep it on course?

As a test bed for modern social democracy, the Blair Government is at an interesting point in its history. At the time of writing, it is nearly into its third year, but it is still not clear whether it is predominantly a liberally-minded, democratising government, or an authoritarian, centralising government. Will it shift one way or another before the next election? Or does the 'third way' demand that it tries to maintain a tortuous path between the two—in which case, how on earth can it keep all the players on message? If the whole social democratic project is not to implode, ways must be found of building and sustaining a mature relationship between those who steer and those who row, built on mutual confidence and respect. By courting the middle ground too assiduously, or by appearing to have more spin than substance, the Blair Government could risk losing the confidence of those it most needs to help deliver its agenda.

In any event, we are likely to see new Labour growing more confident as it gets used to being powerful and to the idea of winning a second term. This confidence (which has taken a long time to develop, considering the size of Blair's majority) could cut either way. It could make new Labour more at ease with the idea of openness and power sharing, or it could make it more arrogant about its capacity to push through its policies, and to prod all of us dumb beasts into action.

## Notes

1 D. Osborne and T. Gaebler, *Reinventing Government*, Reading, MA, Addison Wesley, 1992, pp. 25–49.
2 U. Beck, *Risk Society*, London, Sage, 1992. J. Franklin, ed., *The Politics of Risk Society*, London, Polity/IPPR, 1998.
3 T. Blair, *The Third Way: New Politics for the New Century*, London, Fabian Society, 1998, p. 7.
4 Department of Health, *Our Healthier Nation*, London, CM 2852, 1998, p. 29.
5 Ministers for Women and Department for Education and Employment, *Meeting the Childcare Challenge*, DfEE, London, CM 3959, 1998, p. 14: 1.30.
6 DETR, *Modern Local Government in Touch with the People*, London, CM 4041, 1998, p. 82: 8.2–4.
7 Social Exclusion Unit, *Bringing Britain together: a national strategy for neighbourhood renewal*, Cabinet Office, London, CM 4045, 1998, p. 54: 4.7.
8 D. J. Hunter, *Managing for Health: Implementing the new health policy agenda*. London, IPPR, 1999.
9 A. Coote and J. Lenaghan, *Citizens' Juries: Theory into Practice*, London, IPPR, 1997.
10 C. Delap, *Making Better Decisions*, London, IPPR, 1998.
11 N. Gowman, *Healthy Neighbourhoods*, London, King's Fund, 1999.
12 W. Maloney, G. Smith, and G. Stoker, *Social Capital and Urban Governance: Adding a More Contextualised 'Top-Down' Perspective*, paper prepared as part of ESRC Research Programme on Cities: Competitiveness and Cohesion, 1998.
13 C. Leadbeater, *The Rise of the Social Entrepreneur*, London, Demos, 1997.
14 M. Wann, *Building Social Capital*, London, IPPR, 1995, p. 103.
15 E. Kendall, *Local Inequalities Targets*, London, King's Fund, 1999, pp. 28–37.
16 M. Barnes et al., *Citizen Participation: a framework for evaluation*, School of Public Policy, Birmingham, 1988. P. Connell, A. C. Kubisch, L. B. Schorr and C. H. Weiss, eds., *New Approaches to Evaluating Community Initiatives: Concepts, Methods and Concepts*, Washington, DC, The Aspen Institute, 1995.

# Social Democracy in a Small Country: Political Leadership or Management Consultancy?

JAMES McCORMICK AND GRAHAM LEICESTER

FOR those searching for a form of social democracy fit for the times, Scotland offers a tempting prospect. Its perceived cohesion and collectivist culture, its rejection of Thatcherism, suggest a distinct moral economy which will provide more fertile ground for modernising the left than was available to Tony Blair in the early 1990s. Blair had to win a general election in order to progress 'the project'. That meant pouring the new wine of his social democracy into some very old bottles favoured by the comfortable majority in 'Middle England'. In Scotland there is also an election to be won, but it will be fought on new terms, under new rules, and for a completely new institution. It is a moderniser's dream.

That is the theory. The reality is very different. In practice, the run-up to the establishment of a Scottish Parliament has turned out very differently. There have been visible tensions both within the Scottish system itself and in the relationship between political change in Scotland and in the rest of the UK. It is puzzling, for example, that the Government's commitment to 'joined-up' working should be accompanied at the same time by a tangible fragmentation in the machinery of government when it comes to cross-border issues. It is ironic too that the title of the first major report of the Social Exclusion Unit, *Bringing Britain Together*, in fact served only to feed the forces trying to break Britain apart: the Unit's remit does not extend to Scotland. And it is curious that the much vaunted 'new politics' that devolution and PR is supposed to bring in its wake has in fact brought out public displays of party in-fighting on a scale scarcely witnessed before, even in Scotland (principally over the selection of candidates).

The ground is littered with paradox. Perhaps the biggest paradox of all is the fact that there has already been far greater change in the political system in Whitehall and Westminster since May 1997 through the classic medium of a first past the post landslide, than is expected through a complete refashioning of the system in Scotland. It is worth considering why that is so, since there will be valuable lessons from the Scottish experience for guiding 'the project' in London through a more thorough reform of the political system in Westminster—PR, Lords reform, London government, the euro—in the years ahead.

This essay explores and tests the proposition that Scotland, because it is refashioning its political system, and because of its attitudes, political history

© The Political Quarterly Publishing Co. Ltd. 1999
Published by Blackwell Publishers, 108 Cowley Road, Oxford OX4 1JF, UK and 350 Main Street, Malden, MA 02148, USA

and relative size, will be well placed to develop a new model of social democracy. As progressives in North America grow increasingly suspicious of political and fiscal devolution, social democrats in Britain have placed their faith in political renewal through constitutional reform. We test the basis for that faith against the reality of an uninspiring political debate in Scotland on the eve of its first devolved elections. We conclude with some thoughts on how the best of Scotland's old politics and new Labour's pragmatic managerialism might be combined in a truly original social democratic government.

## Different Attitudes?

Scotland's distinctiveness is fairly well understood. On core political attitudes, Scots appear to be modestly but consistently different from the British average. They are more social democratic in outlook and voting behaviour than much of England, or at least significantly less likely to vote Conservative. There is little difference in relative priorities for government action: lower unemployment, better health, lower crime and better education. Where Scots seem to differ is over how they are prepared to achieve those ends. There has been more suspicion of private sector provision and greater faith in the value of public services, an apparently greater willingness to consider using taxation for redistribution to the worse off. This is coupled with a more critical response to privilege and patronage. On some matters of personal morality and family policy, the centre of gravity is closer to traditional values than the Southern English norm.

The sense of a distinctive Scottish politics has inevitably been heightened by the dynamic of devolution. It could be argued that, while new Labour has disavowed old-style tax and spend, the New Deal represents tax and spend on a grand scale. It is far more ambitious than the party's proposals in 1987 or 1992. As such it should have been applauded by a Scottish audience. Yet a palpable sense of disappointment was evident in Scotland less than a year after the successful devolution referendum. As the SNP pulled ten per cent ahead of Labour in the opinion polls in summer 1998, a different set of rules from Westminster clearly applied in Scotland. Just as in England, Labour had promised modest reform while in opposition, could claim to be delivering on rather more after a year in government—including the establishment of a Parliament—yet the Scots seemed unwilling to give the government much credit.

The precise cause of this disappointment with Labour in Scotland is hard to discern. But perhaps it is ultimately down to the largest attitudinal difference of all: political identity. There is a consistent and widely-shared identification with Scottishness, while a sense of what it means to be British has weakened in recent decades. This may turn out to be the most important dynamic in Scottish politics. Social democrats much further afield have had difficulty coming to terms with identity politics and lower-case nationalism. There is every sign that new Labour will struggle to adapt as well.

Commentators have speculated on the reasons for this struggle. Some conclude that the effort of delivering devolution has delayed progress on the key pledges on schools, the health service, crime and welfare-to-work. If Scottish Labour makes progress on these, it is assumed that the party's fortunes will improve. Others argue that devolution fundamentally alters the political context. The focus will increasingly fall on the battle between Labour and the SNP (constitutional politics aside, two flavours of social democracy) and who can secure the best deal for Scots. This will inevitably turn on how Scottish aspirations are articulated. For example, it is argued that Tony Blair's vision of equality of opportunity is too weak and Gordon Brown's 'quiet redistribution' too quiet for Scottish tastes, but it is difficult to distinguish short-term attitudes towards the Prime Minister from longer-run beliefs or values. We simply do not know whether most Scots would prefer the language of traditional Labour values to be emphasised more clearly. Or if many Scots have an ambivalent attitude towards success, being in favour of it for themselves and their families but reluctant to appear too ambitious. Or if an unspoken belief remains that there is a place for everyone as long as everyone knows their place and no-one has ideas too far 'above their station'.

These questions are difficult to answer, because so much political effort for two decades has been devoted to trying to defend Scotland against unpopular Conservative governments (and in the process uniting excluded groups with a large section of middle class voters offended by Mrs Thatcher's policies and approach). The idea that 'Scotland stuck with Labour' is only partly true (Labour had a modest seven-point lead over the Conservatives at the 1983 General Election) and is an example of how Scottish politics struggles to accommodate diversity and pluralism within.

Considerable effort has gone into exploring how Scotland ought to project itself on an international stage, with the rest of Britain as just one reference point among many. The organisation 'Scotland the Brand', established long before re-branding became fashionable, has conducted an in-depth analysis of how others view Scotland and the Scottish character and how perceived strengths can be turned to business advantage. What is needed, and has not been conducted, is a similar exercise of Scotland looking in the mirror to form an accurate picture of the country. Such an exercise would identify the contradictions of a society which stresses its commitment to social cohesion, yet runs some of the widest inequalities in health and well-being in Europe, and has some of the most stunning physical landscapes as the backdrop to some of the worst pockets of blight and poverty. The perception of Scotland as a beautiful, clean, socially cohesive and talent-filled nation is an ad-man's dream, but it can also foster a dangerous complacency in Scotland itself about the need to change.

Scotland knows better what it does not want to be—not 'a Westminster of the North' for example—but has been avoiding for too long deciding what it aspires to be. In order to make the best use of the greater autonomy the Parliament will offer, Scotland needs to become both more self-critical and more self-confident at the same time. We will need to open up a political space in which that painful yet creative self-examination can seriously take place.

## Scottish Policy: the Space Between

In Scotland, as in any other country, getting to grips with the reality of new patterns of diversity and inequality is more difficult than clinging to familiar stories cast on a broad canvas. These emphasise sharply contrasting differences, between 'Labour Scotland' and 'Conservative England' for example. They misrepresent the degree of pluralism existing within both and fuel a misunderstanding of each other's politics. While there may be a greater sense of security for political parties when differences are exaggerated, they fail to illuminate the importance of the intermediate positions—the political space between—that require more subtlety from us all and offer the prospect of lasting change. The Prime Minister's concept of the Third Way and earlier expressions of the Stakeholder Society have the potential to forge a new model of social democracy. Critics may seek to close down these ideas, because they do not guarantee a strategy for the centre-left, but they at least accept that there is a shared responsibility to find better solutions to economic and social problems. Throwing out that means of creating a possible new model is as risky as assuming that the new social democracy is whatever new Labour happens to do in government. Neither option is of much value.

While government seeks to blur the boundaries between public and private, the dichotomy between the two spheres appears wider in Scotland than in the rest of Britain. The Private Finance Initiative (PFI) for instance has had a rougher ride from public sector unions. The pragmatists have struck an uneasy deal, arguing that reform of the PSBR rules would be better than PFI, but PFI is better than waiting for a time that is not coming—not even with a Labour Scot in charge of the Treasury. In Scottish political debate, public and private sit together uneasily. Levering private money for capital projects in the NHS and schools tends to go against the grain, reflecting doubts that it represents long-term value for money and fears that it paves the way for private funding and delivery of core public services. PFI highlights how the Scottish political system is likely to act as a lens through which new Labour (and other) thinking will pass, being changed in the process, so that making reform coherent across the UK will be a daunting challenge. The UK government will have to concentrate on creating the environment in which new choices are possible, rather than expecting to be able to force them through from the centre.

The challenge for Scottish governance is to sharpen the focus of the lens to promote clarity of thinking and awareness of the options. In particular it should look further than the labels attached to new ideas. Glasgow City Council's proposal to transfer its housing stock to community ownership has been condemned as privatisation. A poorly-designed transfer which failed to achieve value for money, for tenants as well as the city budget, should have no part in a strategy for social democracy. Yet a straight defence of the *status quo* would not only mean insufficient money to improve the worst of the housing stock, but would also overlook the highly innovative models of municipal enterprise developed by some local authorities on the strength of their own bargaining powers with the private sector. Similarly, there are new ways of applying the traditions of mutualism to the provision and funding of local government services. Thus we need to open up a political space in Scotland seriously to explore questions of ownership and how 'profits' are shared between citizens, rather than clinging to a rigid distinction between public and private which neither sector any longer recognises in practice.

Tony Blair's attempts to prise open that space in Scotland have not gone down well. His argument that there is a space between to be called 'Middle Scotland' has been viewed by critics as the extension of an essentially English concept to the different political environment north of the border. There is little resistance to the idea of more Scots aspiring to move up the income ladder, having better jobs, education and more opportunities to learn and to own their homes. But the language and the political labelling suggests a conversion to middle class values and by implication less concern for those who never make it to Middle Scotland.

There is no future, political or otherwise, in preaching and policy-making only for the middle class. There is plenty of evidence that the dislocations in society affect all of us, not just the less well off. 'Ask not for whom the economic inequality bell tolls', as one Canadian commentator has put it, 'it tolls for thee'. Political parties must design policies which recognise that fact, and which seek to build a lasting coalition between what the Scottish Council Foundation has called the Three Nations: 'Excluded Scotland', 'Insecure Scotland' and 'Settled Scotland'. In doing so, we may conclude that the space between 'old' and 'new' Labour is more promising than either end of the spectrum, and we may come to discover that this position, which we call 'critical modernisation', is where most of the Parliamentary Labour Party is located. We might equally begin to explore the space between devolution as defined in the legislation establishing Holyrood and independence, spurred by an attitudinal shift at the centre which recognises for the first time that we live (and always have done) in a union state, not a unitary one. It is not self-evident that these spaces can co-exist or would prove stable: reinventing social democracy, as with remaking the British constitution, is a process with an unknown destination.

# Scottish Institutions: Closing the Space Down?

There are exciting opportunities in Scotland to carry that process forward significantly. Yet, as we noted earlier, the paradox is that, faced with such prospects, the Scottish debate is turning back rather than looking forward. Perhaps at the root of the paradox is the suspicion that, for the purposes of modernising the political system, the Scottish Parliament is the wrong kind of institution at the wrong time. It takes its place in a context in which, the world over, regions, localities and communities are taking greater control of decision-making, in which subsidiarity is being put into effective practice, and in which political processes generally are at least paying lip service to greater individual and local autonomy—'bottom up politics'. Yet the expression of this movement in Scotland is curiously backward-looking. There is a strong whiff of the Restoration about Scottish devolution: the first Scottish Parliament for 300 years, the repatriation of powers formerly held in Edinburgh, the chance to reverse the trends and the policy of the years of Conservative government. This is not the stuff of a forward-looking environment, nor a 'young country'.

There are many trends which are reshaping the world of government. There is a move beyond government to governance, for example, which recognises that government is only one of many actors and often not the most important one. There is a recognition that the role of government is changing, from controlling to facilitating, from refereeing to coaching. There is the trend too from pure representative to more participative forms of democracy: citizens' juries, deliberative polls, referendums, people's panels. Elected governments are having to find new ways to restore trust in their performance and to maintain public support for their programme between elections. Mechanisms of accountability are changing to accommodate the trends, with the government's first 'Annual Report' borrowing from the world of business. Public and private forms of accountability and corporate governance are mixing and learning from each other.

Then there is the knowledge-driven economy, a global trend which is reshaping the way we think about assets, regulation, work, value and almost everything else. It is an economy with new rules, not yet written, characterised again by paradox. 'Collaborate to compete', said the DTI White Paper on competitiveness at the end of last year, share knowledge and experience in order to learn, be open with research and development in order better to exploit it. These are deeply counter-intuitive messages, and their application has consequences beyond the top line of the hi-tech economy.

This is a rich and intoxicating environment in which to take over the levers of power for the first time in eighteen years. It is an environment in which (almost) everyone accepts that the world is changing, and it is a short step in the intellectual and the political argument to say that we must therefore change as well. If change is the context, change is also the imperative.

In such a climate the mantra 'what matters is what works' can carry a good deal of confidence. New Labour's eclectic form of non-ideological policy making, drawing on many sources and a range of individuals from Madsen Pirie to Alan McGee via Martin Taylor, seems to be pragmatic and defensible. It is based simply on problem-solving. Likewise the commitment to experiment, the numerous 'Zones' where normal rules are suspended in order to test different ones, must be right in a world losing touch with the old certainties, although it would be easier to defend if there were a real commitment to independent evaluation and learning before the 'experiments' are forced into the mainstream. And the Government's 'new managerialism' also strikes an appropriate note in a context dominated by the challenge of managing change. We argue below that this approach is insufficient and lacking a vital ingredient: vision. But there is no denying that it is necessary.

It is equally necessary in Scotland, and indeed there are some very good examples of it at work. But there is little evidence of this approach taking root in the machinery of central government in Scotland, either in the political parties or in government itself. The Government's lead economic development agency, Scottish Enterprise, for example can justly claim to have discovered the knowledge economy and the benefits of high technology clustering years before the DTI White Paper brought them to prominence in the UK debate. Scottish Enterprise also led the way in establishing a Strategic Future Team—scanning, scenario planning, thinking deeply about long term trends in the economy and society—an idea now mirrored in the new Future Unit in the DTI. Yet the one element missing from Scottish Enterprise's public statements about their vision of the future has been any new thinking about the role of government and the political process. Because it has for so long not had any coherent and identifiable shape, Scottish government has lain largely outside the debate about managing Scotland.

The legacy of those years, in which Scotland gained more and more administrative devolution without the political power or institutions to go with it, is a densely institutionalised landscape which mitigates against change. In the past, the best way to maximise the autonomy afforded by administrative control in Scotland of policies determined in London was to bolt down autonomy in new institutions, new government agencies which could make the most of an administrative (as opposed to a policy) remit. Hence the plethora of bodies such as Scottish Enterprise, Scottish Homes, Scottish Natural Heritage—all natural expressions of a distinction between policy and implementation which we now know can never be made to stick and which they were set up partly to exploit.

Now there is to be a new institution, a Parliament. It will be different from the others. The Parliament will express the devolution of real political power and policy-making. It will be elected by a new voting system. It has the capacity for politics as well as management. Yet, because it is an institution, and because the Scottish polity is richly experienced in indulging in institutional debate, it is the second of these attributes which has dominated the debate in the run up to the Parliament's establishment, rather than the first. The politics is almost entirely about management: how will the Parliament operate, what will the committee structure look like, how will it relate to local government, what are the consequences for other institutions such as the quangos, what is the constitutional difference between a devolved Parliament and an independent one, and what is the mechanism for making the transition?

Against the trends already identified as emblematic of modernism, the debate in Scotland has gone into reverse. The focus is now firmly on the Parliament, a classical representative institution, which people look to for leadership and agency, for intervention and social re-engineering. Against all the wider and more powerful global trends, the Scottish debate is fixated on the coming of the Parliament as the only trend that matters. Changing incentives and behaviour in order to change outcomes hardly registers.

Hence the growing sense of incomprehension between the processes of political modernisation in Scotland and the rest of the UK. Blair, like Thatcher before him, has ruthlessly by-passed the institutions, the establishment, the representative bodies, in order to promote change. From the moment he appealed to the grass roots membership of the party in order to overcome opposition to the reworking of Clause 4, to the present campaign to reach the people directly through their media in order to secure popular support for the euro, his tactics have been consistent in working around traditional forms and forums where necessary. It is no exaggeration to say that the opposite has become true in Scotland. Even the doughty Helen Liddell, travelling North with a reputation for dynamism and iconoclasm forged in sorting out pension mis-selling, has run up against the rock of the education establishment. Institutional inertia is alive and well, and positively encouraged by the Scottish interpretation of what the 'new politics' means. It was boasted, for example, that the consultation paper on how the new Parliament should operate had been sent by the Scottish Office to nearly 800 representative organisations for comment. It is another world.

## New Labour—and Caledonia—Dreaming

So what are the lessons from Scotland, both for reinventing social democracy in a small country and for transmitting energy into the wider debate? Perhaps it comes down to the vision thing. A recent issue of *Renewal* suggested in its editorial that, for all its technical and managerial success, the government is still in need of a dream.[1] Having been elected on a general promise that 'things can only get better' it now needs to paint a picture of what things will look like when they do. What is the project for?

David Marquand made the same point in his ESRC annual lecture in October last year. 'In place of ideology or myth [new Labour] has a rhetoric— an ahistorical (not to say anti-historical) rhetoric of youth, novelty and a curiously abstract future. . . . Its attractions are obvious. . . . But it lacks emotional and moral resonance. There is nothing noble about it, nothing to create a sense of common endeavour in a glorious cause. . . . It is the rhetoric of a management consultant, advising a company to design its products, not of a political leader, mobilising his followers for a rendezvous with destiny.'[2]

We see that progression, from political leader in a glorious cause to management consultant with nothing but rebranding and media relaunches in his kitbag, uncannily and precisely charted by the Scottish Secretary Donald Dewar over the period of his term of office, peaking at his own rendezvous with destiny when the devolution White Paper was published in July 1997.

Since then it has been the SNP that has cornered the market in what Marquand calls 'emotional and moral resonance'. Their appeal has been couched firmly in terms of the date with destiny, the grip of history, and an appeal to voters based on the heart-warming tryptych of 'democracy, enterprise and compassion'. Theirs is an appeal for commitment, for enthusiasm, for an emotional attachment to the sentimental ballad that has become their campaign theme tune, 'Caledonia'. By contrast, Labour's message is an institutional one: 'better off together, worse off apart'. It plays to a concern for the pounds in our pockets and the fate of the British constitution. This is an achingly rational argument in what is an emotional debate. It is time new Labour, in Scotland as much as England, had a dream.

## The Vision Thing

This is the missing link. It is, as *Renewal* and Marquand suggest, the one ingredient which could lift the 'project' out of the mire of managerialism. With a vision, the incoherence and contradictions in the programme will seem like work in progress, constructive tensions on the road to change. Without it they provide too easy a target for those sceptical about constitutional reform, cross-departmental working, and other changes in the machinery of government.

'What matters is what works' is a necessary corrective to the line that some things were beyond the pale even if, or indeed especially if, they worked better than the *status quo*. But it provides no adequate guides for the thinking about the future. The new Edinburgh Business Park boasts an elegant series of rectangular artificial lakes, bedecked with reeds, ducks and the like, which give the impression of a river flowing through the site. It is a triumph of landscaping. Except that before they started there actually *was* a river flowing through the site, but it was so noxious and polluted that they buried it underground and built a better one on top. The new pragmatism in politics must not make the mistake of burying the river.

In fact, there is a false distinction between the pragmatic and the visionary. We are merely talking about degrees of vision: one imaginative enough to bury the river, the other committed to cleaning it up. In practice there can be no action without a vision of sorts. The question is whether it is a long term, strategic one. This is something that is too dimly perceived at present in the Government's commitment to 'joined-up government'. It is easy to join things up for pragmatic reasons—avoiding duplication, saving administrative costs, improving efficiency, avoiding giving with one hand while taking away with the other—but that is to miss one of the essential elements in this style of governing: the desire to bring a variety of departments and other actors together to work towards a common set of strategic goals. That allows a much more inventive and inclusive approach to policy design, and also permits a shift to longer term investment in prevention. It is the centrality of a vision, a purpose, driving policy development and action which distinguishes 'holistic' from 'joined-up' government—perhaps the reason why most Ministers prefer the latter term.

It follows from this that the most effective government will be one which is both well organised and motivated by a vision of the good society which carries an emotional and moral appeal. It is for this reason that the report by Sir Donald Acheson on inequalities in health published in 1997 was so important. It argued, in essence, that an unequal society is an unhealthy society, and that in future all policy should be skewed towards helping the less well-off in order to correct that. It was an argument for redistribution.

That report can be seen as a test of both the managerial competence and the moral commitment of a modern social democratic government. The first test is to ask, given that the report deals with every area of policy in an holistic manner (although always with a focus on health outcomes), whether there is any way of the machinery of government dealing with such a document? On that score changes in the machinery in Whitehall since the election have made a great difference, with an enthusiastic and dedicated Minister for Public Health in an environment committed to 'joined-up government'.

But, as the tobacco advertising row perhaps suggested, the strategic vision and the moral commitment are less clear. Health is a powerful, hard indicator. There is no amount of massage that can disguise mortality figures, which now stand proxy for a number of other indicators of poverty and deprivation. A commitment to tackling inequalities in health is a commitment to tackling inequalities in society generally, qualitatively different from the language of 'equality of opportunity' in other policy areas. A government determined to reduce inequalities in health has taken on a very big and a very visible challenge. It has a dream: we need to see it more clearly articulated and more broadly owned.

We have argued that there is evidence of a stronger commitment to the moral purpose of tackling inequality in society in Scotland than exists in the South East of England. The message of the Acheson report should have been better received in Scotland, revealing as it did no more than Scots know already in their bones. There is no question about the idealism and commitment of the old politics in Scotland. What is missing is the competent managerialism of the new politics. The government is not joined up and so cannot yet become holistic. There is nowhere to put the Acheson Report, both because it tackles too many policy areas at once, and because the remit of the Inquiry extended only to England, even though its findings are relevant to the whole of the UK and deal with policies such as income redistribution which can only occur on a UK-wide level. There are issues here about 'joining-up' across the border which need to be addressed.

More important, though, is the need to take the opportunity that devolution offers to refashion the machinery of government in Scotland, to permit a form of policy-making which is both guided by a strategic vision and reflects the complexities of the modern world. Scotland's size should facilitate the former. The strong idealistic tradition in Scottish politics needs to be reinvigorated to supply the vision to fuel the latter. Both elements are necessary; perhaps we shall see them come together effectively in a devolved Scotland. If so, the constitutional reformers will have succeeded in opening up a political space in the UK where the critical moderniser can thrive and in which the machinery of government is wedded to a deep moral purpose. That is a heady brew, which promises a genuine and creative social democracy. But it cannot happen 'in one country': it can only prosper as an articulation of a vision shared at the centre.

# Notes

1 Neal Lawson, 'New Labour's Field of Dreams', *Renewal*, Vol. 7, No. 1.
2 David Marquand, *Will Labour Win?*, London, ESRC, 1998, extracted in *New Statesman*, 23 October 1998.

# New Approaches to the Welfare State

JULIAN LE GRAND

THE welfare state lies at the core of social democracy. Social security, education, health, housing, social care: policies towards all these are essential elements of the social democratic project. Any rethinking of social democracy must therefore involve some re-assessment of the welfare state: its aims, its finance and its methods of provision.

Under the Conservative administrations of the 1980s and early 1990s, the principal debate over the welfare state concerned the last of these: methods of provision, particularly so far as social services were concerned. Should public services such as health and education continue to be provided, as in the traditional social democratic welfare state, through monolithic state bureaucracies: soviet-style command and control economies, with resources allocated by managerial fiat? Or should they be decentralised in operation, with the purchaser split from the provider? Should the providers of social services, such as hospitals or schools, be given operational freedom? And, yet more controversially, should they be encouraged to compete with one another in a quasi-market environment? What should be the role of the state in such a situation? And so on.[1]

Although these debates have not gone away, the focus of political attention has shifted. The major issues relating to public services now concern their finance, rather than their provision. This has been the principal concern of the Labour Government elected in May 1997. One of that Government's major electoral planks was a tax to be levied on the privatised utilities to finance programmes for the long-term unemployed. It also set up a Royal Commission to investigate the finance of long-term social care (that published its Report in February 1999);[2] and a review team on pension finance (that published a Green Paper at the end of 1998).[3] More generally, it initiated a debate over welfare reform primarily concerned with financing the ever-growing cost of social security. Although there have been major reforms in the organisation of the National Health Service[4] and in public health,[5] it is not these that have captured public attention; instead the chief issue has been the resources going into it and how these are to be paid for.

This chapter therefore concentrates on financial issues. However, it does not pretend to review all the financing problems that confront social democratic governments with respect to the welfare state. Instead, it offers a brief discussion of some of the dilemmas over financing welfare; then it suggests a possible way of overcoming those dilemmas, with specific reference to the problem of financing long term care. The latter is developed in some detail, not only because it is an important issue in and of itself, but also because I

Published by Blackwell Publishers, 108 Cowley Road, Oxford OX4 1JF, UK and 350 Main Street, Malden, MA 02148, USA

believe it is important for policy analysts not only to point to problems, but to put forward specific proposals for dealing with them.

## Financing Welfare: a Dilemma

Concern over the public finance of the welfare state stems from two sources. One is deeply familiar to anyone who has studied or worked within the public sector: the apparently inexorable growth in the demand placed on social services and benefits, especially so-called 'universal' ones such as the National Health Service and state pensions, and the pressures this puts on the public purse. Although governments of all political persuasions have struggled with this issue, it presents particular difficulties for social democratic governments who were in many cases the founders of the universal welfare state, and with most of their politicians and supporters retaining a strong ideological commitment to its survival. The current Labour Government is not exempt from that pressure; however, it is also committed to shedding the 'tax-and-spend' image of past Labour governments and, understandably, it faces real difficulties reconciling the two.

The second worry about public finance is also of ancient lineage, although its adoption by Labour is newer. It concerns the influence of publicly financed benefits and services on the behaviour of individuals and families. In the 1980s what we then described as the 'New' Right rediscovered the old Victorian concern about the impact of the welfare state on behaviour.[6] It was argued that the availability of financial support from the state for those in adversity discouraged people from making their own arrangements for supporting themselves—or, worse, precipitated the kind of behaviour that created the problem in the first place. So unemployment benefit and income support made it easier for employers to make workers redundant, while at the same time discouraging the unemployed from looking for work; too generous invalidity or disability benefits encouraged people to define themselves as disabled or incapacitated, and again prevented them from working; single parent benefit encouraged family break-up and out-of-wedlock births; state pensions discouraged private pensions or other savings.

In fact these arguments were part of a broader attack on the social democratic welfare state: that it was based on some naive assumptions about human nature. In particular, social democrats and others on the left ignored the importance of individual self-interest as a motivating factor in human behaviour. Instead they assumed that welfare recipients were essentially passive, that beneficiaries would simply accept whatever they were offered, and would not react to any incentive structure that faced them. Even where people were not passive, it was assumed that they were principled or altruistic: that they would not take advantage of the welfare system on moral grounds, even if it offered them golden opportunities for self-enrichment.[7]

Despite its provenance on the right, this argument was taken up by many of the participants in the new Labour project, including, most notably, Frank

Field. They argued that individuals are not passive 'pawns', not simply victims of the system. They do react to the environment in which they find themselves and they do respond to incentives. Therefore those incentives have to be structured in a way that works 'with the grain of human nature'—that is, by appealing to their self-interest.[8]

Now these two anxieties about the uses of public finance—the cost, and the impact on behaviour—can lead in opposite directions so far as policy towards welfare is concerned. Worries about cost tend to focus on the financial demands of the universal services and benefits: the NHS, pensions, child benefit. And the proposed remedy usually involves compromising or indeed even eliminating their universal nature, either by introducing means-tested charges or benefits where none existed before, or by tightening up the relevant means tests where they already exist.

But the concern about the impact of the welfare state on behaviour—or the more general concern about shaping policies so as to recognise the import-ance of self-interest—does not lead to a rejection of the social democratic ideal of universal services and benefits. This is for two reasons. First, the alternative of means testing offers precisely the wrong set of incentives, both from the point of view of the individual and from that of the society. As well as helping the genuinely needy, means tests also reward those who choose not to make provision for themselves: the feckless, the improvident, the workshy. Those who work hard, or those who save for the future, are penalised through rendering themselves ineligible for any benefit. Means tests also reward the avoider and the evader. Although universal benefits can also have an impact on incentives, the impact is nothing like as profound or pernicious as that of means tests.

Secondly, universal benefits have the advantage of appealing to the self-interest of the middle class and hence in retaining their support for tax finance of benefits and social services. Many studies have shown how crucial is that support for the development and maintenance of the welfare state;[9] and even if one's principal concern is with the welfare of the poor it is unwise, to say the least, to throw that support away through excluding the middle classes from welfare benefits.

So new Labour—or, more generally, new social democracy—faces a dilemma. Should it recognise cost imperatives, jettison universality and embrace yet more means-testing? Or should it recognise the damaging effects of means tests, both on the individuals who are subject to them and on middle class support for the welfare state? Put another way, is it possible to preserve universality while restructuring incentives to appeal to self-interest and keeping down the cost to the taxpayer of public services?

An answer to the problem in the context of pensions put forward by Frank Field, both in and out of office, is to rely on compulsion. Individuals could be compelled to save a portion of their income for their pensions either through existing private institutions, or, as Field would prefer, through mutuals or co-operative institutions. This is part of what elsewhere I have termed 'legal' welfare: using the regulatory or legal system as an instrument of distribution rather than the fiscal (tax and social security) system.[10]

The problem with this idea is that that any system of compulsion sets up similar 'corrupting' effects on behaviour as do means tests. Individuals have an incentive to duck and weave, to evade and to avoid. In essence, of course, Field's proposals amount to little more than an income tax by another name; and income tax is the ultimate means test.

So is there any other way around the dilemma? I believe there is, one that relies on the (quite new Labour) notion of partnership. The next section provides an illustration of how such a scheme might work in the context of financing long-term care.

## A Partnership Proposal

There is an approximately one in four chance that anyone currently under the age of 65 will need some form of long-term residential care after they pass that age. Such care is expensive: in 1996 it was around £275 per week on average for ordinary residential care and £320 for nursing care. State aid is available to meet those charges; however, it is means tested using both an income and a savings cut-off.

It is clear that, in order to provide an adequate level of long-term care, it will be necessary to continue relying on private resources, both in financial terms and in terms of time and effort provided by informal carers. The trick is in some way to mobilise those resources (or to continue to mobilise them) in a fashion that: (a) generates enough combined resources (public and private) to provide at least a minimum level of care for those who need it and preferably a higher level as appropriate; (b) allows for users and carers to make appropriate choices over the kind and level of care provided; and (c) does not provide incentives for evasion and avoidance.

The problem with the present means-tested system of state assistance is that it meets none of these conditions. The level of provision of long-term care is universally regarded as inadequate, especially for the less well-off, and offers little in the way of choice to those involved. At the same time the means test, which requires the running down of assets until their value falls below a certain level, seems to penalise those who have had the foresight to save for their old age or for their children's inheritance. It is viewed as punitive and exploitative and encourages evasion and avoidance. As an alternative, the Royal Commission on Long Term Care has recommended a universal system of free personal care funded by taxation. However, this would be very expensive (one estimate of the cost is £6.4 billion annually by the middle of the next century). Indeed, the proposal is so expensive that it has been rejected by two of the Commission's own members in a Note of Dissent.

An alternative to the Royal Commission's proposals would involve introducing what might be termed a 'partnership' funding arrangement. This would involve a minimum level of public funding coupled with a system of matching grants for expenditure over that minimum. Under this system each person assessed as being in need of care would be entitled to a minimum level of care met from public funds. This minimum, although adequate, would be basic. For the payment of care above the minimum, the state would undertake to match £ for £ (or at some lower rate) the resources that individuals or their relatives can mobilise for their own care. To keep spending under control, there would be an overall limit on the total amount of grant that could be received by any individual.

Take the following example as an illustration of how the scheme might work. An elderly person currently living at home is assessed by a social worker as in need of residential care. For everyone so assessed, the state will automatically pay a minimum of, say, £150 per week. There are a number of possible homes in which she could be accepted, each offering different standards at different charges, from one providing a basic level of care at the government rate of £150 per week, to others offering higher quality but charging above that rate. If she (or her relatives) opt for the home with the lowest charge, the state minimum payment will meet the charge and she does not have to pay for anything out of her own resources. However, if she chooses a more expensive home, then the state will match any extra resources she puts in herself.

Now suppose she chooses a home somewhat superior in quality to the minimum, but which charges £300 per week. Then the state will pay £150 (the minimum), plus half the difference between the minimum and the charge, that is £75; the total amount paid by the state would then be £225, with the elderly person contributing £75 out of her own resources.

In this case the state is matching contributions at a £ for £ rate. However, it could choose to do so at a lower rate: say 50p or 25p per £ personally contributed. In the 50p per £ case the elderly person paying an overall charge of £300 would contribute £100 out of her own resources, while the state would contribute £150 (the minimum), plus £50 as a matching contribution: £200 in total. In the 25p per £ case, she would contribute £120, while the state would contribute £150, plus £30 as a matching contribution: £180 in total.

A major advantage of schemes such as these is that participation in them is co-operative, rather than, as with a means-tested scheme, adversarial. People have no incentive to hide their assets, to give them away, or to engage in other forms of evasion and avoidance. Rather, they have an incentive to produce their own resources, resources that can be used in partnership with the state to improve their long-term care situation. If, on the other hand, people preferred not to contribute everything to their own care, but to set aside some of their resources for their children to inherit or whatever, then they are at perfect liberty to do so; the only penalty is not benefiting from the matching grant that they otherwise would have received.

A related advantage of such a scheme would be that the means test would be completely abolished. The intrusive, demeaning and costly administrative apparatus of means tests could be entirely dispensed with. More importantly, those who did have the foresight to save and were prepared to contribute, instead of simply losing their savings as under the means-test, would be rewarded for doing so by getting better community care. The stick would be replaced by the carrot: arguably, both better social policy and better politics.

The scheme is also quite practical. In particular, it is hard to see many difficulties in either introducing the system or administering it. It does not require an elaborate apparatus for assessing people's means, for these are contributed voluntarily.

The scheme would provide more benefit to those who paid more, and thus will be less targeted on the poor than the present means-tested scheme. But *any* reform proposal that involves a move away from means testing (including, for instance, the Royal Commission's proposals) will have this feature. Moreover, this scheme would be 'progressive' at least in the sense that the more expensive the care chosen, the lower would be the proportion of the cost met from public funds. For instance, in the £ for £ example given above, three quarters of the cost is met from public funds. If the elderly person had chosen a home that charged £500 instead of £300, then she would have paid £175, and the state would have paid £325: just less than two thirds of the cost.

There is an extra point here. Strictly, it is not correct to say that the partnership scheme automatically gives more to the better off. Rather, *the scheme gives more to those who are prepared to contribute more of their own resources to their own care.* Indeed, this is one of its perceived advantages: that it helps those who help themselves. Now often, of course, those helped in this way may be the better off; but they will not always be so. For instance, relatively poor childless individuals may decide to spend more on their care than better off individuals with a family who wish to keep their children's inheritances intact. Spending on care, as with spending on anything else, is determined by needs and wants, as well as by income; and the distribution of support under the scheme will depend on that spending, not on income per se.

A possible disadvantage is that, under the scheme, the state might end up funding aspects of care of which the state would not approve. If this did look like being a problem, institutional accreditation or 'approved expenditure' procedures could help resolve it. However, it is also important to recognise that people do have different needs and wants for long-term care. In this situation most universal schemes are faced with an unpalatable choice. They can either provide a very basic minimum to everyone, thus keeping costs down, but satisfying nobody; the consequence is likely to be a residualist scheme with the poor unhappily left at the minimum and with those who can afford it trying to buy themselves out. Alternatively, a universalist scheme can provide a higher quality and quantity of care, meeting the requirements of those who want or need rather more than the basic minimum, but at an exorbitant cost to the public purse. In contrast, the partnership scheme offers both a minimum *and* help to those who want or need a higher quality and quantity of care; and, since it encourages people to volunteer their own resources, it can do so at less expense than a high quality system with full state funding.

A final concern is over provider incentives: would not providers have an incentive to raise their prices in the knowledge that the state would be meeting some of the cost? Housing benefit has had this effect on rents. However, this scheme is different from housing benefit in key respects. Housing benefit has the feature that, under some circumstances, a £1 rise in rent is met by an increase of £1 in the amount of benefit, obviously offering an incentive for providers to raise rents at no cost to the benefit recipient. However, the partnership scheme does not have this feature. Even under the most generous version of the partnership scheme (the £ for £ matching rate), an individual would have to bear half of the cost of any increase in charges; under the less generous versions, they would have to bear two-thirds (50p per £ scheme) or four-fifths (25p per £ scheme) of the increased cost. These costs would be sufficient to constrain providers from any system-busting increases in charges and also to prevent users and providers colluding to defraud the system.

## Refinements

The scheme could be refined in various ways. Some suggestions follow: none, of course, are an essential part of the central idea.

The *progressivity* of the scheme could be enhanced by dividing the difference between the charge and the minimum into different bands and reducing the matching ratio from band to band, perhaps eventually to zero. For instance, instead of being uniformly 1:1 as in the above example, the public/private matching ratio could be 3:1 for the first £100 of the difference, 1:1 for the second £100, 1:3 for the third £100, and zero for the fourth £100. In that case, the elderly person in the example would pay £50, and the government £250: 83 per cent of the cost. If she had chosen the £500 home, then she would have paid £200 and the government would have paid £300: 60 per cent of the cost. This is more progressive than in the example, with a uniform 1:1 ratio, with the government paying a higher proportion of the total cost for the cheaper option and a lower proportion of the more expensive one.

The scheme could (and should) be *cash-limited*. One move in this direction already mentioned is to limit the total amount of grant that could be awarded to any individual. However, this would not be sufficient on its own to ensure the scheme remained within cash-limits; it would also be necessary to have some mechanism for limiting the number of individuals who were eligible for the scheme. This could best be done through the assessment process by which individuals are judged in need of care, and needs are compared with available resources. Indeed, in the spirit of case-management, the assessors could hold the budget for the scheme. They would then have a strong incentive to ensure that eligibility decisions were compatible with available resources.

## Partnership Schemes and Tax Relief

Finally, it is worth noting that it would be possible to obtain some of the advantages of this scheme through tax-relief. Tax relief for own contributions to care costs are a form of partnership scheme involving government assistance to people making their own provisions, in a fashion not wholly dissimilar to the scheme proposed here. However, tax reliefs have several disadvantages. They are only open to those who pay taxes; and their value increases with the marginal tax rate. Hence they disproportionately benefit the better off. They are not transparent; they appear in the form of tax not being paid, and the people in receipt of the relief may not be aware that there has been a reduction in their tax bill because of it. Moreover, even those who are aware of the tax reduction may not see it as a form of government assistance; rather they may see it as the government taxing 'their' money less and hence as involving a reduction in government malevolence rather than an increase in state beneficence. They are inflexible, with the amount of aid being determined by the parameters of the tax system, such as marginal tax rates, themselves determined by factors unrelated to the need for long-term care. And they are relatively unaccountable, since they do not come under either Treasury or parliamentary oversights of direct public spending.

## Conclusion

A partnership scheme of the kind proposed here would have many advantages as a means of providing government help towards the funding of long-term care. It would provide a strong incentive for individuals and their families to mobilise their own resources to meet care costs, through positive not negative incentives. Unlike the present system, there would be no means test with all its disincentives and distortions; unlike social insurance or compulsory private insurance, it is based on voluntarism and willingness, instead of compulsion and evasion; it keeps the middle classes in (again unlike means-tested schemes); and although it may benefit the better off, it is likely to do so much less so than other kinds of partnership schemes such as tax relief on savings or insurance contributions. Moreover, unlike tax relief, it would be transparent, flexible and accountable; and, since it would go to non-taxpayers as well as taxpayers and because its value would not depend on the marginal rate of tax, it would be much less regressive. Last but not least the scheme would be relatively easy to implement.

More generally, partnership schemes of this kind help solve the problems with which this chapter began. They are universal, retaining involvement of the middle class and without perverse incentives. And because they involve individuals using their own resources in partnership with the state they are less expensive than conventional universal schemes.

Partnership forms part of the rhetoric of the Third Way and can suffer from the fashionable vagueness that characterises that debate. However what has been suggested here is a concrete proposal incorporating the concept that, whatever its demerits, is far from vague. Moreover, the essence of the idea can be applied to other welfare areas, such as pensions.[11] It is to be hoped that it can thereby contribute in an innovative way to the project of shaping a new social democracy.

# Notes

1 Together with colleagues I have discussed these developments extensively else-where. See, for instance, J. Roberts, W. Bartlett and J. Le Grand, eds., *A Revolution in Social Policy*, Bristol, Policy Press, 1998.

2 Royal Commission on Long Term Care, *With Respect to Old Age*, Cm. 4192–I, London, HMSO, 1999.

3 Secretary of State for Social Security (1998) *A New Contract for Welfare: Partnership in Pensions*, Cm 4179, London, HMSO, 1998.

4 Secretary of State for Health, *The New NHS—Modern, Dependable*, Cm 3807, London: HMSO, 1997.

5 Secretary of State for Health,) *Our Healthier Nation*, Cm3852, London, HMSO, 1998.

6 C. Murray, *Losing Ground*, New York, Basic Books, 1984

7 For further discussion of these points see J. Le Grand, 'Knights, knaves or pawns? Human behaviour and social policy' *Journal of Social Policy*, 26, 149–169, 1997.

8 F. Field, (1995), *Making Welfare Work: Reconstructing Welfare for the Millennium*, London, Institute of Community Studies, 1995, p.20.

9 P. Baldwin, *The Politics of Social Solidarity* Cambridge, Cambridge University Press, 1990; F. Pampel and J. Wiliamson (1989) *Age, Class, Politics, and the Welfare State*, Cambridge, Cambridge University Press, 1989. J. Le Grand and D. Winter, 'The middle classes and the welfare state under Labour and Conservative Governments', *Journal of Public Policy*, 6, 1987, pp. 399–430.

10 Le Grand, *op.cit*

11 See Phil Agulnik and J.Le Grand 'Tax relief and partnership pensions' *Fiscal Studies*, 19, 1998, pp. 403–28; 'Partnership versus compulsion' *New Economy*, 5, 1998, pp. 147–52.

# True Blood or False Genealogy: New Labour and British Social Democratic Thought

MICHAEL FREEDEN

WHEN Tony Blair traced some of the ideational roots of new Labour back to early and mid-20th century liberals, as well as when he put out organisational feelers of co-operation towards the Liberal-Democrats, he dared make explicit a central feature of British progressivism. In contrast to the overt politics of confrontation and the tactics of exclusion that have typified the public face of British political culture, with its assumption of a one-to-one association between party and political values, the ideology of social and political reform has cut across party boundaries ever since Labour was formed. Although Liberalism and social democracy have frequently displayed diverging sub-currents, they have been for the past century overwhelmingly involved in a complex series of intertwined relationships, overlaps, and parallel growth. This mutual succour has created a peculiar blend of ideas and programmes distanciated both from classical liberal and from continental socialist positions. Within this broad family there have evidently been unhappy partnerships, black sheep and even conscientious objectors. Indeed, its resemblances are far more obvious to the external analyst than they have been to most of its members.

But this raises a problem with regard to the relationship between new Labour and its heritage. The iconic status that Blair has accorded liberal thinkers and practitioners such as Hobhouse, Lloyd George, Beveridge and Keynes suggests that their input into the progressive tradition from which new Labour draws has been a crucial counterweight to the statist and group-oriented character of British socialism. To the contrary, as will be shown here, the work of assimilating some of the most advanced ideas of liberalism had already been accomplished by central social-democrats *within* the Labour movement, in the spheres of personal liberty, economic co-operation between state and individual, theories of human welfare and growth, and the mobilising of a democratic and regulatory, not bureaucratic and overbearing, state.

The problem is, however, slightly more complex than that. It is not a question of establishing a liberal and social-democrat common ground: on a superficial level that can be demonstrated to the satisfaction of all but the most rigid students of politics. The real issue is the identification of a large number of common-ground configurations in which the notions of community, liberty, welfare, and the sphere of the state are mutually related. Each little

© The Political Quarterly Publishing Co. Ltd. 1999
Published by Blackwell Publishers, 108 Cowley Road, Oxford OX4 1JF, UK and 350 Main Street, Malden, MA 02148, USA

shift in emphasis, in prioritising one value over another, in associating some of these ideas more closely and separating others, results in a different ideological balance.[1] Within this rich field of interpretations and influences, an open society can choose from a plethora of social-democratic constructs, and it is against that kind of backdrop that new Labour must be evaluated.

The so-called centrist-left position of new Labour's 'Third Way' is hardly new in its desire to stake out a common ideological ground among apparently disparate political convictions, but it is entirely misguided in implying that such a common ground is monolithic and clearly defined and that, consequently, new Labour can appropriate the totality of its substance. Indeed the emerging issue is rather different: if at all, new Labour is positioned somewhat outside the field of the welfare state progressivism that has been Britain's most notable ideological contribution to the political thinking of the twentieth century. To that extent it has abandoned key facets of the social democratic inspiration emanating from its own past ranks by moving *away* from the liberal and, no less significantly, the communitarian tenets on which even British liberals had prided themselves.

## The Progressive Crucible

Strictly speaking, then, there is of course no such thing as social democracy, if by that label is meant a singular fixed list of beliefs and practices. Nor has 'social-democracy' been a term much in favour in the history of British labour thinking. Rather, Labour appropriated the term 'socialism', because in the British context socialism had already been tamed and domesticated. Before the advent of the Labour party in 1900, it had not even been a party-political word. It signified instead the recognition, shared among progressives in general, that society was an interdependent structure and that the regulated co-ordination of social life was essential in order to abolish, or reduce, unacceptable material conditions. The Rainbow Circle, one of the most important discussion groups to straddle the ostensible divide between liberalism and socialism, and a vital crucible of progressive thought, illustrates this ideological compound admirably. In the early years of its formation, employing a rhetoric which uncannily resonates with the new Labour of exactly one century later, Herbert Samuel identified a 'third social philosophy' located between the liberalism of Bentham and Adam Smith and the socialism of the Social Democratic Federation and the Fabians. The root idea of this 'New Liberalism' was 'the unity of society—complex in its economic, cooperative, ethical and emotional bonds' employing a view of the State as a partnership. The Rainbow Circle was no stranger to the view that divisions among progressives were institutional, not ideational; that 'the cleavage between the new Liberalism & Socialism is not to be found in their ideas of property but in the ordinary political possibilities of the two parties'. On the eve of the foundation of the Labour party, J. A. Hobson reminded the Circle, in the presence of one of its most illustrious members, Ramsay MacDonald, that the principles upon which a joint Progressive party should be based 'are already in evidence in the form of widely held intellectual affinities which as a matter of fact place the leaders of the Radical, the Socialist & the Labour groups much nearer to each other than their followers imagine.'[2]

The liberalism which John Stuart Mill bequeathed to his intellectual successors was based on the free development of individuality, on a specific configuration of these three concepts in a mutually sustaining framework. It focused on the centrality of responsible human choice in a setting of personal growth and which acknowledged the constraints of social life as well as the dual benefits to society and the individual of nourishing differences. Some of the features of social-democracy emanated from the logic of liberalism itself: an increasing sense of sociability, the rational desirability of social harmony, and the promise of continuously improving control over the conditions of human development—a possibility attached to a hopeful view of social evolution and of the future. It was also located at a crucial transformative juncture when human nature was no longer perceived solely in terms of action to which unreasonable hindrances had to be removed, but also in terms of processes of intellectual, moral and emotional development which had both to be unblocked and enabled, by means of individual endeavour as well as external assistance. The new liberal theorist L. T. Hobhouse put this succinctly when he asserted that 'the sphere of liberty is the sphere of growth itself' and that 'mutual aid is not less important than mutual forbearance, the theory of collective action no less fundamental than the theory of personal freedom.'[3]

## Well-being and Welfare

Combined with these emerging features of advanced liberalism was a subtle but persistent shift in the language of utilitarianism—a theory by no means dead with the fall from grace of Bentham's hedonistic calculus and maximisation of individual pleasures. Utilitarianism had recognised human beings as loci of fundamental interests and needs that required satisfaction, and this heritage underwent refinement as its core idea moved from pleasure to happiness and well-being, and finally to welfare. Moreover, this discursive change was interlinked to the rise of the 'social' as an analytical unit, so that social welfare and even the welfare state gradually entered the progressive vocabulary.

Here already was ample room for the fertile pluralism of British progressive thought. While the old Hobbesian understanding of liberty as the absence of impediments to individual action had been severely truncated, progressives in the main transplanted liberty into a soil nourished either on the idea of natural human growth, or on the idea of social self-expression. The first remained focused on the benefits liberty conferred on an individual, but did not rule out any intervention genuinely conducive to removing barriers to personal growth and welfare. The second concentrated on the benefits liberty conferred on society, developing the Marxist notion of emancipation to include human realisation only through a full immersion in social life.

Concurrently, the concept of welfare was locked into a dual ideational environment. On the one hand, it was linked in three senses to pervasive images of health. First, the rhetoric of rights was intriguingly married to an extensive range of individual functional requirements which included personal health. Secondly, social entities were discovered to have needs partially separate from those of their members. Thirdly, those needs were addressed in terms of structural and relational normalities, and came to be best described in the language of health and disease. This intellectual cocktail lay at the root of welfare thinking as it developed in early twentieth century Britain. On the other hand, welfare was linked to intricate notions of community. These could in turn be broken down into a harmony of individual welfares, a focus on raising the material welfare of the dispossessed as central to the process of bestowing full social membership on them, or an emphasis on the flourishing of collective life. However, the confluence of welfare and health could also be retained as a second order issue, one which could only be addressed indirectly by removing bad housing, enforcing reasonable working hours, and protecting against dangerous trades. Behind that lurked a far more instrumental view of personal health as conducive to individual wealth-production.

Hints of this conceptual indeterminacy within progressive ranks may again be detected through the Rainbow Circle minutes. The discussants disagreed on whether the presence of materialist arguments weakened or strengthened social-democracy; on whether the same concept of property was entertained by liberals and socialists; on whether society could or could not be described as an organism; on whether individuals sensitive to social needs were the most valuable and whether communal benefit was most furthered by placing individuality at its disposal; on whether progress was attributable to individual achievement or whether such achievement resulted from what society had placed at the disposal of such individuals; on whether the ideas of fraternity and equality were distinctively socialist; on whether nationalisation would reduce inefficiency or be replaced with physical, moral, intellectual and artistic efficiency. But these variations were all accommodated within agreed parameters of reformist political discourse: they constituted competitions over the correct combinations of the elements to be found in a shared pool of ideas.

## Social Democratic Strands

### A. The Fabians

British socialism in the meantime, arriving on the scene while liberalism was undergoing significant internal change, was itself a multi-layered phenomenon, although already well-attuned to its native culture. Calls for aesthetic and ethical fellowship, demands for radical changes in the conditions of life and labour, an insistence on workers' control through nationalisation and a crude economic reading of Marx filled the space of public debate, edging out the more revolutionary continental rhetoric of class conflict and social upheaval. The language of socialism introduced some additional notions into the public domain: equality as a material rather than legal concept; labour as a human attribute and expressive requirement, not merely an activity; and the existential situatedness of individuals in groups, to the point where some groups were seen to adopt a persona of their own. It is striking that the ideological architecture of British socialism contained much of the structure of its advanced liberal counterpart even if, as emphasised above, the internal configuration of ideas varied from ideological family to family, and from case to case, and their application could follow different routes.

Three of the socialist strands between the 1880s and 1930s are of major consequence in the mainstream ideological development of the social-democratic tradition in Britain: the Fabians, the views initially epitomised by Ramsay MacDonald and which underwent further modifications as the century progressed, and the pluralists in the inter-war years. The Fabians were social-democratic in a number of senses: first, though they were notoriously elitist in organisation and in the role they assigned to expertise, they were democratic in their pioneering recognition of mass political education and the need to convince an electorate of the rightness of their programmes rather than the wisdom of their political leaders. Secondly, they assimilated the dominant cultural icon of evolution into the notion of gradualism, expecting a transformation through the ballot box. Thirdly, they discarded individualistic atomism in favour of a concern with social categories. This involved the redefinition of individuals as constituting clusters of group attributes, rather than vehicles of narratives of growth. Fourthly, and here the Fabians shared a crucial belief with other socialists, as well as with the new liberals, they regarded the state as the agent of reform and social justice, the only social agency, in fact, possessed of the power, the prestige, the benevolence and the disinterested non-sectarianism that could attract political loyalty, transcend conflict, underpin citizenship, and effect the redistribution of wealth required to repair the social costs of the industrial revolution. Sidney Webb referred to the 'fourfold path of collective administration of public services, collective regulation of private industry, collective taxation of unearned income, and collective provision for the dependent sections of the community'.[4] For many socialists, though not for all, the logic of state activity was conceptually attached to the nationalisation of key public resources and services, but it could concurrently be employed to enlist state supervision and control of other important social practices. Notably, the liberal concern with the state as a source of potentially arbitrary and unaccountable power was largely removed from Fabian understandings.

## B. *State Socialism*

MacDonald's socialism well illustrates the common discursive field with liberalism, as well as one particular arrangement of social democratic concepts. For MacDonald, the organic analogy was attractive for the same reason that new liberals had adopted it: not merely because it focused on groups, but because it made one think 'of the whole of Society as well as of the separate individuals who compose it.' It was in fact, he insisted, capitalism whose productive processes imposed a deadening uniformity, allowing less play for individuality: 'Nothing is, indeed, more absurd than an argument in support of the present state of society, based on the assumption that as we move away from it in the direction of Socialism we are leaving individuality and individual liberty behind.' Individuality was conjoined in a social framework with well-being, and MacDonald gave prescient expression to the evolving concerns of social-democracy when he speculated that '[i]t appears to be the special task of the twentieth century to discover a means of co-ordinating the various social functions so that the whole community may enjoy robust health, and its various organs share adequately in that health. But this is nothing else than the aim of Socialism.' MacDonald's socialism shared with liberalism an abhorrence of class as a divisive sectionalism, ripe for replacement by national and communal growth, and it even retained a vision of 'civil society'—smaller groups such as trade unions, churches and families—whose importance would increase as safeguards of material and spiritual needs.[5]

On the question of equality it is even more difficult to prise MacDonald away from broadly liberal and pluralist notions. Socialists, he argued, understood by the concept 'that the inequalities in the tastes, the powers, the capacities of men may have some chance of having a natural outlet'. This would both ensure, in liberal terms, that for the individual personality 'opportunities should be given to it to advance in certain directions' and, in socialist terms, that each may have 'an opportunity to contribute their appropriate services to society'—a foreshadowing of R. H. Tawney's views on social function.[6] In standard Millite terms, MacDonald linked individual growth and welfare by interpreting equality as '"I have an equal right with you to self-development" and even that is limited to a development upon lines consistent with individual and social well-being.' Hence, also, MacDonald argued the case for limited private property 'in those things which personality requires for its nourishment', objecting mainly to the misuse of monopolistic concentrations of property as constraining individual liberty, a well-rehearsed liberal argument harking back to 19th century liberalism.[7]

It was however on the issue of liberty that fissures between the socialist and liberal traditions could be seen. MacDonald diverged from his liberal colleagues in the Rainbow Circle by setting liberty more firmly than they would have dared within a communal framework. The result was a curious fusion, employing developmental language to insist that the liberty of socialism was the 'liberty of a man to fulfil his true being—the being which has ends that are social, that relate to Society, and that are not merely personal.' This left little space between the concepts of individuality and community, a lack of space reproduced in Amitai Etzioni's communitarian views and their intimations of social control and social duty, which have been influential in new Labour circles.

## C. The Pluralists

Nevertheless, the seeds of social democracy had been sown, and the ensuing diet of the Labour intellectual tradition was identifiably one from which liberals had partaken. Similar themes are present in the writings of Tawney and G. D. H. Cole. Tawney ascribed a powerful sense of altruistic fellowship to an ethically construed idea of community. But he also insisted that the free disposal of personal possessions was the condition of a healthy and self-respecting life and sought to distribute property rights more widely. Property, albeit, had to be accompanied by special obligations and was hence conditional. This ensued because human activities and practices were valorised, not only as expressions of self, but also in terms of the social functions they performed. Here one can identify the early hint of a motif which new Labour have replicated, but only up to a point: the grounding of reward and remuneration on the basis of service to the community. The liberal appreciation of excellence in performance was closely associated with a recognition of the community as the ultimate norm-setter for what counted as useful work.[8] Nevertheless, throughout his writings Tawney not only paid tribute to aspects of the liberal tradition but insisted that the only version of socialism that stood a chance of success was the one that accepted liberal notions of fair play: personal liberty, freedom of speech, tolerance and parliamentary government. Individualism and voluntarism were key concepts for both Tawney and Cole. Indeed, as has recently been argued, their notion of function entailed little more than the socialist emphasis on human productivity, but lacked the primacy organic perspectives harnessed to serving distinct social needs.[9] And whereas liberal and socialist organicists were confident about the state's ability to act as the guardian of human interests, the guild socialists—quite contrary to the Fabians, and more typical of the old liberals than the new—displayed a fear of the state's unadulterated power.

Socialism for Tawney was henceforth social democracy. And beyond this 'political' liberalism, as Tawney stated in 1949, was an 'ecumenical liberalism' which 'profoundly affected' socialists. For, although they rejected the 'arid provincialisms' of the Manchester School, socialists acknowledged as the goal of political effort the free development of human personality, unimpeded by class, capricious inequalities of circumstance or arbitrary despotism. The moral challenge to socialism was therefore 'to work out a new social synthesis which may do justice both to the values of the Liberal era and to equally important aspects of life, to which that era, for all its virtues, was too often blind.' Here was already the mark of another 'third way', located between capitalism and communism. Specifically, Tawney positioned social democracy in an area hewn out between the denial of political liberty by both fascism and communism, and the denial of equal economic opportunities by the plutocracies of the West.

## Revisionism as Mainstream: Crosland

A generation later, Anthony Crosland, reacting to the temporary rise of Marxist arguments in the 1930s, attempted to revise the socialist creed. That revision was in effect a reassertion of mainstream British social-democracy; it was, as Crosland himself admitted, 'hallowed by an appeal to the past'. Crosland vaguely recognised a crucial feature of ideological structure, namely, that what one group may assert as first principles, another will regard as contingent and ephemeral expressions of deeper core concepts. Thus, he identified a contest between nationalisation of the means of exchange, and the labour theory of value as merely reflecting 'the underlying aspiration towards equality'. Echoing the views of interwar centrist-liberals, Crosland resurrected the importance of incentives as a psychological constituent of human activity. Previous socialists had objected to profits as corrupting, or at the very least had kept quiet about them. But once profits were subsumed under the broader category of incentives, they could not be singled out from practices which social-democrats—as distinct from Marxists—would be willing to endorse. The 'psychologisation' of profit thus redeemed it as an aspect of human nature which respect for individual needs would have to legitimate.

Crosland had already reflected the process of narrowing the concept of welfare that is so conspicuous in new Labour language. He bracketed the welfare state together with the paternalist tradition, a categorisation that would have disturbed new liberals: the state had certain responsibilities towards its citizens for preventing poverty and distress. Paternalism was a response to a series of demands for social security and a guaranteed national minimum. Social welfare was now targeted at a specific deprived sector of the population, rather than interpreted as a general attribute of human flourishing. The fundamental needs which welfare had to satisfy were reduced to addressing need in the sense of primary and secondary deprivation, thus significantly decoupling welfare from a broader idea of equality underpinned by the free and universal provision of social goods. Nevertheless, Crosland defined a socialist as one who accorded welfare exceptional priority over other claims. That is to say, welfare retained a prime position in the conceptual configuration of social-democrats, but only as an etiolated redistributive version of the fuller concept available to them.

In addition, individual rights for workers had replaced more participatory applications of the socialist concepts of work and community, the latter being demoted to 'an ideal of fraternity and co-operation' and to the practice of 'collective responsibility'. The mixed economy was signalled by the refusal to dismiss capitalism, merely its inefficiencies. Yet the state was still the prime mover: government had to allow space for private corporations, but it needed to manage them as a reflection of democratic responsibility and popular control. Liberty was simply taken for granted, for 'it would never have occurred to most early socialists that socialism had any meaning except within a political framework of freedom for the individual'. But which conception of liberty? Crosland offered a glimpse in the conclusion to his book, in which he advocated a more expressive view of liberty, supported by a culturally qualitative increase in the choice of life-styles—in effect a pluralist version of the Millite avowal of self-development. Taking on the Fabians, Crosland observed that much legislation in matters sexual and in the area of censorship 'should be highly offensive to socialists, in whose blood there should always run a trace of the anarchist and the libertarian, and not too much of the prig and the prude'. Socialism was not about the sacrifice of private pleasure to public duty. Nor was it, importantly, about the suppression of dissent.[10]

## Health as Liberation: Titmuss

Finally, some brief reflections on Richard Titmuss, whose contribution to British social democratic thinking has not been adequately recognised. Returning to the theme of welfare as health, Titmuss persevered with the metaphor of society as an organic whole composed of interdependent parts, with its corollary that many human needs were social in origin and collective in the means for their satisfaction.[11] But he was also sensitive to the claims of individual liberty which he specifically applied to the relationship between patient and doctor. Titmuss related liberty to two major factors. The first was that of lifestyle choices, inasmuch as health had now been reinterpreted by radical reformers, not merely as social well-being, but as a subjective constituent of an individual's own understanding of his or her capacity to function. Liberty was consequently linked to psychological states of mind which required recognition and assistance through the fundamental altruism of others. Need, welfare and liberty were connected at a more basic level than the motivation for incentives. The second was that of power relationships, now discovered in the internal logic of professional structure. Whereas liberty had traditionally been conceived as the emancipation of class from class, or as the limitation of state intervention in the private sphere, Titmuss transferred its focus to new ground. He was alert to the mixed blessings of professional expertise. Science may have encouraged the growth of a critical spirit, but it also was fast becoming a technology with new authoritarian implications. The new linchpin of the medical profession—the general practitioner—was in danger of being squeezed between the bureaucratic demands of socialised medicine and the power of the medical specialist. Hence this crucial group of

GPs, on which free access to medicine depended, had itself to be allowed to exercise its own judgment which the development of science had opened up. In other words, where knowledge had become the province of a few, its free and fair dissemination was a function of according new rights to its middlemen.

In the language of such rights, doctors required and obtained the freedom to choose which medical technologies to administer, as well as to choose the nature of their association with the state. Concurrently, patients secured access to health services for all who wanted to use them. Hence for Titmuss, health care was not only a question of *equal* access for all, but of *free* access, including the freedom to choose which health services to use and whether to use them.[12] The defining classical liberal choice-right had reappeared: 'The emphasis on the social rights of all citizens to use *or not to use* as responsible people the services made available by the community in respect of certain needs which the private market and the family were unable or unwilling to provide universally.' (My emphasis.) This liberal aspect of Titmuss's creed prioritised individual choice over the social insistence on the scrupulous discharge of a duty to be healthy. Both doctors and patients were therefore endowed with the essence of liberal interaction: the possibility of opting in and out of constitutive social relationships. However, the intention of Titmuss's argument was not to reintroduce a new exclusivist contractualism into social relationships. Titmuss rightly regarded the emergence of these rights—as did progressive liberals and social democrats—not as the product of a conflict between individualism and collectivism, but as reflecting a dispute over different degrees of freedom. And, as did so many of those progressives, Titmuss aspired to 'release the individual (whether, in this context, doctor or patient) from unalterable dependence on any particular social group'.

## New Labour and Liberty

The analysis of some of the theoretical constructions of British social democracy has of necessity been selective, though far from arbitrary. It does, however, assist in adumbrating certain parameters of the field within which new Labour professes to be located. Party rhetoric, instructive and central as it is to understanding how a political system works, rarely aspires to the heights of complex ideological arguments, nor can it if it is to act as a mobiliser of public opinion. But new Labour rhetoric is ambitious, and it has laid claim to being the inheritor of a social-liberal, or centre-left, position in British politics. And it is on that claim that it has to be judged as a set of ideological and philosophical positions.

The focus on liberty has for a while been notable in Labour discourse, in the writings of Roy Hattersley and Bryan Gould, as well as in the official voice of Neil Kinnock, whose statement 'at the core of our convictions is belief in individual liberty' graces the preface to Labour's 1992 manifesto. To be sure,

Kinnock positioned liberty firmly in the context of equalising social and economic opportunities provided by the community, but he distinctly prioritised it. Although the role of liberty in the social democratic tradition has been acknowledged in new Labour writings and speeches, that emphasis on liberty has been muted. Talk of self-development and growth has been replaced by a more minimalist notion of equality of opportunity, of life-chances, moving away from the emancipatory tone of many past British socialists. The recognition of social interdependence as a mechanism of releasing individuals from socio-economic fetters gave way to limited promises of a Freedom of Information Act, now receding from the Governmental agenda. Free will, on Blair's understanding, is associated with religious undertones of individual responsibility, not the growth of personhood.[13] Interdependence may still relate to employing collective power to advance individual interest, but this is 'an enlightened view of self-interest [that] regards it, broadly, as inextricably linked to the interests of society'.[14] Gone is the libertarian space carved out by Crosland and the emphasis on individual personality of the pluralists; back comes the fusion preferred by MacDonald. There is nothing on individuality in Blair's preface to the 1997 manifesto, except for a reference to the abilities of individual pupils; the preferred and fundamental social unit is the group, the British people, the community. Strikingly, Blair has declared that 'families continue to be society's most important unit'—a statement which would fit into conservative, not liberal or socialist, discourse. It is the source of the unifying sense of responsibility which cements a society, though it also is a modernised family in that women are equal to men. Only one individual activity is singled out, that of 'successful entrepreneurs'. Significantly, liberty is not located in proximity to self-development, as in new liberal and much social democratic argument. Instead Blair wishes to retrieve from an older and more capitalist version of liberalism 'the primacy of individual liberty in the market economy'.[15] The skills individuals need to develop are instrumental and marketable ones that will increase their employability, rather than their autonomy or well-being.[16]

## The Particularisation of Community

The concept of community has undergone the most intriguing changes of all. On one dimension, it has lost the inclusive, organic nature typical of mainstream social-democracy and has become startlingly majoritarian. One of the most allusive passages of the manifesto talks of 'a government that will govern in the interest of the many, the broad majority of people who work hard, play by the rules, pay their dues and feel let down by a political system that gives the breaks to the few, to an elite at the top'. But the sub-text of this passage, borne out in other utterances, is that there may also be others, on the marginalised outreaches of society, who do not—in the language of socialist expectations—work hard, who do not—in the language of conservative conventionalism—play by the rules, and who do not—in the language of liberal contractarianism—pay their dues. Communal membership is not ascribed, but earned; it is not a status but an activity.

This is spelled out more unequivocally on a second dimension. 'The assertion that each of us is our brother's keeper has motivated the Labour movement since the mid nineteenth century', thus Blair in his *New Britain*. Individual responsibility is linked not to autonomy but to duty to others and to the community, it is 'a value shared'. Indeed, the potential pluralism of social democracy recedes before the establishing of a 'sense of values, of common norms of conduct'. A singularity of moral purpose spells out a holism, not an organic unity of parts: 'The only way to rebuild social order and stability is through strong values, socially shared, inculcated through individuals and families'. This rhetoric of unified and virtuous authority represents a breach with the conceptual structures of social democracy, even with Fabian dirigisme. In its echoing of the 'one nation' of paternalistic conservatism, its rediscovery of natural harmonies and the decent institutions that underpin them, and its contraction of the role of politics, it jettisons the mechanically segmented, yet statist, nature of Fabianism. It resonates, of course, with the theories of Etzioni in which a plethora of rights has to give way to a new emphasis on obligations-cum-responsibilities, not of others towards yourself but of yourself towards others; and in which a community is the local repository of culturally inherited and preserved ways of life to which compliance is required. Sometimes this notion of mutual rights and responsibilities is expressed as a market relationship, 'a modern notion of social justice—"something for something",' a rather starker rendition of Tawney's functionalism. Being human is comprehended neither in liberal terms of development nor in socialist terms of nourishing fundamental needs, but in terms of responsible conduct. The fundamental unconditionality of full social membership is hence repudiated.

More often, though, as seen through the revealing phrases of new Labour's principal ideologues, the balance tips heavily in favour of the community away from the permissive, individualist and loosely regulatory fraternity of Crosland: 'New Labour builds on the traditional Labour ideal of social cooperation and expands it into a more dynamic view of the need for a strong society and an active community to help people succeed. This new tough concept of community, where rights and responsibilities go hand in hand, enables new Labour to reclaim ground that should never have been ceded to the right.'[17] It therefore intersects with liberty as a value constrained, not only by harm to others or by socio-economic obstacles, but (as Blair said in *The Third Way*) by shared values 'promoting tolerance within agreed norms'.

## A Partnership of Equals?

The mixed economy emerges in an altered form under new Labour. It is centred around an ambivalence concerning human nature, the site of a fragmented self unrecognisable to earlier progressives. That nature is co-operative as well as competitive, selfless as well as self-interested. People require groups—families and local communities—as a nourishing bed of their moral powers, and multi-cultural differences must be acknowledged within a framework of equal human worth. But the most prominent (and desirable) characteristics of men and women are 'talent and ambition, aspiration and achievement'. Hence government appears, not as a manager and overseer, but as a co-equal, arguably even minor, partner with business and industry. The partnership is no longer one in which pockets of private enterprise are permitted as long as they do not unduly serve private ends. The social-democratic state that demanded compliance, indeed subservience, to demo-cratically-established social aims, has vanished. Instead, new Labour fully recognises that 'the private sector, not government, is at the forefront of wealth creation and employment generation'. Competition is the norm where possible, regulation the reserve restraint where necessary. Or, put even more succinctly, 'New Labour welcomes the rigour of competitive markets as the most efficient means of anticipating and supplying customers' wants, offering choice and stimulating innovation'. The internal balance of the social-liberal and social-democratic ideational configurations has been discarded. Any hint of a struggle between the public and private sphere, or of their different functions and purposes, is elided. The battle is declared over. Instead, a politics that combines 'ambition with compassion, success with social justice', is mooted. New dichotomies are formed, but their synthesising mechanisms are assumed rather than constructed. The 'stakeholder' phrase, redolent of 'shareholder', signifies a society in which seizing opportunities, achievement and merit are the main bases of social justice, while need is a secondary criterion. In this vision of boundless property owners, wealth is crucially spread, not redistributed—a term that new Labour avoids if at all possible.

## The Constriction of Welfare

How is the notion of welfare interpreted in new Labour understandings? Here again, important slippages have occurred in relation to the social democratic tradition. In the visionary heights of that tradition, welfare evolved as a view of optimal human and social flourishing alongside the idea of citizenship as an attribute of the entire community participating in and prospering on a full range of social goods. New Labour, however, has pressed further with the shrinkage of welfare back to the more modest and minimalist conception that has run in parallel to that major theme. The particularism of welfare is evident in a number of ways. It is limited in the population it addresses, aiming 'to provide for those at the bottom'. It has refocused on poverty as the main form of social exclusion, and on care for vulnerable groups such as the elderly. It sees the virtues of the welfare state as transformative for the less well-off, but also as cost-effective. It is defined, as Giddens has put it, as 'a pooling of risk rather than resources'.[18] It has adopted a critical perspective concerning welfare dependency, replacing it with the aim of making people more independent and responsible and regarding welfare as functional for wealth creation. It has scrapped Titmuss's faith in human altruism and in the liberating force of welfare for all. Curiously, it sees as part of the welfare brief the 'insecurity of middle income Britain'—that insecurity being a fear of crime. And most tellingly, because welfare is no longer thought of as universal, but has been reduced to a 'hand-up' to the poor, it has consequently assimilated the American notion of workfare in the phrase 'from welfare to work'—thus indicating a dichotomy that cuts loose from the more inclusive socialist views of work as welfare, as the essence of well-being, and redefining the status of welfare as instrumental to other ends.[19]

While pride in and allegiance to the welfare state is still tendered, the concatenation of 'welfare' and 'state' causes an additional difficulty for new Labour. One finds the odd glimmering of the role of government through providing work and education to help people to help themselves, but even that falls short of former social-democratic aspirations. More often, the ascending revival of civil society, not only as a supplement, but a substitute for state activity signals a reallocation of institutional power and responsibility. This differs, however, from MacDonald's approval of the role of voluntary groups. New Labour has ceased to believe in big, centralised government as the framework within which civil society operates. It would dissociate itself from MacDonald's assertion that 'the Socialist considers that the state is as essential to individual life as is the atmosphere' and that the evolution of political democracy was directed at creating 'a state which could respond to the common will.'[20] New Labour's state is not only a partner but an institution that no longer wishes to assert universal control over the various spheres of society. Indeed, public/private partnerships are identified as a distinct way of establishing citizenship itself, of 'reconnect[ing] people to the political system'. Community is firmly detached from both state and government rather than expressed through them. Localisation suggests an emphasis on communities rather than an overarching community.

New Labour thinking certainly cuts across ideological and party boundaries, but its reinterpretation of key social values and the patterns in which they are packaged represents the strongest deviation from the social democratic tradition of mainstream British progressive thought to date. Its Fabian dirigisme is expressed, not in its love of state bureaucracy, but in its claim to the monopoly of political wisdom, to conceptual and epistemological certainty. Its belief in human improvability is not located in an open-ended view of social evolution but in the belief that the future has already arrived, that the millennium (courtesy of new Labour) virtually signifies the end of history and the final attainment of modernity. Its view of society is less organic and more structurally (though not value) pluralist, but some of that organicism is displaced to smaller units such as the family as motors of social co-ordination, while the direct link between individual and society is toned down. Social rewards are handed out less for good citizenship or for a life of service, and more for achievements in fields of material productivity and independence from social support. Its nod in the direction of individual choice is vitiated by its transferral of bureaucracy to the level of civil society itself, with its new managerial ethos of the competitive assessment of professionals. New Labour is undoubtedly centre-left, as it is unquestionably reformist. But its parentage cannot simply be sought in the hundred years social liberal tradition nourished in Britain, a tradition that now appears to have been as vulnerable as it is rich.

# Notes

1 For an analysis of ideology in these terms, see M. Freeden, *Ideologies and Political Theory: A Conceptual Approach*, Oxford, Clarendon Press, 1996.
2 M. Freeden, ed., *Minutes of the Rainbow Circle 1894–1924*, London, Royal Historical Society, 1989, pp. 28, 29, 68.
3 L. T. Hobhouse, *Liberalism*, Williams and Norgate, 1911, pp. 147, 124.
4 S. Webb, 'Modern Social Movements', in *The Cambridge Modern History of the World*, XII, Cambridge, Cambridge University Press, 1910, p. 760.
5 J. R. MacDonald, *Socialism and Society*, London, Independent Labour Party, 1905.
6 J. R. MacDonald, *The Socialist Movement*, London, Williams and Norgate, 1912, p. 139.
7 J. R. MacDonald, *Socialism and Government*, London, Independent Labour Party, 1910.
8 For a development of this argument see M. Freeden, *Liberalism Divided: A Study in British Political Thought 1914–1939*, Oxford, Clarendon Press, 1986, p. 315.
9 M. Stears, 'Guild Socialism and Ideological Diversity on the British Left, 1914–1926', *Journal of Political Ideologies*, vol. 3 (1998), 289–305.
10 C. A. R. Crosland, *The Future of Socialism*, rev. edn., New York, Schoken Books, 1963; see also A. Crosland, *Socialism Now*, London, Jonathan Cape, 1975.
11 R. M. Titmuss, *Essays on 'the Welfare State'*, London, George Allen and Unwin, 1963.
12 R. M. Titmuss, *Commitment to Welfare*, London, George Allen and Unwin, 1976, p. 237; *Essays*, p. 141.
13 T. Blair, *New Britain: My Vision of a Young Country*, London, Fourth Estate, 1996.
14 T. Blair, *Socialism*, London, Fabian Society, 1994.
15 T. Blair, *The Third Way*, London, Fabian Society, 1998.
16 For a further discussion of some of these issues see M. Freeden, 'The Ideology of New Labour', *Political Quarterly*, vol. 70 (1999), 42–51.
17 P. Mandelson and R. Liddle, *The Blair Revolution: Can New Labour Deliver?*, London, Faber and Faber, 1996.
18 A. Giddens, *The Third Way*, Cambridge, Polity Press, 1998, p. 116.
19 Blair, *New Britain*, pp. 142–3; *The Third Way*, pp. 5, 14; Interview in *The Guardian*, 17 January 1998; Mandelson and Liddle, *The Blair Revolution*, pp. 72–3, 142–3; Giddens, *The Third Way*, p. 117.
20 MacDonald, *Socialism and Society*, pp. 133–4.

# 'Rights and Responsibilities': A Social Democratic Perspective

STUART WHITE

## Introduction

At the heart of new Labour's self-understanding lies a doctrine of civic responsibility, a doctrine that 'rights must be balanced by responsibilities', that, in the words of the new Clause 4, 'the rights we enjoy reflect the duties we owe'. This doctrine of civic responsibility is deeply controversial. For some on the left, new Labour's enthusiastic espousal of such a doctrine, and its willingness to enforce alleged civic responsibilities, notably in the area of work, represents a break with the traditional libertarian values of British social democracy. For others, however, the commitment to balance rights and responsibilities expresses a conception of fairness and mutuality that has deep roots in the social democratic tradition. Who is right? As I shall explain below, new Labour's rhetoric of civic responsibility is compatible with a variety of different philosophical positions, making it extremely difficult to give a clear and firm answer to this question. Recent discussion of the so-called Third Way has not done much to clarify matters for it marks out a very broad conceptual terrain, one that can accommodate a number of rival political philosophies and their very different understandings of the civic responsibility doctrine. My aim here is to offer an interpretation and defence of the doctrine of civic responsibility from the standpoint of a specifically social democratic public philosophy, a philosophy centrally defined by its commitment to three core values: the values of reciprocity, equal opportunity, and autonomy.

There is no need to invent a new social democratic philosophy from thin air. British social democrats already possess a rich philosophical tradition, the tradition of 'liberal socialism', which finds classic expression in the works of Leonard Hobhouse, R. H. Tawney, and Anthony Crosland. For the liberal socialist, economic justice is centrally about satisfying a principle of reciprocity according to which entitlements to income and wealth are properly linked to productive contributions. The liberal socialists were right to emphasise the importance of this reciprocity principle; and a coupling of certain rights and responsibilities in the economic sphere is certainly consistent with (if not required by) this principle. To this extent, new Labour's emphasis on civic responsibility can be seen as rehabilitating an important liberal socialist value (and not, as is often alleged, as a departure from liberal socialist values). Also central to liberal socialism, however, are egalitarian and libertarian values that must temper our understanding of civic responsibility in a number of important ways.

In the economic sphere, for example, egalitarian values require that we pay close attention to the background distribution of opportunity against which citizens' putative reciprocity-based obligations are enforced: universal enforcement is unjust, from a liberal socialist standpoint, unless certain background conditions first obtain. Secondly, a legitimate concern for civic responsibility must be clearly distinguished from a concern to promote or enforce a sectarian conception of personal morality (as might be derived, for example, from a particular set of religious beliefs). Drawing on their liberal inheritance, contemporary social democrats should endorse a principle of autonomy that affirms each citizen's right to follow the life-style of his/her own choice subject to the condition that they do not significantly harm their fellow citizens. Enforcement of reciprocity-based economic obligations is quite consistent with this principle of autonomy. But the principle requires us to make (or attempt to make) a clear distinction between the claims of civic and personal morality and to refrain from policies that do no more than express the moral prejudices of one section of the population. In many areas, such as perhaps drugs and family policy, this is likely to support less public interference in individuals' lives than some new Labour rhetoric about balancing rights and responsibilities might suggest.

## The Ambiguity of the Third Way

There can be no doubt that a doctrine of civic responsibility lies at the centre of the cluster of ideas that have framed the Government's recent attempt to articulate a so-called Third Way philosophy. Stated in very general terms, the doctrine is simply that citizens have certain responsibilities towards their fellow citizens and that the state has a legitimate, indeed essential, role in cultivating the disposition to act on these obligations and, in some cases, in directly enforcing them. The doctrine of civic responsibility is complemented in Third Way thinking by a doctrine of real opportunity: that citizens must have real opportunity for acquiring income, wealth, and other essential requirements for pursuing the good life. The recognition and enforcement of civic responsibility is one side of a social contract which, on its reverse side, provides each citizen with the rights necessary to enjoy real opportunity.

This Third Way conception of citizenship is surely unobjectionable as it stands. And it is not entirely vacuous either. Any credible account of what constitutes real opportunity, for example, and of what institutions and policies are necessary to secure it, will almost certainly rule out any strong form of classical liberalism or right-wing libertarianism. Nevertheless, it is clear that what we have here is a very general and loose conception of citizenship, one which can be elaborated in a number of different ways, indeed in ways that point towards very different, opposing political projects. This is why the Third Way cannot really be presented as a new public philosophy, as some of its proponents maintain, but rather represents a very broad conceptual terrain which adherents of genuine and rival public philosophies will interpret in different ways. The Third Way doctrine of civic responsibility is itself subject to such rival interpretations. Elsewhere I have distinguished, very loosely and schematically, between 'liberal' and 'communitarian' interpretations of this doctrine. Liberals wish to identify a short list of discrete civic obligations and to confine the role of the state to the enforcement of these specific obligations. The people I am calling communitarians believe that there is a much wider range of behaviours for which individuals can reasonably be held responsible to the community and which, therefore, the state may potentially regulate.

A fundamental weakness of much Third Way and cognate philosophising lies in the tendency to regard basic concepts such as 'civic responsibility', or 'fairness', or 'social justice', as having self-evident and clear, univocal meanings. The working assumption, all too often, is that you do not have to say exactly what you mean by these values: it is enough merely to invoke them (e.g., to define the Third Way as 'social justice in a market economy'). This is profoundly mistaken. Political theories compete over the interpretation of these concepts, and one cannot claim to have articulated a clear public philosophy until one has indicated how one understands them: e.g., whether one understands 'social justice' in egalitarian, meritocratic, or classical liberal terms. I shall try to outline and defend a clearer, more determinate conception of civic responsibility, a conception grounded in the liberal socialist tradition of political philosophy and which accordingly draws on three core values: reciprocity (doing one's bit for the commonwealth in return for the rights and opportunities it provides); equal opportunity (roughly speaking, equal access to income, wealth, and other material requirements of the good life); and autonomy (freedom to pursue the good as one perceives it providing that one does not harm others).

## The Reciprocity Principle

Many—though not all—contemporary claims about the need to 'balance rights and responsibilities' are made in the context of welfare policy. Typically, the claims are made to defend a proposal which would make the enjoyment of a socioeconomic right more tightly conditional on satisfying a corresponding productive obligation. The paradigm is the proposal to link welfare benefits more tightly to work-related activity as, for example, in the Government's 'New Deal' programme for the young unemployed. Now one might try to defend such proposals on a number of grounds, but one ground that is often appealed to, more or less explicitly, is that of economic fairness or, in the language of political philosophy, *distributive justice*. Distributive justice is widely thought to require respect for a principle of economic reciprocity according to which: *those who willingly share in the economic benefits of social cooperation have a corresponding obligation to make, if so able, a personal and relevantly proportional productive contribution to the community in return for these benefits*. Connecting eligibility for welfare benefits to activities that indicate the recipient's willingness (and/or increase his/her readiness) to make this contribution is thought to satisfy this reciprocity principle, and so satisfy the demands of distributive justice. Should contemporary social democrats endorse this reciprocity principle and the attendant idea that citizens may have enforceable obligations to make a productive contribution to the community in return for the economic benefits they receive from it?

Let us first consider this question from the standpoint of philosophical tradition: Would contemporary social democrats be true to the traditional values of social democracy if they were to endorse these ideas? Of course, even if endorsement is consistent with their traditional values, this would not, in itself, make it right for social democrats to endorse these ideas. But inconsistency with traditional social democratic values is often forwarded by critics as a consideration that weighs against policies to obligate welfare recipients and the like, and so it is worth giving this question some attention in its own right.

As I have said, I believe that contemporary social democrats have no need to reinvent their political philosophy. They need only reapply the liberal socialist philosophy associated with the work of Leonard Hobhouse, R. H. Tawney and Anthony Crosland. Now it is striking just how central the reciprocity principle is to the way in which these liberal socialists conceive of distributive justice. For them, it is centrally defined by an opposition to what Tawney termed 'functionless property': to income rights detached from the performance of some socially useful productive function.[1] Taking the lead of Henry George and his followers, British liberal socialists saw the income rights accruing from private property in land as the paradigm case of functionless and therefore illegitimate property. But they quickly expanded the category to include the income rights accruing from inherited wealth, from various forms of 'speculative' capital gains, and the 'rent of ability' that skilled workers enjoy by virtue of the scarcity of their talents. A just state would, they argued, eliminate these various sources of functionless property through a combination of taxes on land rents, wealth transfers, capital gains, and progressive taxes on earnings, and it would then distribute the proceeds back to citizens in the form of various social benefits. In distributing these benefits, however, the state would have to take care not to create other forms of functionless property. As Harold Laski puts it in chapter 5 of *The Grammar of Politics*:

[An individual] can claim . . . such a share of the national dividend as permits him at least to satisfy those primary material wants . . . which, when unsatisfied, prevent the realisation of his personality . . . But the right is relative to a duty. If I receive it must be in order that I return. Society cannot maintain me for the privilege of my existence. I must pay my way by what I do . . . No man . . . has a right to property except as a return for functions performed.[2]

Beveridgian social insurance fitted neatly with this reciprocity-centred conception of distributive justice because of the way it connected welfare entitlements to economic contributions (albeit in a way that we would now regard as insufficiently attentive to, say, unpaid contributions from care workers within the home).

A concern for reciprocity, and a willingness to enforce specific reciprocity-based obligations, is, therefore, by no means inconsistent with the liberal socialist tradition. A tendency to downplay the importance of reciprocity, and to recoil from the enforcement of reciprocity-based obligations, may have been a feature of left-wing political culture in Britain in recent decades; in part, perhaps, an understandable reaction to fears of 'blaming the victim'. But such a tendency can go too far, and this is to be regretted, because the reciprocity principle does seem to capture a deep and widespread intuition about distributive justice. It is unfair for potentially productive citizens to reduce the consumption possibilities of their fellow citizens by 'free-riding' on their productive efforts. Structuring income entitlements to satisfy the reciprocity principle helps to prevent such exploitation.

Some recent research on the subject of distributive justice has underscored the importance of the reciprocity principle. In an influential article written at the start of this decade, the American philosopher Samuel Scheffler suggested that contemporary liberal egalitarian theories of distributive justice, such as those associated with the work of John Rawls, lack resonance outside of academia because they do not run with the grain of popular ideas about personal responsibility. Egalitarian liberalism has floundered as a political project in countries like the US because it has appeared to support policies that contradict 'deeply entrenched ideas about responsibility'.[3] Part of the problem here, I suggest, is the left's failure in recent years to give due weight to widespread notions of *civic* responsibility, notions that can be readily explained and defended by reference to the reciprocity principle. In a similar vein, radical egalitarians Samuel Bowles and Herbert Gintis have argued that popular resistance to the American welfare state derives, not from an opposition to egalitarian redistribution *per se*, but to redistribution that enables citizens to evade the contributive responsibilities that derive from a widely-shared norm of 'strong reciprocity'.[4] The norm of strong reciprocity is, Bowles and Gintis contend, not a contingent cultural artefact that the left can reasonably hope to ignore or to overturn. Drawing on a growing body of cross-disciplinary research in psychology, economics, and evolutionary biology, they argue that adherence to this norm of reciprocity is a deeply entrenched human commitment, one that may well have evolved to facilitate social cooperation, and one that individuals are prepared to suffer for rather than see violated with impunity. They conclude that any project for egalitarian economic reform ignores the norm of reciprocity at its peril. Egalitarians should frame their reforms in a way that explicitly acknowledges and upholds this norm, rather than being indifferent to it.

# Equal Opportunity and Fair Reciprocity

I conclude, then, that social democrats should endorse the principle of reciprocity and the related idea that citizens may have enforceable productive obligations to their community. What matters from a social democratic point of view, however, is not mere reciprocity, but what we may call *fair* reciprocity. Distributive justice is centrally about reciprocity, but not *solely* about it. The reciprocity principle must be elaborated and applied in a way that acknowledges other requirements of distributive justice, including, centrally, a robust principle of equal opportunity.

The individual's putative obligation to make a productive contribution to the community—the obligation that he/she has under the reciprocity principle—will be enforced against some background distribution of assets and opportunities. Is it fair to say that the individual has such an obligation, and to enforce it, regardless of what these background conditions look like? From any recognisably social democratic standpoint, the answer must surely be no; for to assert otherwise is to assert that significantly disadvantaged individuals in a highly inegalitarian society may have an enforceable moral obligation to cooperate in their own exploitation. No social democrat can believe that. (Do we think, to take the most extreme example, that slaves have an enforceable moral obligation to work in a slave society?)

Some threshold distributional conditions must be satisfied, therefore, before we may say that citizens in general have enforceable reciprocity-based obligations to make a productive contribution to the community. If the concern for reciprocity becomes disconnected politically from the struggle to attain these threshold conditions, then, as much of the recent US experience with workfare shows, it can all too easily provide support for purely punitive social policy. It is vitally important to stress that the reciprocity-based contract between citizens and community is a two-sided contract: that the community must do its bit by securing certain threshold distribution conditions, at the same time as the individual citizen is required to do his/her bit.

I shall not try to give a detailed account of the relevant threshold conditions here, but a few general pointers may help us get a concrete sense of what fair reciprocity ('reciprocity plus equal opportunity') is likely to entail. First, as Hobhouse argued, the community must ensure that all those with obligations under the reciprocity principle have access to the work necessary to satisfy these obligations in a meaningful way. This may imply some form of 'right to work', with the state acting as employer of last resort for the long-term unemployed. It surely also implies access, at a high level, to the education, training, and working capital necessary to ensure that citizens have a reasonable range of choice as to how they meet their reciprocity-based obligations. (Current proposals for 'Individual Learning Accounts' and the like can be seen as a modest first step in this direction.) Secondly, the state must ensure that those satisfying their productive obligations receive at least a minimally decent income in return. This points us in the familiar direction of various kinds of in-work assistance to the low paid. Thirdly, if we are going to insist that any one citizen satisfies these obligations, then fairness requires that we apply the same logic to all citizens. It is unfair if *I* have to contribute for my living while *you* do not. This suggests, amongst other things, that it is necessary to tax inheritances and other wealth transfers to prevent economic free-riding by the idle rich. For contemporary social democrats a crucial question, therefore, is whether new Labour is making sufficient progress on these various fronts. They should not repudiate the reciprocity principle, as some imply, but concentrate on ensuring that the conditions for its fair application are met.

It may be instructive at this point to note a crucial difference between a philosophy of economic responsibility grounded in the social democratic ideal of fair reciprocity, and an approach grounded in what U.S. policy thinkers call the 'New Paternalism'. New Paternalist thinkers, such as Lawrence Mead, argue that the community should obligate welfare recipients to do certain things—in particular, to work—because this is (supposedly) in the best interests of the welfare recipients themselves.[5] Distributive justice is not the New Paternalist's concern, and so New Paternalist thinkers do not view the achievement of some background distribution of economic opportunity as a prior condition for, or necessary corollary of, universal work enforcement in the welfare system. Indeed, in his early work, Mead's central argument was that across-the-board enforcement of work is essential precisely because the background opportunities of many welfare recipients are so poor (the available jobs so bad in quality and pay) that they would otherwise rationally opt out of work. (Mead drops this argument in his later work, contending there that enforcement is essential because many welfare recipients are in fact irrational and so will not respond to financial incentives to leave welfare for work.) Social democrats should not, I think, dismiss paternalistic considerations as altogether irrelevant in social policy. But their approach to work obligations will be distinct from that of the New Paternalists because they emphasise equal economic opportunity as an *essential* corollary of work enforcement.

The fair reciprocity approach should also be distinguished from the 'Civic Liberalism' recently advocated by Mickey Kaus.[6] Kaus argues that we should eschew a 'Money Liberalism', targeted exclusively at economic equality, for a 'Civic Liberalism', targeted instead at equality of status. He argues that an individual's status is conditional on productive contribution, and that Civic Liberalism thus supports a policy of replacing welfare with guaranteed public employment. However, unless background inequalities in economic opportunity are addressed, as fair reciprocity demands, it is by no means clear that universal enforcement of work will produce equality of status. Will the rich kid who can live comfortably off the family fortune and the ghetto kid who has to earn a living in the burger bar really feel equal to each other in social status? Though Kaus advocates universal entitlements to health care and education economic and status equality are perhaps more interdependent than he allows. The fair reciprocity perspective calls for more in the way of economic equality than Kaus does, and so may offer a surer basis for status equality. A similar contrast between the fair reciprocity approach and the 'Communitarianism' of Amitai Etzioni could also be made.

The reciprocity principle holds that individual income entitlements should be linked to productive contributions. But what counts as a productive contribution in satisfaction of this principle? Fair reciprocity also requires that we take care not to arbitrarily ignore or privilege some forms of contribution over others. In 1911, Hobhouse could quite comfortably assert that paying single mothers to stay at home and raise their children was fully consistent with the principle that income payment should follow productive service.[7] Even if one does not entirely agree with what Hobhouse says on this point—what he says is surely underpinned by a conception of gender roles that we would today rightly regard as indefensible—we should still acknowledge the status of care work as a form of productive contribution to the community, and the need to frame policy in a way that acknowledges this status. Social democrats, as proponents of fair reciprocity, should beware of reductively equating productive contribution with conventional paid employment. This marks another important point of difference between the fair reciprocity approach to civic responsibility in the economic sphere and approaches like the New Paternalism which focus more exclusively on paid employment.

A final point: in thinking about the claims of reciprocity, and how to satisfy them, contemporary social democrats should keep in mind that there is always likely to be some indeterminacy between philosophical principle and public policy. Principles certainly constrain the range of legitimate policies, but they do not necessarily select out specific policies as uniquely just. Contemporary social democrats should keep an open, pragmatic mind as to the ways in which the reciprocity principle might be satisfied in social policy. Following developments in the USA, we have lately become used to thinking of reciprocity-based social policy in terms of tighter eligibility conditions for welfare benefits combined with the introduction of new in-work benefits, roughly on the model of the US Earned Income Tax Credit, to help 'make work pay'. But there are other possibilities worthy of consideration, particularly Tony Atkinson's proposal for a Participation Income (PI): an income grant paid without any test of means to all citizens but subject, in the case of working age and work capable adults, to a broadly defined condition of productive participation in the community.[8] A PI respects the claims of reciprocity, but does so in a way that does not tie citizens so tightly into the world of formal paid employment. As such, it may do a better job than more narrowly focused employment subsidies at acknowledging other forms of productive contribution, and may also do better at advancing another core social democratic value: autonomy.[9]

# The Autonomy Principle

I have speculated that an aversion to the language and enforcement of civic responsibility may have been a feature of left-wing political culture in Britain in recent decades. New Labour has repudiated this culture, and, to this extent, it can be seen as rehabilitating an overly neglected concern for civic responsibility inherent in the liberal socialist tradition. In reacting against something, however, there is always a danger of going too far in the opposite direction. If we are to ward off this danger, and prevent the new concern for civic responsibility from degenerating into a crude attack on cultural non-conformism, there is an urgent need to clarify what our specifically civic responsibilities are and what the state may do to ensure our conformity to them. Contemporary social democrats need to give close attention here to the liberal dimension of their philosophical inheritance and, in particular, to the legacy of John Stuart Mill.

Our civic responsibilities are, from a neo-Millsian perspective, the responsibilities we have to refrain from activities that produce significant harms to our fellow citizens.[10] We harm our fellow citizens, in the very specific sense that is relevant here, by acting in ways that damage one or more *civil* interests that as citizens we have in common, such as our interests in bodily integrity, in spiritual integrity (in being free to live in authentic accordance with our own view of the good life), and in economic opportunity.[11] The paradigmatic form of harm is direct physical aggression. But we can also damage these shared civil interests, and so significantly harm our fellow citizens, by intimidation, by forms of discrimination, and by economic exploitation. The state may (indeed, should) define a set of civic responsibilities that track these harms, and it may (indeed, should) foster the disposition to respect these responsibilities and, in some cases, even directly enforce the relevant obligations. Doing so is essential to our prospects for a just, or even minimally decent, common life. But within the boundaries set by these civic interests and corresponding obligations, the state must on the whole leave us free to pursue the life-style we choose.[12] Within these limits it must itself respect our spiritual integrity by giving us the autonomy to pursue our own good in our own way. We may refer to this idea as the autonomy principle.

The enforcement of reciprocity-based obligations in the economic sphere is perfectly consistent with this autonomy principle, for the enforcement of such obligations serves to prevent a specific form of harm—the economic exploitation that arises when one citizen opts to free-ride on, and so unfairly curtail the economic opportunities of, his or her fellow citizens.[13] But when the state moves to define, and to make us conform to, an alleged civic obligation we need to be assured:

1 that this is indeed necessary to prevent a genuine harm;
2 that the gain in this respect is sufficiently large and sufficiently certain as to

174

outweigh any damage to civil interests that may result from the state's new policy.

Given where we start from in Britain today, application of such a principle will in many cases point in the direction of reducing state coercion and other forms of intervention relative to the *status quo*, rather than to the imposition of new and/or tougher legal obligations.

Take the case of drugs policy. For some people, the use of certain currently prohibited narcotic substances, so-called 'drugs', is the paradigm of 'irresponsible' behaviour, and so it seems perfectly proper that use of these substances remain prohibited. This is, however, precisely the kind of logic that the autonomy principle challenges. If the use of a given substance by a citizen leads, with a high probability, to that citizen harming fellow citizens in some way, e.g., through physical aggression, then, consistent with the autonomy principle, there is at least a *prima facie* case for prohibiting use of this substance. But the high probability of harm has to be established before prohibition is justified. If this has not been established, then, paternalistic considerations aside, the relevant prohibition simply amounts to one group in the community arbitrarily restricting the freedom of another.

The situation is most inequitable when there is a settled and reasonable consensus in the community to permit the use of one substance with potentially dangerous effects on behaviour while the use of another substance, which appears less dangerous in this respect, remains prohibited. British citizens are currently permitted to use alcohol, for example, despite its potential behavioural effects, but are prohibited from using marijuana which almost certainly does not have as potentially dangerous effects. By failing to hold alcohol and marijuana to the same standard, the state fails to show equal respect for its citizens, unfairly discriminating against those who prefer to use marijuana rather than alcohol. A lengthier analysis would, I suspect, reveal many more examples of similarly discriminatory prohibitions and restrictions, especially in relation to sexuality (restrictions which entail bias against gays, lesbians, and other queer sexualities). To be true to their liberal inheritance, contemporary social democrats should take a firm stand against this form of discrimination. There is a need for a comprehensive 'Liberty Audit' in Britain to identify prohibitions and restrictions of this kind as immediate targets for autonomy enhancing reform.

Consider now the case of family policy. Here a central question at the moment, with obvious implications for individual autonomy, is whether the state ought to discourage the formation of single-parent families. From the standpoint of the autonomy principle the critical first question we need to ask is: Does the single-parent family generate significant harms (relative to two-parent families)? If there were good evidence of such harms then, once again, there would at least be a *prima facie* case for viewing marriage as a civic responsibility and for taking steps to encourage individuals to respect this responsibility (e.g., by making divorce much more difficult or by imposing tax penalties on single-parent families). In the US, Communitarian philosophers like William Galston have pointed out that children from single-parent families there perform, on average, less well on a range of measures (education, employment, income, criminality); and have argued on the basis of this evidence that single-parent families do indeed cause significant harm, both to the children involved and to the wider community which has to bear the costs of their dysfunctionality.[14] The two-parent family, on this view, is an important form of 'social capital' that more effectively nurtures citizens with the virtues and competencies necessary for a healthy liberal society. The state should therefore take a stand in support of the two-parent family over the single-parent family. This 'functional traditionalism', as Galston terms it, is discriminatory; but, Galston would argue, it does not amount to *arbitrary* or *unfair* discrimination because single-parent families do (supposedly) produce harms that two-parent families do not.

While the logical form of this argument satisfies the demands of the autonomy principle, however, the argument marshals empirical evidence on the supposed harm of single-parent families in a questionable way. Is the experience of being in a single-parent family in itself damaging, or is it specific contingent features of life in the average single-parent family, such as poverty and weak labour force attachment, that produce the observed harms? If the latter is the case, then the appropriate policy response is not necessary to discourage the formation of single-parent families *per se*, but to remedy the problems of low income and weak labour force attachment that currently afflict these families. Note that this could conceivably involve obligating single parents in new ways, e.g., requiring single parents on welfare benefits to be more active in the labour market; but it would not involve obligating people in precisely the way recommended by US Communitarians (so as to bolster the two-parent family).

The implications of the autonomy principle will not always be uncontroversial. There is bound to be some reasonable disagreement amongst citizens as to whether a given type of behaviour causes harm in the relevant sense, how much harm, and about how to weigh different harms against each other. But the principle still provides the appropriate framework for approaching issues that have to do with the public regulation of individual behaviour and life-style. The danger to be avoided is that which political philosophers call 'legal moralism': using the law to enforce or otherwise promote a specific conception of morally correct behaviour as an end in itself, simply because a majority, or some supposedly enlightened minority, happens to think that this conception describes the proper way to live. The autonomy principle provides a bulwark against such legislation by insisting that anyone making a proposal to restrict or discourage a certain way of life or behaviour make a reasonable case that this proposal is necessary to prevent significant damage to citizens shared civil interests (and does not itself produce outweighing damage to these same interests). This does not mean that 'morality' or 'ethics' are taken out of politics. It means that civic morality, which specifically concerns the rights and obligations of citizenship, is distinguished from the more comprehensive personal morality that an individual might have as, say, a member of a particular church or religious tradition.

This point is perhaps worth elaborating in view of the alleged influence of Christian socialist ideas within new Labour. This influence has raised concern in some quarters that a new Labour government might try to base public policy on religious values, deploying public authority in a sectarian way that necessarily lacks legitimacy for large numbers of perfectly decent and reasonable citizens who happen not to share these values. Here it is important to distinguish two ways in which religious concerns can enter into and help motivate political action. On the one hand, religious concerns can enhance our commitment to an essentially civic morality of the kind I have discussed above. A civic morality centred on the values of reciprocity, equal opportunity and autonomy obviously requires attitudes of mutual respect, of reverence for others, and solidarity with the disadvantaged. By cultivating our sense of respect for and solidarity with others, participation in a religious tradition can increase our commitment to these civic values. (This does not mean, of course, that the significance of such participation to the individual concerned lies only in the fact that the religion in question happens to support these values.) Contemporary social democrats should not be wary of this liberal religiosity, as one might call it. Indeed, they should welcome it, for, as US commentators such as Michael Lerner have recently argued,[15] a religiosity of this kind may have a vital role to play in countering the ethos of materialism and selfishness that stands as an obstacle to fundamental egalitarian reform of capitalist societies.

On the other hand, the religious individual may desire to use state power to enforce or promote his or her religion, or the way of life endorsed by this religion, as an end in itself, without regard to any distinctively civic morality. Contemporary social democrats should unequivocally oppose this form of religious intervention in politics. Note that it is not a matter here of getting religious individuals to adopt particular policy positions which social democrats tend to support, such as a more libertarian position on the law's treatment of certain sexualities. Rather, it is a matter of insisting that religious leaders and their followers respect civic values when making a case for legal restrictions on some form of behaviour of which they disapprove. It is not enough for the Archbishop of Canterbury to say, 'I oppose lowering the age of consent for gay sex, because this violates my understanding of Christian values', for to restrict the liberty of a fellow citizen on these grounds is legal moralism pure and simple. To be consistent with the autonomy principle, the Archbishop must, in his capacity as a citizen attempting to offer a justification for the exercise of political authority to other citizens, make the case that lowering the age of consent for gay sex is undesirable because doing so would result in some form of harm to citizens' shared civil interests. If, as I suspect, he cannot make a credible case for restricting sexual liberty in these terms, then he must give up his political opposition to this reform. Contemporary social democrats should regard it as a basic civic responsibility that one respect the claims of civic morality, and limit the political or legal promotion of one's religion, in this way.[16]

## Summary

The doctrine of civic responsibility, that 'rights must be balanced by responsibilities', occupies a central place in the nascent philosophy of new Labour. I have argued that contemporary social democrats—'new social democrats', if one likes—should not repudiate this doctrine, but that they should elaborate and apply it on their own terms. Drawing on the liberal socialist philosophical tradition of Hobhouse, Tawney, and Crosland, I have sought to outline and defend a distinctively social democratic understanding of this doctrine, grounded in three core values: reciprocity, equal opportunity, and autonomy.

The principle of reciprocity captures an important requirement of distributive justice and suggests that it is legitimate to connect economic entitlements with the performance of productive obligations, to balance these rights with responsibilities. But what matters from a social democratic perspective is not simple reciprocity, but fair reciprocity, which requires radical action on society's background distribution of assets and opportunities. Enforcement of reciprocity-based work norms is punitive and unjust if this distributional condition is not met. Generous in-work subsidies, generous educational entitlements (subsidised 'lifelong learning' and the like), public job guarantees for the long-term unemployed, heavy taxation of inheritances and other wealth transfers, may all be necessary in practice to meet it. Finally, our civic responsibilities must be defined in a way that is sensitive to our shared interest in freely pursuing the good life as we individually perceive it. To this end, we must show, in order to justify the imposition and enforcement of a specific civic obligation, how this serves to prevent an activity that would otherwise result in some demonstrable and significant harm to other citizens (where harm implies damage to a civil interest that citizens have in common, such as their civil interests in physical integrity and economic opportunity). Application of this principle in present circumstances is likely to justify an expansion of freedoms and rights relative to the *status quo*, as much as the coining of new enforceable responsibilities.

## Notes

1 R. H. Tawney, *The Acquisitive Society*, New York, Harcourt Brace Jovanovich, 1948 [1920], pp. 52–83. See also Leonard T. Hobhouse, *Liberalism and Other Essays*, Cambridge, Cambridge University Press, 1944 [1911], pp. 81–102, and Anthony Crosland, *The Future of Socialism*, New York, Macmillan, 1957, p. 208.
2 Harold Laski, *A Grammar of Politics*, London, Allen and Unwin, 1925, p. 184.
3 Samuel Scheffler, 'Responsibility, Reactive Attitudes, and Liberalism in Philo-

sophy and Politics', *Philosophy and Public Affairs* 21, 1992, pp. 299–323, specifically p. 301.

4 Samuel Bowles and Herbert Gintis, 'Is Egalitarianism Passé? Homo Reciprocans and the Future of Egalitarian Politics', *The Boston Review* 23, December/January 1998/1999, pp. 4–10.

5 For a recent statement of Mead's views, see Lawrence M. Mead and Frank Field MP, *From Welfare to Work*, London, Institute for Economic Affairs, 1997. The classic early exposition is Lawrence Mead, *Beyond Entitlement: the Social Obligations of Citizenship*, New York, Freee Press, 1986.

6 Mickey Kaus, *The End of Equality*, New York, Basic Books, 1992.

7 According to Hobhouse (*Liberalism*, p. 87), 'if we take in earnest all that we say of the rights and duties of motherhood, we shall recognise that the mother of young children is doing better service to the community and one more worthy of pecuniary remuneration when she stays at home and minds her children than when she goes out charing and leaves them to the chances of the street or to the perfunctory care of a neighbour'.

8 Anthony Atkinson, 'The Case for a Participation Income', *The Political Quarterly* 67, 1996, pp. 67–70. Activities that satisfy Atkinson's participation condition include: paid work; some forms of care work, e.g., care for an infirm relative who needs full-time attention; full-time education or training; job search; and various approved forms of voluntary work.

9 For costings of a participation income scheme, and discussion of its progressive distributional effects, see Carey Oppenheim, 'Welfare Reform and the Labour Market: A Third Way?', paper prepared for conference on 'Labour in Government', Center for European Studies, Harvard University, November 13–15, 1998.

10 I do not mean necessarily to restrict the scope of civic morality only to fellow citizens. Foreign citizens and (though this is more controversial) animals also have basic interests that we may have enforceable responsibilities to respect and protect.

11 To be exact, one harms a fellow citizen, in the sense here relevant, by denying them *fair* economic opportunity: the opportunity to which they are entitled as a matter of distributive justice. A full account of the autonomy principle thus presupposes a theory of distributive justice. My comments on equal opportunity and the reciprocity principle only begin to sketch out such a theory here.

12 I add the qualifier 'on the whole' to this sentence because I do not wish to imply that all paternalistic interventions by the state (interventions to prevent self-harm) are necessarily illegitimate. For a useful discussion of the special circumstances in which paternalism may be legitimate, see Gerald Dworkin, 'Paternalism', in Richard Wasserstrom, ed., *Morality and the Law*, Belmont: CA, Wadsworth, 1971, pp. 107–26.

13 For relevant discussion, see J. S. Mill, *On Liberty*, Penguin, Harmondsworth, 1985 [1859], chapter 4, p. 141.

14 William Galston, *Liberal Purposes*, Cambridge, Cambridge University Press, 1991, pp. 283–88.

15 Michael Lerner, *The Politics of Meaning*, New York, Perseus Books, 1996.

16 For further discussion of this idea, see John Rawls, *Political Liberalism*, New York, Columbia University Press, 1993.

# Index

Acheson Report 140–1
agriculture 114
anti-Europeanism 24–5
Ashdown, P. 13
Asia 87–8
Atkinson, A. B. 46, 173
Attlee, C. 27
Austria 28
autonomy 167, 174–78

Babel, A. 11
Bad Godesberg Programme 20
Balladur, E. 31
Barber, B. 11
Beck, U. 114
Belgium 22, 34–5
Benn, T. 10
Berlin, I. 13
Berlinguer, E. 20, 21
Bevin, E. 10, 27
Binmore, K. 100
Black, C. 25
Blair, T. 3, 12, 21, 69, 79, 81, 104, 111, 119,
    133, 138
    European policy 25
    on ideas and values 44, 48, 151
    individuals and groups 161
    and Scotland 135
    and the USA 26–7
    see also Labour Party; New Labour
Bowles, S. 170
Brandt, W. 20
Brown, G. 101, 103, 104, 133
Brundtland Report 106
Bundesbank 24

Callaghan, J. 27
capital 88
    mobility 87, 90
capitalism
    and democracy 14–15
    management of 97–8
    renaissance 10–11, 13–14
    and socialism 13

capitalist class 74–6
    political power 76
care work 173
Charter 88 13
China 27
Chirac, J. 22
Christian socialism 177–8
Ciampi, C. A. 31
citizenship 5, 15, 46–50, 124, 166–78
    and rights 54–6
Clarke, P. 16
class politics 71–83
Clinton, B. 27, 60, 61
coalition government 22–3, 82
Cole, G. D. H. 157
commercial banks 86
commercialism 65
Commission on Social Justice 37
community, nature of 161–2
community-based action 123–28
Community Fund 61–2
constitutional change 34–5
co-operatives 62
corporatism 42
Cossuta, A. 23
Craxi, B. 19, 21
Crosland, A. 10, 16, 99, 158–9, 166, 169
Crouch, C. 42
Czech Republic 88

Dahrendorf, R. 10, 13
D'Alema, M. 21, 22, 30, 31
decentralisation 34–5
defence policy 25
Delors, J. 38, 41
Denmark 25, 91–2
Dewar, D. 139
distributive justice 43–6, 48, 168–73
Dini, L. 31
drugs policy 175

eco-efficiency 107–8
economic policy 28–32
education policy 80

employment policies 29, 37, 38–39, 44–6, 69–70
environmentalism 105–16
  fiscal policy 108
  and governance 113–15
  industrial policy 109
  international economic management 109–10
  new technologies 109
  quality of life 110–13
environmental taxes 108
equality 48–50, 54, 128, 156
  of choice 49
  of opportunity 54, 161, 167, 171–3
  merit goods 57–8
  of status 172–3
Etzioni, A. 157, 162, 173
European Central Bank (ECB) 24, 41–2
Europeanism 23
European Union 11–12
  convergence 29–32, 37–40, 50
  economic policy 28–32, 40–3
  industrial relations 32–4
  institutions 15–16, 41–2
  macroeconomic policy 40–3, 89
  and multinational companies 110
  national elections 19–20
  regulatory competition 93–5
  tax policy 24, 43
  and the USA 25–8
exchange rates 89, 101

Fabianism 16, 154–5
Fairness at Work Bill 103
families 37, 72, 161, 175–6
Field, F. 143–4, 145
financing welfare 142–50
Fischer, J. 26
foreign direct investment (FDI) 85
France 22, 28, 29–30, 30–1, 33, 35, 94
Friedrich Ebert Stiftung 37, 38
fundamentalism 11

Gaitskell, H. 10, 16, 27
Galston, W. 176
game theory 100–1
general practitioners 159–60
genetic modification 114
George, H. 169

Germany 26, 28, 33, 35, 85–6, 115–16
  energy taxes 29
Giddens, A. 10, 40, 42, 71, 87, 163
Gintis, H. 170
Gladstone, W. E. 69
globalisation 29, 84–95
  or Europeanisation 40–3
González, F. 19, 26
Gould, B. 160
governance 4–5
government borrowing 64
Gray, J. 10, 13, 87, 90
Greece 22, 30
green politics 105–6
Greenspan, A. 42, 61
growth theory 101, 103

Hattersley, R. 160
Hayek, F. von 14, 17
healthcare 60–1, 119
Hemerijck, A. 92
Hobhouse, L. T. 153, 166, 169, 171, 173
Hobsbawm, E. 14
Hobson, J. A. 152
Holland 21, 29, 30, 42, 46, 90, 92
Holtham, G. 63
Hong Kong 86
Hutton, W. 13

image-making 20–3
inclusive society 44–6, 55
individuality 156
inflation 29
Independent Commission on Social Justice 13
industrial relations 32–4
Institute for Public Policy Research 79, 81
internationalisation of financial trading 86
International Monetary Fund (IMF) 28, 110
Italy 20–1, 26, 28, 30, 33, 35, 92–3

Japan 27, 85–6, 89, 90
Jenkins Commission 34
Jospin, L. 12, 21, 24, 29, 30, 31, 33, 35
Juppé, A. 30

Kaus, M. 172–3

Kay, J. 13
Keynesianism 40–3, 50, 99–100
Kinnock, N. 21, 160–1
Kohl, H. 24
Kok, W. 21, 29

labour market
  changes 71–2
  flexibility 28
  participation 44–6
  policies 38
Labour Party 74, 116
  Clause IV 4, 20, 166
  and Europe 23–5
  general election 1997 2–3, 69–71
  labour market flexibility 28
  and the USA 25–8
  see also Blair, T.; New Labour
Lafontaine, O. 15, 22, 24, 41
Laski, H. 169
legal moralism 176–77
legal services 57
Le Grand, J. 49
Lerner, M. 177
liberalism 152, 156–7, 166, 169–70
liberty 153–4, 159
  and health 159–60
  and New Labour 160–1
Liddell, H. 138
Liddle, R. 162 (quoted)
Lipponen, P. 21
local action 123–28
  evaluation 125–6, 128–9
Local Agenda 21 114
local government 126

Maastricht Treaty 69–70
MacDonald, R. 152, 155, 161, 164
macroeconomic policy 40, 41–3, 89
Major, J. 24
Manchester School 157
Mandelson, P. 32, 162 (quoted)
Mankiw, G. 100
market reforms 21–2
market regulation 14–15, 89, 101
Marquand, D. 138–9
mass media 66–7, 118
Matthew, C. 69
Mayer, C. P. 63

Meade, J. 61
Mead, L. 172
means testing 144
Meidner Plan 20
Meidner, R. 91
merit goods 57–8, 60
middle England 76–9
Mill, J. S. 18, 153, 174
Mitterrand, F. 19, 21
modernisation 12
moral goods 113
multi-national companies 85–6
Murdoch, R. 25

National Childcare Strategy 119
natonalisation 30
NATO 25, 26
neo-liberalism 53
  and public ownership 63
Netherlands see Holland
New Deal at Work 46–7, 70, 103, 168
New Deal for Communities 119, 124
New Labour 3, 10, 12–14, 79–83, 98–100,
    102, 103–4, 117–18, 137
  and capitalism 99, 103
  concept of community 161–2
  education policy 80
  environmental policy 116
  industrial relations 32–4
  institutional reform 34–5, 119, 131
  and Liberalism 69–70
  and liberty 160–1
  and local action 124, 125, 128–9
  partnerships 162–3
  social base 74, 78–9, 80
  and welfare 57, 163–5
  and women 78
  see also Blair, T.; Labour Party
non-government organisations 120–1

Occhetto, A. 31

Papandreou, A. 19, 21, 26
participation 44–6, 136
Participation Income 173
partnership funding 145–50
  tax relief 149
partnerships 120–1, 162–3
Party of European Socialists 38

paternalism 172
pension funds 86
pensions 57, 81, 92–3, 144
Persson, G. 28
Phelps, E. S. 45, 46
Plant, R. 46–7, 55–6, 57
pluralists 157–8
Polanyi, K. 11
Popper, K. 18
Portugal 35
poverty rates 45–6
power sharing 129
pragmatism 139–40
price changes 100
private enterprise 31–2
    and education 80–1
Private Finance Initiative (PFI) 134
private service sector 38
privatisation 30–1, 63–4, 76
productivity gap 107–8
profits 158
property
    functionless 169
    rights 156, 157
proportional representation (PR) 131
public debate 114
public investment 103
public ownership 4, 59–60, 62–4
    economic efficiency 62–3
public participation 119–20, 122–3
public/private partnerships 102, 164
    in Scotland 134–5
public provision 57–9
    Community Fund 61–2
public service 15

quality of life 111–12

Radcliffe, R. 64
Rainbow Circle 152–3, 154, 156
Rawls, J. 100–1, 170
reciprocity 47, 166, 168–73
religion 177–8
Renewal 138, 139
residential care 145–9
responsibility 46–50, 166–78
    image-making 20–3
Rhodes, M. 94

Rodrik, D. 90
Romer, D. 101
Royal Commission on Long Term Care
    142, 145

Samuel, H. 152
Sassoon, D. 37, 40, 50
Scharpf, F. 41, 87, 93, 94
Scheffler, S. 170
Schröder, G. 12, 22
Scotland 131–41
Scottish Council Foundation 135
Scottish Enterprise 137
Scottish National Party (SNP) 132, 139
Scottish Parliament 136, 137–8
self-esteem 44–5
Simitis, C. 21, 22, 26
Singapore 81, 85, 86
Smith, J. 10, 13
social democracy
    in changed world 1–2
    as political movement 2
    rebirth of 11–12
social entrepreneurs 126–7
Social Exclusion Unit 104, 119–20, 131
social goods 111–12
socialism 97, 152, 154–65
social mobility 127–8
social pacts 90, 94, 101, 102
social rights 54–6
    autonomy 174–8
    and obligations 55, 56, 99
    reciprocity 166, 168–73
social science 16
Solow, R. M. 45
Spain 35
stakeholding 163
state, the
    and autonomy 174–8
    and civil society 17
    environmental issues 113–15
    role of 98, 101–2, 104, 159, 164
Strauss-Kahn, D. 24, 32
subsidiarity 15
sustainable development 106–7, 111
Sweden 21, 25, 28, 90, 90–1
    welfare state 29

Taiwan 85

Tawney, R. H. 156, 157–8, 166, 169
taxation 29, 38, 56, 112
  coordination in Europe 43
  environmental taxes 108
Thatcher, M. 24, 65
'Third Way' 40, 98-9, 102, 103–4, 117–18, 152
  ambiguity 167–8
  and social democracy 86–7
Thompson, G. 84
Titmuss, R. 159–60, 164
trade unions 32–3, 73, 74, 82, 98, 103
trust 118
Tsohatzopoulos, A. 22

United States of America 85–6, 89, 173
  relations with Europe 23, 26
  relative poverty rate 45–6
  workfare 171
utilitarianism 153

values 43–4, 54–6, 164, 177–8
van Aartsen, J. 26
Vandenbroucke, F. 55
Veltroni, W. 26
vision, need for 139–40
Visser, J. 92

Walzer, M. 15
Webb, B. 18
Webb, S. 17, 155
welfare
  and community 154
  as health 154, 159–60

welfare benefits 38, 56
  means testing 144
  merit goods 57–8
  pensions 57
  universalism 39, 56, 57, 144
welfare reform 29–30, 37
welfare rights 55–6
welfare state 37, 39
  adaptation 88–93
  cost 143, 144
  finance 142–50
  and globalisation 88–93
  impact on behaviour 143
  and paternalism 158
  and taxation 43, 93
well-being 15, 111–12, 153–4
  collective 112–13
Williams, R. 105
Wilson, H. 21, 27
women
  and care work 173
  employment 37, 77
  political agenda 77–8
  voting patterns 77–8
work 171–2
  modern problems 71–2
  New Deal 46–7, 70, 103, 168
  right to 171
  value of 64–5
working class decline 73–4, 98
Working Families Tax Credit 47, 103, 104
World Bank 28, 110
World Trade Organisation 110
Wright, T. 48 (quoted)